THE STUDY AND
OF GLOBAL LEA. ⎯ ıⅰP

THE STUDY AND PRACTICE OF GLOBAL LEADERSHIP

Edited by

GAMA PERRUCI
Marietta College, USA

United Kingdom – North America – Japan
India – Malaysia – China

Emerald Publishing Limited
Howard House, Wagon Lane, Bingley BD16 1WA, UK

First edition 2022

Reprints and permissions service
Contact: permissions@emeraldinsight.com

British Library Cataloguing in Publication Data
A catalogue record for this book is available from the British Library

ISBN: 978-1-83867-620-9 (Print)
ISBN: 978-1-83867-617-9 (Online)
ISBN: 978-1-83867-619-3 (Epub)

ISSN: 2058-8801

ISOQAR certified
Management System,
awarded to Emerald
for adherence to
Environmental
standard
ISO 14001:2004.

ISOQAR
REGISTERED

Certificate Number 1985
ISO 14001

INVESTOR IN PEOPLE

This book is dedicated to Dr Gamaliel Perruci. His legacy lives in his students, family and friends, and his wonderfully insightful books, like this one. Gama was a courageous and kind leader, and we are fortunate to have had him in our lives. Gama's mantra waś "give back the gift." And he certainly did through his service as board chair for the International Leadership Association. This book was his last gift to the leadership field. In his native Portuguese, we say: 'Muito Obrigado, Gama!'

CONTENTS

PART II – THE STUDY OF GLOBAL LEADERSHIP

PART III – THE PRACTICE OF GLOBAL LEADERSHIP

ABOUT THE CONTRIBUTORS

Marco Aponte-Moreno is an Associate Professor of Global Business at Saint Mary's College of California. His research in global leadership looks at how the arts can be used to develop leadership skills in cross-cultural settings. He obtained his PhD from the Graduate Center of the City University of New York, focusing on leadership discourse analysis. He has a BA in languages from the University of Paris (Sorbonne-Nouvelle) and is originally from Caracas, Venezuela.

Jeff Bourgeois is an Assistant Professor of Global Leadership at the Indiana Institute of Technology. Previously, he taught Leadership Studies in China, Rome, and San Diego. His research agenda highlights cultural implications on leadership education, university presidents, and transnational higher education. Recent publications explore the experiences of and support for foreign-born leadership educators. He received his PhD in Leadership Studies from the University of San Diego. Correspondence can be sent to jeffb@sandiego.edu

Michael Cox, PhD, is a Professor Emeritus in Leadership and former Director, Center for Studies in Leadership at the University of Guelph. He is experienced in complex leadership initiatives in defense, government, NGO, health and United Nations Development Program; Canadian International Development Agency; Canada-China Management Program and Visiting Fellow in collaborative leadership research at the Australian Defence Force Academy. He can be contacted at: drmcoxfaculty@gmail.com

Kathleen A. Curran, PhD, is a Global Leadership Development Researcher, Coach, Facilitator, and Consultant; and Principal of Intercultural Systems, established in Singapore in 1996 and active worldwide. As an Institute for Social Innovation Fellow at Fielding Graduate University, she focuses her praxis on global leader identity and global talent development. Recent publications include "Developing Global Resonance for Global Leadership" (*Leadership and Power in International Development*) and "Global Identity Tensions for Global Leaders" (*Advances in Global Leadership*).

Beth Fisher-Yoshida is a Professor of Professional Practice, the Director of the MS in Negotiation and Conflict Resolution program, the Director of the Youth, Peace and Security Project, all at Columbia University. Her main areas of practice, research and writing involve women and negotiation, intercultural communication, narrative, youth leadership and CMM. She received her PhD in Human and Organizational Systems and MA in Organization Development from Fielding Graduate University and is a Certified Clinical Sociologist (CCS).

Trisha Gott, PhD, is an Assistant Professor and Associate Director at the Staley School of Leadership Studies at Kansas State University. She teaches undergraduate, graduate, and professional coursework related to the ethical dimensions of leadership and leadership development. Since 2016, she has served as Co-PI and Co-director for the Mandela Washington Fellowship Civic Engagement and Leadership Institute at Kansas State University.

Mikinari Higano, PhD, established the very first in Japan academic leadership program for undergraduate students at Rikkyo University in 2006. In 2016, he moved to Waseda University and started another program to start from scratch. Now he consults many other universities on the introduction of leadership education curricula. He wrote a chapter on "New Leadership Education and Deep Active Learning" for the anthology *Deep Active Learning: Toward Greater Depth in University Education* (Springer).

Brett Hinds is Ford Motor Company's global Chief Engineer for electrified vehicle battery systems. He has been with Ford's global powertrain operations since 1990 upon graduation from Lawrence Technological University with a BSME degree. He later earned a MS in Engineering Management from Oakland University (1996) and a PhD in Leadership from Benedictine University (2020). His doctoral dissertation focused on understanding global leaders' power with global followers.

Tina Huesing is a Chief Consultant at Wyrmwood Consulting, a networked consulting company specializing in helping people and organizations be their best. Previously, she was the Senior Director Six Sigma for Motorola EMEA and is a certified master black belt. She holds an MBA from Thunderbird, Global School of Management and a PhD from Benedictine University's Center for Values-Driven Leadership. She has lived and worked in Europe, The Middle East, India, China, and New Zealand.

Amber A. Johnson is a Strategy Consultant who helps organizations enhance collaboration, shape culture, improve communication, and drive results. She completed her Ph.D. in Values-Driven Leadership at Benedictine University in 2020. Her doctoral dissertation focused on how global organizations can lead successful change initiatives. Previously, she spent 11 years with the Center for Values-Driven Leadership at Benedictine University, 7 years with global humanitarian organization World Vision, and was a US Peace Corps volunteer.

Brandon W. Kliewer is an Associate Professor of Civic Leadership in the Mary Lynn and Warren Staley School of Leadership Studies at Kansas State University. He studies leadership in organizations and democracy through the lens of civic capacity, leadership coaching, group dynamics, dialogic process consulting, democratic theory, and systems change. He holds a PhD from The University of Georgia in political science. He can be reached at bkliewer@ksu.edu

Wanda Krause, PhD, is the Program Head of the MA in Global Leadership Program and an Associate Professor in the School of Leadership Studies at Royal Roads University. Her work focuses on Middle East politics, civil society, human rights issues, evaluation, women's participation, and global leadership. Her books include *Civil Society and Women Activists in the Middle East: Islamic and Secular Organizations in Egypt* and *Women in Civil Society: The State, Islamism, and Networks in the UAE.*

Sean Lee is a Writer and Illustrator of the human condition. His current project *Homo Ubuntu: Our Paleolithic Legacy in the 21st Century* is the second in a series *The Algorithmocene*. His pre-pandemic career was in technology, innovation, and sustainable development, holding a variety of research, management, and consulting positions within public, private, small, and large institutions. He holds several patents and a PhD in Physics from the University of Florida.

Kaitlin Long is an Administrator for Student Programs at the Mary Lynn and Warren Staley School of Leadership Studies at Kansas State University. She manages global and local service-learning programs and leadership programs to prepare students for the transition post-graduation. She earned her master's degree from Ball State University and serves on the management team for the Leadership in Civic Engagement Institute for Mandela Washington Fellows at Kansas State University. She can be reached at KaitlinL@ksu.edu

James D. Ludema, PhD, is the Dean of the School of Business at Calvin University. His book *The Appreciative Inquiry Summit: A Practitioner's Guide for Leading Large-Scale Change* is widely considered a classic in the field. He has lived and worked in Asia, Africa, Europe, Latin America, and North America and has served as a consultant to a variety of organizations including GlaxoSmithKline, BP, McDonald's, US Cellular, the US Navy and many local and international NGOs.

Wendy E. Rowe, PhD, is a Professor in the School of Leadership and the Founder of the MA Global Leadership program, Royal Roads University. She teaches strategic leadership, organizational change, international development, action research, and research methods. She has a 30-year history of leadership practice and research within the United States, Canada, Kenya, Ecuador, Dominican Republic, India, New Zealand, and Australia, using models of collaboration, transformational change, and developmental evaluation to enhance organizational and leadership capacities.

Lorraine Stefani, PhD, is Emeritus Professor of Higher Education at the University of Auckland, an accredited leadership coach, and independent researcher. She has an impressive publication record including books and book chapters on a range of academic and leadership development topics. She has provided leadership consultancy in many countries including projects for the NZ Ministry of Health and the Ministry of Higher Education in Saudi Arabia. Currently, she coaches individuals in New Zealand, Australia, and Pakistan.

Randal Joy Thompson (PhD, Fielding) is a Fellow with the Institute for Social Innovation, Fielding Graduate University. Her publications include:

Reimagining Leadership on the Commons: Shifting the Paradigm for a More Ethical, Equitable, and Just World; Proleptic Leadership on the Commons: Ushering in a New Global Order; Leadership and Power in International Development: Navigating the Intersections of Gender, Culture, Context, and Sustainability; many book chapters; and articles in journals.

Mary Tolar, PhD, serves as the Director of the Staley School of Leadership Studies, Kansas State University, providing learning experiences aligned with the mission of "developing knowledgeable, ethical, caring, inclusive leaders for a diverse and changing world." Her teaching, research, and service center on the art and practice of civic leadership development. She supports the Mandela Washington Fellowship Civic Engagement and Leadership Institute at Kansas State University as institute faculty and in her administrative role.

Yulia Tolstikov-Mast, PhD, is a Global Leadership Scholar, Doctoral Faculty, Consultant, and Author. Originally from Russia, she was a Founding Faculty Indiana Tech's PhD in Global Leadership Program and is a Global Mindset Inventory Certified Facilitator with wide consulting experience. Her scholarship appears in *Advances in Global Leadership* and the *Journal of Leadership Education*, among others. She led a multi-stage study of Russian followership and is the Co-Investigator in Russia for the GLOBE 2020 Project.

Éliane Ubalijoro, PhD, is the Executive Director of Sustainability in the Digital Age and the Future Earth Montreal Hub. She is a Professor of Practice at McGill University and a Research Professor at Concordia University. She is a Member of Rwanda's National Science and Technology Council and Presidential Advisor Council. She is a Member of the Impact Advisory Board of the Global Alliance for a Sustainable Planet as well as the Capitals Coalition Supervisory Board.

Michael Useem, PhD, is a Professor of Management and Faculty Director of the Leadership Center and McNulty Leadership Program at the Wharton School, University of Pennsylvania. His teaching includes MBA, executive-MBA, and executive courses on management, leadership, and governance. He is the author of *The Leader's Checklist, The Leadership Moment,* and *The Edge: How Ten CEOs Learned to Lead – and the Lessons for Us All,* and he can be reached at useem@wharton.upenn.edu

Jennie L. Walker, PhD, is an Associate Professor and Lead Faculty for Business Leadership at Forbes School of Business & Technology at University of Arizona Global Campus. She specializes in developing leaders and organizations for success in complex, diverse, and increasingly global environments. For the past 20 years, she has provided professional education and coaching in leadership development, talent management and organizational effectiveness for multinational organizations and as a Professor and Executive in higher education.

James Warn, PhD, is a Visiting Fellow and Former Interim Head, School of Business, Australian Defence Force Academy at the University of New South Wales. He is experienced in developing and delivering leadership education at a Masters level and providing professional leadership development to career professionals. He has consulted on projects addressing organizational change and published on leadership and immigrant entrepreneurship. He is currently working as an organizational psychologist and can be contacted on LinkedIn.

Brett Whitaker is an Associate Professor and Chair in the Department of Leadership Studies at Fort Hays State University (FHSU). He holds a PhD in Global Leadership from Indiana Tech. His research and teaching interests include global leadership, global issues, leadership education, and curricular design. He may be reached at blwhitaker@fhsu.edu

ABOUT THE EDITOR

Gama Perruci, PhD, was the Dean of the McDonough Center at Marietta College in Ohio and served as a Leadership Education Consultant for *The New York Times*, a Facilitator for the Young African Leaders Initiative, and a Facilitator for the leadership programs at Dartmouth College's Rockefeller Center. He was also a frequent guest on the *BBC* and served as a Member of the Ronald Reagan Presidential Library's Academic Advisory Council and as the Board Chair of the International Leadership Association. He is the author of several books including *Global Leadership: A Transnational Perspective*; *Teaching Leadership: Bridging Theory and Practice* with Sadhana Warty Hall; and *Understanding Leadership: An Arts and Humanities Approach* with Robert M. McManus.

INTRODUCTION

When we first began this book project, little did we know that it would be deeply impacted by a global epidemic. At the time, globalization seemed to be a giant seemingly unstoppable force changing the international state system (Stearns, 2020). Then the COVID-19 virus hit, borders closed, and the global market collapsed.

It would be tempting to see recent global health events as undoing all of our understanding of globalization in the past decades. However, even a global pandemic cannot hide the reality of a highly interconnected world. It took a ship running aground in the Suez Canal in March 2021 for us to be reminded that the world continues to be highly dependent on global trade and that the web of interconnectedness still shapes Global Leadership. The ship, Ever Given, was owned by a Japanese company, registered in Panama, operated by a Taiwanese transportation organization, managed by a Germany company, and at the time it ran aground, staffed by a crew of 25 Indians. For almost a full week (March 23–29), the Ever Given traffic jam dominated global news and led to – by one estimate – $900 million in "damages," including lost revenue and compensation for the labor and equipment used to free the ship (Farzan, 2021).

The global pandemic also accelerated the use of communication technology to challenge closed borders. Despite lockdowns, Zoom became a verb, and working remotely gained wide acceptance (Haag, 2021). While the pandemic disrupted air travel, organizations found ways to collaborate across borders in new and significant ways. It will be interesting to see whether the traditional view of working in the office will go back to "normal" after the global pandemic ends.

This book serves as a reminder that Global Leadership will continue to be relevant as an area of study and practice. The topics in this edited volume are broken down into three sections. First, we will examine how globalization is impacting human relations in the new millennium.

Leadership is examined as a process that has five components – leaders, followers, goals, context, and norms (McManus & Perruci, 2019). As a human phenomenon, it involves leaders and followers pursuing a goal. Since the 1950s, we have recognized that the organizational context shapes the character of the leader-follower relationship (Northouse, 2013). At the end of the twentieth century, our focus turned to the new global context that globalization has brought about. We are now paying close attention to the different cultural norms and values that are influencing the leader–follower relationship (Mendenhall et al., 2018). We can no longer assume that leaders and followers will be using the same cultural map when making decisions. Managing intercultural conflict has become a key issue in Global Leadership (Perruci, 2019).

We are now searching for a new shared narrative of leadership. Global leaders must find ways to increase the level of collaboration across the cultural divide. Technology can help by creating opportunities for collaboration. However, leaders still need to use communication skills to form effective bonds with their followers. We may need new modes of communication that will foster a sense of community among the leadership participants. In this volume, we suggest that maybe we are experiencing the rise of the "homo ubuntu," a reference to the traditional African perspective of communitarianism.

Globalization is also giving rise to new sources of identity, as leaders seek to connect with their followers at the transnational level. Issues, such as climate change, resonate with individuals across continents. Leaders who have a global mindset are more apt to closely connect with followers from different cultures who share similar concerns about these issues. In this book, we do not assume that the development of this global mindset happens accidentally. That is the product of the study and practice of Global Leadership.

In the second section of the book, we focus on the study of Global Leadership. In recent decades, Western higher-education institutions have expanded the number of programs that are designed to prepare leaders for this new global context. Western-based leadership programs have been exported to different parts of the world. In this book, we highlight such an initiative in China. We also stress the importance of students having an international experience that allows them to expand their global-leadership skills. While the main focus has been on undergraduate study-abroad experiences, this book takes a different view by examining the impact that study abroad has on graduate students. The study of Global Leadership is not solely a Western phenomenon. In this book, we explore the rise of leadership education in Japan, as an example of a non-Western development shaped by the rise of globalization.

The third section of the book focuses on the practice of Global Leadership. When examining the practice of large corporations from different cultural traditions, we notice that some common practices emerge that transcend local cultural traditions. However, the data also show that leadership also continues to reflect the national setting. In other words, we should not be ready to discard the local/national context because of globalization. The picture that emerges from this analysis is a complex combination of the new with the old. Global leaders must develop new skills that can incorporate an intercultural perspective as the "new language" of Global Leadership. We need to develop adaptive transformational systems, while at the same time exhibiting a complex "global consciousness."

We use key issues as illustrative of how the Global Leadership agenda is shifting away from the Western-dominated individualistic perspective. Globalization is dramatically expanding the movement of both capital and human resources. Immigration is not just highlighted by refugee crises, but also the way technology is driving the rise of new industries that are shifting talent at a transnational level. Global women leaders also are emerging as important players on the global leadership stage. We conclude the book by highlighting some of the leadership challenges that global leaders will face in this century. We call this new crisis context "leadership at the edge of experience."

The general picture that should emerge from the chapters in this edited volume is one of hope. While the challenges are immense, we do not disregard human ingenuity and our ability to transform our human systems to adapt to the new reality. For those who see the end of the global pandemic as a return back to "normality," the following pages may come across as dissonant. When crises arise, the world is transformed – by design and by inevitability – to the extent that we never go back to the way it once was. Rather, a new world emerges, and we once again learn its "new language" and come to see it as the new normal (Ashton & Toland, 2021). For those who thrive whenever we move into a new normal, this book will serve as a path forward to explore the possibilities that await us!

REFERENCES

Ashton, J., & Toland, S. (2021). *The new normal: A roadmap to resilience in the pandemic era*. HarperCollinsPublishers.

Farzan, A. (2021). Egypt seizes the Ever Given, saying its owners own nearly $1 billion for Suez Canal traffic jam. *The Washington Post*, April 13. Retrieved April 25, 2021, from https://www.washingtonpost.com/world/2021/04/13/ever-given-seized-egypt/

Haag, M. (2021). Remote work is here to stay. Manhattan may never be the same. *The New York Times*, March 29. Retrieved April 25, 2021, from https://www.nytimes.com/2021/03/29/nyregion/remote-work-coronavirus-pandemic.html

McManus, R., & Perruci, G. (2019). *Understanding leadership: An arts and humanities perspective* (2nd ed.). Routledge.

Mendenhall, M., Osland, J., Bird, A., Oddou, G.R., Stevens, M.J., Maznevski, M., & Stahl, G.K. (2018). *Global leadership: Research, practice, and development* (3rd ed.). Routledge.

Northouse, P. (2013). *Leadership: Theory and practice* (6th ed.). SAGE.

Perruci, G. (2019). *Global leadership: A transnational perspective*. Routledge.

Stearns, P. (2020). *Globalization in world history* (3rd ed.). Routledge.

PART I

THE CONNECTION BETWEEN LEADERSHIP AND THE GLOBAL CONTEXT

1

THE GLOBAL DIMENSION OF LEADERSHIP

GAMA PERRUCI

INTRODUCTION

We live in an increasingly interdependent world that pulls us together – through the forces of economic, political and cultural integration – while at the same time we battle the forces of fragmentation (Barber, 2001). While it is true that technological innovation builds connections across borders, leaders can also use new means of communication to divide and conquer through nationalist fervor. These are indeed conflicting times for the study and practice of Global Leadership. We laud leaders who create a compelling vision for their followers, but quite often those aspirations create an "us" versus "them" dynamic that challenges peace and stability.

This chapter provides an overview of the global dimension of leadership. The rapid pace of globalization is forcing us to confront the growing influence of the cultural context on the leader–follower relationship. We can no longer assume that the two sides (leaders and followers) will use the same cultural map. Global leaders must transcend local and national cultures and lead at the transnational level (Perruci, 2018).

The first section of the chapter reviews the empirical study of leadership. Over the past century, there has been an evolution of our thinking about the word "leadership" – moving from being synonymous with "leader," to a complex process that involves many components, including the cultural context. Following this historical overview, the chapter introduces the Five Components of Leadership Model, which serves as a framework for studying Global Leadership. We will use this model to discuss the interplay between the historical context and the influence of cultural values and norms in the leader–follower relationship. The chapter ends with an examination of key historical developments (e.g., the rise of the Westphalian international system; globalization) and how they have created four different scopes of leading (local, national, international, global). We live in a challenging new century in which all four scopes are vying for relevance. We are only beginning to grasp the full meaning of these conflicting forces of collaboration and competition.

THE EMPIRICAL STUDY OF LEADERSHIP

Why is Global Leadership a thriving academic area today? There are two ways of looking at this question and their concomitant answers – one focused on the evolution of the theoretical field, and the other focused on the practice of leadership. In this section, we will look at the first perspective (the theory), while the next section will look at the practice (the historical forces that are shaping our interest in Global Leadership).

The Evolution of Theory-Building

When we trace the evolution of the empirical study of leadership, an interesting pattern emerges. It has gone from a simplistic focus on the leader, all the way to a consideration of the complex influences of context and culture. The traditional leadership literature breaks down this evolution into five general phases. In the late 1800s, leadership was associated first with the traits of leaders – the Trait Approach (e.g., Ferris, 1889). To study leadership meant the identification of the ideal characteristics of great leaders (The Great Man Theory). In practice, aspiring leaders hoped to find ways to imitate these ideal traits. Bibliographies were a common way to promote leadership development. We expected leaders to be well versed in the lives and accomplishments of historical figures from the ancient (Western) world.

By the 1930s, scholars were frustrated by the lack of consensus around those ideal traits. Great leaders seemed to come in many forms and shapes. After all, how could one reconcile the "empirical" observation of a leader's height (suggesting that leaders tended to be taller than non-leaders) with

Napoleon Bonaparte's successful military campaigns? By putting great leaders on a pedestal, did leadership scholars paradoxically make them inaccessible? How could anyone possibly become the next George Washington? From a theory-building standpoint, these great leaders may have had common traits – e.g., fortitude, calmness under pressure, clear communication, integrity – but how do we translate them into maxims? Do they work in all circumstances?

The Behavioral Revolution in the 1940s and 1950s widened the scope of the leader-centric approach by considering the interaction between leaders and followers (e.g., Stogdill & Coons, 1957). Scholars, in this second phase of the empirical study of leadership, began to pay attention to how leaders behaved (leadership styles) and the impact that their behavior had on outcomes (goal achievement). During the second phase, followers began to appear in the literature as an actor (albeit limited and secondary) in leadership. Another aspect of the Behavioral Approach was the consideration of the goal in leadership. As leaders motivated followers to accomplish certain goals, a common definition of leadership emerged – albeit still leader-centric.

By the 1950s and 1960s, scholars introduced the importance of context in the leader–follower relationship – the third phase in the empirical study of leadership. Fiedler (1967), one of the best-known Contingency Approach theorists, argued that there is no single best leadership style, as proposed by the trait and behavioral approaches. Rather, effective leaders are able to adapt their styles according to different situations. Fiedler's research yielded three situational variables – the strength of the relationship between leaders and followers (leader–member relations), the clarity of the task (task structure), and the degree to which a leader has legitimate power (position power). The interplay of these three variables, Fiedler argued, defined the degree of a leader's effectiveness. Ideally, effective leaders have a strong relationship with their followers, are able to define clear tasks and structures, and hold strong legitimate power.

By the 1970s, scholars paid closer attention to the leader–follower relationship – the fourth phase in the empirical study of leadership. They moved away from a leader-centric approach to consider the ways both leaders and followers contributed to successful outcomes. Burns (1978) became a pioneer in the study of Transformational Leadership, in which both leaders and followers play a significant role in the leadership process.

The growing importance of followers in leadership gave rise in the 1980s to the study of Followership as a legitimate theoretical inquiry in the literature (e.g., Chaleff, 2009). Followers were now full participants, endowed with power and fully capable of contributing to the leader–follower relationship.

By the end of the 1980s, leadership was no longer viewed through the eyes of the leader. Instead, leadership was conceptualized as a "process" in which different components played a role. But we were not finished with the evolution. The 1990s brought on the fifth phase of the empirical study of leadership – the focus on how cultural norms influence the leader–follower relationship. Globalization played a significant role in this new preoccupation on culture (Braman & Sreberny-Mohammadi, 1996; Rhinesmith, 1996). As economic and cultural integration intensified, intercultural conflict also became salient. Scholars became not only interested in comparing how different cultures viewed leadership, but also on the skill set that leaders needed in order to become effective at the global level (e.g., Lustig & Koester, 1993).

By the beginning of the twenty-first century, the study of Global Leadership had become a critical subfield of Leadership Studies (Mendenhall et al., 2018). Leadership could no longer be studied without considering the cultural context of the leader–follower relationship (Henson, 2016). This book is a product of the global processes that have given rise to the importance of using culture as a variable in our understanding of leadership. We can no longer assume that leaders and followers are using the same cultural map in their leadership. In fact, many of the conflicts between the two arise from their different cultural perspectives.

It may seem obvious at the beginning of our new century that the world is made up of many cultures, but for the scholar living at the beginning of the twentieth century, the Western world was treated as the standard for examining leadership. We have moved away from the Western leader-centric approach. The study and practice of leadership has become a complex, multifaceted tapestry that invites a wide variety of theories, models, and interpretations. This explosion of intellectual exploration may seem daunting and hopeless for those who would hope for the development of a cohesive theory of leadership, but on the bright side, the rise of Global Leadership has opened the field to creativity, innovation, and deep learning. The West has much to learn from non-Western approaches, and vice-versa.

The Five Components of Leadership Model

In the previous section, we were able to trace the evolution of our under-standing of leadership from a simplistic approach (leadership as synonymous to leader), to a more complex perspective (leadership as a process). During each phase, we noted that different components were added to the equation. By the time the new millennium rolled around, five components had emerged as important ingredients of the leadership process – leader, follower, goal, context, and cultural norms/values.

Burns (1978), highlighted in the previous section, offered a clear definition of leadership involving leaders, followers, and goal. McManus and Perruci (2015) expanded on it and included two more – context and cultural norms. The emerging definition ties all the five components together into a single definition:

> *Leadership is the process by which leaders and followers develop*
> *a relationship and work together toward a goal (or goals) within*
> *an environmental context shaped by cultural norms and values.*
> *(McManus & Perruci, 2015, p. 15)*

There are some key aspects of this definition that are important to highlight. First, there are arrows pointing both directions from the leaders' and followers' circles – emphasizing the mutuality of the relationship. Two circles, representing leaders and followers, were also deliberately made the same size. Power differentials between the two would dictate the relative sizes of each, but that depends on the context, which surrounds all three components – leaders, followers, and goals. In a crisis situation, we expect the leader to exert more control of the situation. However, in a democratic election, we assume that power flows from the voting constituents (followers) to the candidates (aspiring leaders). In that case, the circle representing the followers would be larger than that of the leader.

Second, the contextual circle enveloping the leaders, followers, and goals captures the idea that leadership does not take place in a vacuum. A few years back when I was co-teaching an International Business course with the CEO of a global enterprise based in Canada, we asked our students to develop a business plan for a new product to be introduced in a particular country. As part of the assignment, we asked our students to research (and incorporate the information into their business plan) the historical, economic, and political context of the chosen country. The students seemed troubled by that request. After all, in their minds, they were taking an international business course. The CEO was adamant – how can you understand the local market without uncovering the historical forces that are shaping the country today? Furthermore, how can you consider the likelihood of success without taking into consideration the political and economic climate of that country? The lesson became clear – we cannot look at one issue (introducing a product to a new market) in isolation. We have to connect several dots in order to gain a deeper understanding of the context.

Third, the context circle is enveloped by yet another circle – representing cultural norms and values. Everything we do involves culture. We in the West sometimes fail to recognize this important linkage between leadership and culture. I am always amused when my students are studying abroad and say – and meaning it – how much culture that country has. All countries, including theirs, are "culture rich." From our perspective, our behavior is "normal"; therefore, it is often seen as devoid of cultural roots. When we step out of that cultural setting and enter another cultural environment, the degree of difference clouds our judgment as to how much culture a country "has." In reality, the biggest culture shock for many of my students takes place not when they go abroad, but when they come back to the United States and begin to interpret their own behavior through a new set of cultural lenses.

Global Leadership pays close attention to the two enveloping circles – context and cultural norms. On the context side, there is the recognition that transnational forces in the new millennium are changing the global context. The emergence of China, for instance, as a dynamic economic power has considerably changed the political and economic environment at a global level. The move toward political and economic integration among the European countries has had a significant impact on transnational migration and business enterprises. The rise of high technology mega-corporations, such as Google, Facebook, and Amazon, affects communication, commerce, social interaction, and information sharing across the globe. The climate change debates are not taking place in a geographical vacuum. They are part of dramatic shifts in biodiversity, climate patterns, and health, among other issues, that transcend national borders.

Based on these changes, I have slightly modified the McManus and Perruci definition of leadership to offer a definition of Global Leadership:

> *Global leadership is the process by which global leaders seek to develop a relationship with their followers in order to accomplish common goals shaped by a global context with competing cultural norms and values. (Perruci, 2018, p. 33)*

This definition draws attention to a *global* (transnational) context, and it does not take for granted that leaders and followers uphold the same cultural values. In fact, the definition assumes that Global Leaders, by leading in a transnational environment, deal with competing cultural norms and values. The new global context is fueling the two conflicting forces – globalism and nationalism – that are pulling global organizations and societies in opposite directions. On the one hand, globalization is creating global norms that sometimes challenge local values. For instance, anti-corruption campaigns fostered by international institutions can change local practices rooted in centuries old norms and values. On the other hand, populist leaders can also energize local constituents to rise against "cultural imperialism." This nationalist backlash does not take place in developing economies only. In the United States and parts of Europe, charismatic leaders have demonized globalization as having a negative effect on local industries – e.g., the coal industry, basic manufacturing, small businesses. The fear that local cultural norms are being assaulted by global processes beyond the control of individual societies is real – and it generates palpable anger, resentment, and parochial sentiments.

THE GLOBAL DIMENSION OF LEADERSHIP

In the previous section, we stressed the importance of understanding why we now focus on theories that involve cultural norms and values. Our fascination with cultures has a historical basis – in other words, it is not accidental. In this section, we move from the theoretical (the Five Components of Leadership Model) to the application side – explaining how we got here historically.

We have grown accustomed now to the phrase "we live in an increasingly interconnected world," but this world was not created overnight. It is the product of many political and economic transformations. In this section, we highlight two, in particular. On the political front, we have a system of sovereign states that prize independence and the national interest. On the economic front, the forces of globalization move individuals, organizations, and states to collaborate and compete. The combination of these two dynamics creates paradoxical forces – fragmentation and integration – all happening at once. How does one lead effectively in this complex context? That is the key question of the twenty-first century.

The Westphalian International System

The world today is divided into political units called states (Miller, 1994). They have borders, a government, a population (citizens), and are recognized as sovereign. We can quibble over the fact that some states have borders that are not clearly delineated (e.g., border disputes between warring states), or the legitimacy of a government to speak on behalf of a particular population (e.g., dictatorships), or even whether a particular population should have its own state, but the international system that we have today is generally viewed as sacrosanct – as if it was always so.

In reality, we know from history that indeed that was not always the case. The Roman Empire ruled the known world for centuries before it was challenged and overthrown in 476 CE. Much of the stability that western Europe enjoyed during the Pax Romana period was thrown into disarray as regional rulers vied for power. Centralization of power was achieved once again with the rise of the Roman Catholic Church, which brought European monarchies under its authority. For roughly 1,000 years, the Church ruled with an iron fist and provided stability in the continent.

As the power of the Church began to decline in the 1400s, local monarchs saw this as an opportunity to exert greater influence. The Protestant Reformation in the 1500s further divided Europe into competing powers (Larkins, 2010). By the early 1600s, Europe was primed to face a major conflagration. For 30 years (1618–1648), European monarchs fought one another in a complicated tapestry of alliances that did not always align with religious affiliation. The Thirty Years War, as the conflict became known in history, did not result in a decisive victory for any sides. In the end, exhausted and economically drained monarchs signed the Peace of Westphalia as a recognition that fighting did not offer any advantage.

All sides agreed to pull back and leave one another alone – under certain conditions, of course – and thus emerged in 1648 the "Westphalian" international system (Croxton, 2013). The monarchs agreed to recognize one another as sovereign, with delineated territorial borders. The immediate impact of that peace arrangement was the clear division between domestic and foreign affairs. Each "country" was given the right to adopt any laws that could not be challenged by the others. Another important aspect of this newly developed international system was the assumption of "equality" among all the countries. Regardless of their economic power, each country had the right to exist as an independent political unit.

This European creation is still the standard for political relations at the international level. We know that in reality, countries compete for power and at times violate the sovereignty of other states. The Westphalian international system, however, is still considered the legitimate legal framework today. Much of our discussion about globalization, as the next section will cover, centers on the perceived decline of sovereignty and territorial borders. Some have suggested that we are entering a post-Westphalian period (Jacobsen et al., 2008; Kegley & Raymond, 2002), but it is too soon to tell. States are still considered the basic unit of international relations. However, the system has come under considerable pressure under globalization, the next topic for discussion.

The Rise of Globalization 3.0

Just as the Roman Empire and the Catholic Church exerted great influence over a vast territorial expanse, Globalization now has become a true transnational force. This time, however, the power center is invisible. There is no central government that speaks for Globalization. Even its own beneficiaries, such as the United States and parts of Europe, rail against it. Everyone is affected by it.

Globalization is not a new process. Friedman (2005) actually argues that we are witnessing the third wave of globalization. The first wave, Globalization 1.0, dates back to the late 1400s, as European explorers sought new routes to Asian markets. As the Middle East experienced the rise of Islamic rulers – often hostile to Western monarchs – explorers looked for ways around it through the seas. The accidental "discovery" of the Americas fueled the expansion of trade and colonialism, which opened new markets for the extraction of resources. As Europe became more dependent on raw materials and commodities from its colonies, the world became more integrated under European cultural influences. The rise of the international system, outlined in the previous section, was in fact a product of Globalization 1.0 – a European invention that went global.

The rise of nationalism – another European invention – in the 1700s only stoked interstate rivalries, as they competed for economic and political power. National identity came to be associated with the sovereign state.

Important national symbols, such as the flag and currency, served as unifying representations of the nation masked by the sovereignty of the state. To be powerful politically, militarily, and economically as a state meant to be respected as a nation. Under Globalization 1.0, the two (nation and state) became closely intertwined.

By the 1800s, the Industrial Revolution had a significant impact on global economic relations. As the British Empire emerged as an economic and political powerhouse, large corporations, under the guise of "free trade," connected economies across the globe. That process was accelerated in the early 1900s, as the United States emerged as a new global economic and political superpower. Multinational corporations (MNCs) ushered in what Friedman called Globalization 2.0. MNCs rose as important players on the global stage because of their transnational operations (Bassiry, 1980; May, 2006). Some, in fact, rivaled the gross national product of countries in the developing world. In certain regions of the world, Western MNCs wielded great power against local governments, sometimes shaping elections and social movements.

MNCs intensified the global economic integration process not only through trade (e.g., the exchange of commodities and manufactured products) but also through the flow of capital and human resources. Executives from developed countries traveled extensively on a global scale, particularly after World War II, as the United States promoted the stability of markets and expansion of investments across borders. Global travel, obviously, existed under Globalization 1.0, as the commercial exploits in the Americas, Africa, and Asia would attest. However, the difference now laid in the dramatic increase in the volume of transnational relations.

By the end of the twentieth century, as technological changes enveloped the world with revolutions in communications and transportation, Friedman argues that we began to experience the third wave of Globalization (3.0). The Internet had a revolutionary effect on the way individuals were able to collaborate across borders. Once again, the volume of exchange is what made this new phase so stunning. The world "shrank" – or became "flat," in Friedman's words.

The beginning of the new millennium posed a new challenge to the international system. The neat world of sovereign states came under attack. MNCs, with their growing global supply-chain production, relied on porous borders to sustain the flow of information, capital, goods, services, and ultimately, people. The global view of MNCs clashed with the states' national interests. As many MNCs moved to low-wage production sites in the developing world, national governments questioned the national allegiance of MNCs. More and more, MNCs built their business strategies using a global view, as opposed to specific countries.

Globalization 3.0 also freed the individual to become an important actor on the world stage. This wave challenged the association of national identity with individual states. Migration emerged as a key issue in the third wave. The Silicon Valley, for instance, relies heavily on foreign-born engineers to support the growth of high-tech start-ups. International students make up a sizeable chunk of the graduate-school population of Western universities, particularly in STEM (science, technology, engineering, and math) fields. As individuals cross borders and clash with local values, we observe two phenomena – cultural shifts (adaptation by local cultures) and cultural backlash (rejection of the immigrant's cultural norms). Both forces (integration and fragmentation) are now part of the new reality for global leaders.

We see both forces at work in the global pandemic. Countries have closed their borders and imposed restrictions on the free movement of their citizens. At the same time, their economies were severely affected by the economic slowdown on a global scale. Disruption of the supply chains negatively affected production across continents. As travel was curtailed, communication technologies, such as Zoom, became new standards of information sharing at the transnational level. The end of the global pandemic will not mean a return to the old "normal." Globalization will bounce back, but the individual countries will have to assess their level of vulnerability to corporations that show loyalty to a global (as opposed to a national) context. At the individual level, work has gone remote, which allows human capital to become separated from local communities.

Leading in the New Millennium

Leading in the new millennium is not for the faint-hearted. The three waves of globalization described in the previous section continue to play a role in Global Leadership. The sovereign state is still a powerful actor in the international system. MNCs continue to play a preeminent role in the global economy. Individuals also have more options to move around and use new means of communication and transportation to impact the world.

Friedman's three waves of globalization suggest the emergence of four types of leaders who are playing a role in the new millennium. First, local leaders have always been important at the community level. Globalization impacts local communities, and its leaders mobilize support for or against it. The rise of the Westphalian system of sovereign states created two other categories of leaders – national and international. By slicing territories into discrete units with borders, we created an artificial separation between domestic and foreign affairs. Much of the backlash against Globalization 3.0 today has been led by national leaders who view globalization as damaging to their country's national interest.

In this chapter, I make a distinction between an "international" and a "global" leader. The former refers to a leader of a sovereign state who leads at the interstate level. For instance, the German chancellor and the French president have played an international leadership role through the European Union. The US president after World War II played an international leadership role by rallying the Western states against the Soviet Union. Much of the discussion about the Trump administration's foreign policy (2016–2020) centered on the notion that "America First" deviates from the post-World War II role that the United States played as an international leader.

The term global leaders, however, refers to those who play a role at the transnational level – leaders in organizations that transcend national borders. In particular, I have in mind leaders of MNCs and nongovernmental organizations (NGOs) who have operations at the global level. Global leaders have become particularly salient in transnational issues. For instance, poverty impacts global migration patterns. A single country cannot solve global poverty. States depend on international (e.g., United Nations) and transnational (e.g., the Red Cross) institutions to address it. Oxfam, for instance, describes itself as

> *a global movement of people who are fighting inequality to beat poverty together. We tackle the inequalities that make and keep people poor. We save and protect lives in times of crisis, work with people to build resilience and rebuild their livelihoods and, because we want lasting solutions, we campaign for genuine, durable change. (Oxfam International, 2020)*

As the world becomes more complex and interdependent, all four categories of leaders (local, national, international, and global) will become critical players in finding solutions to pressing issues. Global leaders are not going to solve world hunger, climate change, and the collapse of biodiversity alone. However, they can help mobilize resources by working with local, national, and international leaders. The challenge for Global Leadership lies in the ability of those four types of leaders to collaborate, rather than competing to the detriment of the global common good.

CONCLUDING REMARKS

In this chapter, I have defined Global Leadership as a process that transcends national borders. Globalization 3.0 has empowered individuals to use the latest technological tools to affect issues on a global scale (e.g., movements to bring global awareness against climate change). Social media quickly disseminates information (and disinformation) across borders at a dizzying pace. Events in the corners of the globe quickly spread across regions and create a global dynamic outside the control of local and national leaders.

To focus our theoretical attention on Globalization 3.0, however, does not take away the continuing importance of other actors in the international system (e.g., sovereign states, MNCs); and that is what makes Global Leadership so vexing in the twenty-first century. States are still critical players in the global context. They possess a military capability that cannot be ignored. The difficult relations between the United States and Iran serve as a reminder that the international system has not gone away. Large MNCs have paid close attention to the economic tension between the United States and China, because their investments in both countries are at stake. Local and national leaders are increasingly voicing their dissatisfaction with Globalization 3.0 because of economic dislocation and the impact that it is having on the local job market.

Global leaders – both in the for-profit and nonprofit sectors – are called to forge new alliances with local communities in order to develop solutions to global challenges. On the for-profit side, corporate social responsibility (CSR) has increasingly allowed MNC leaders to invest in communities on a global scale. On the nonprofit side, NGO leaders are forming alliances with local communities to develop solutions that are most appropriate to local needs. At the same time, they are sharing lessons learned that can be applied to other regions of the globe. Through new technologies, successful experiments at the local level can be quickly "exported" to other communities, irrespective of their location in the world. Global leaders can play a catalyst role in bringing different players together to address local, national, international, and global problems.

REFERENCES

Barber, B. (2001). *Jihad vs. McWorld*. Ballantine Books.

Bassiry, R. (1980). *Power vs. profit: Multinational corporation-nation state interaction*. Arno Press.

Braman, S., & Sreberny-Mohammadi, A. (1996). *Globalization, communication and transnational civil society*. Hampton Press.

Burns, J. M. (1978). *Leadership*. Harper & Row, Publishers.

Chaleff, I. (2009). *The courageous follower: Standing up to & for our leaders* (3rd ed.). Berrett-Koehler.

Croxton, D. (2013). *Westphalia: The last Christian peace*. Palgrave Macmillan.

Ferris, G. (1889). *Great leaders: Historic portraits from the great historians*. D. Appleton and Company.

Fiedler, F. (1967). *A theory of leadership effectiveness*. McGraw Hill.

Friedman, T. (2005). *The world is flat: A brief history of the twenty-first century*. Farrar, Straus and Giroux.

Henson, R. (2016). *Successful global leadership: Frameworks for cross-cultural managers and organizations*. Palgrave Macmillan.

Jacobsen, T., Sampford, C., & Thakur, R. (2008). *Re-envisioning sovereignty: The end of Westphalia?* Ashgate.

Kegley, C., & Raymond, G. (2002). *Exorcising the ghost of Westphalia: Building world order in the new millennium*. Prentice Hall.

Larkins, J. (2010). *From hierarchy to anarchy: Territory and politics before Westphalia*. Palgrave Macmillan.

Lustig, M., & Koester, J. (1993). *Intercultural competence: Interpersonal communication across cultures*. HarperCollins College Publishers.

May, C. (2006). (Ed.). *Global corporate power*. Lynne Rienner.

McManus, R., & Perruci, G. (2015). *Understanding leadership: An arts and humanities perspective*. Routledge.

Mendenhall, M., Osland, J., Bird, A., Oddou, G.R., Stevens, M.J., Maznevski, M., & Stahl, G.K. (2018). *Global leadership: Research, practice, and development* (3rd ed.). Routledge.

Miller, L. (1994). *Global order: Values and power in international politics* (3rd ed.). Westview Press.

Oxfam International. (2020). About us. Retrieved January 14, 2020, from https://www.oxfam.org/en/what-we-do/about

Perruci, G. (2018). *Global leadership: A transnational perspective*. Routledge.

Rhinesmith, S. (1996). *A manager's guide to globalization: Six skills for success in a changing world* (2nd ed.). Irwin Professional Pub.

Stogdill, R., & Coons, A. (Eds.). (1957). *Leader behavior: Its description and measurement*. Bureau of Business Research, College of Commerce and Administration, Ohio State University.

2

IN SEARCH OF A SHARED NARRATIVE OF LEADERSHIP

BETH FISHER-YOSHIDA

INTRODUCTION

Organizations need leaders, and effective leadership styles need to fit the demands of the organization. The increase in diversity within organizations makes this more challenging. Narratives differ about what makes a good leader, and there are debates on whether leaders are born or made (Marques, 2010; Northouse, 2016). There is some consensus that more than one style of leadership is needed over time.

This chapter will focus on the challenges diverse organizations pose to leaders as they search for ways to be effective across diversity. Mainly, the challenge in developing a shared narrative of good leadership. Differences in norms, values, customs and practices shape how leadership is seen from various cultural lenses. Diversity will be looked at from the rise of multinational enterprises (MNEs); cultural dimensions and how they show up in the workplace and shape organizational culture; leadership, cross-cultural leadership and the role of narratives on people and leaders; creation of conflict in the workplace that arises from cultural clashes; and suggestions for creating a shared narrative on leadership.

INCREASINGLY DIVERSE ORGANIZATIONS

Globalization and increased diversity in the workforce are not something new. Multinational corporations (MNCs) have grown in number and size since World War II – the increase in overall mobility with access to faster, less expensive and more efficient transportation (Auto Tech Review, 2018; UN.org, 2018); the rise of internet usage and social media becoming more popular and mainstream spreading cultural information to a wider audience (Smart Insights, 2019); and more organizations using virtual work platforms to connect staff members around the world to save time and money on costly business travel (Global Workplace Analytics, 2017).[1]

Increased globalization brings anticipated benefits and challenges and unintended consequences. MNCs are motivated to reach beyond their national borders for a variety of reasons through strategic decision-making operationalizing for sustained growth and viability (García-Canal & Guilleén, 2015). As Garcia-Canal and Guilleén note,

> *the core explanation or the existence of MNEs remains, namely, that in order to pursue international expansion, the firm needs to possess capabilities allowing it to overcome the liability of foreignness; no firm-specific capabilities, no multinationals. (García-Canal & Guilleén, 2015, p. 20)*

Managerial competence was referenced, but the focus is on the agility of doing business in foreign domains from an operational perspective, not a cross-cultural orientation.

The following examples of a few well-known MNCs serve to illustrate just how global they are. ABN AMRO is a Dutch bank existing in five continents of Asia, Europe, Australia, North America, and South America. Adidas, a German clothing company, outsources most of its production to 55 countries. Ford Motor Company, an American car company, manufactures or distributes automobiles across six continents with about 175,000 employees and more than 65 plants worldwide. Hankook Tire and Technology Group is headquartered in South Korea, yet has manufacturing facilities located in South Korea, The People's Republic of China, Hungary, Indonesia, and the United States and technical centers in South Korea, United States, Germany, Japan, and China. SONY Group has its headquarters in Japan and more than 114,000 employees worldwide, consisting of fewer than 50% Japanese and the rest from the United States, Asia-Pacific, China and Hong Kong, the Middle East, Africa, Latin America, and Canada.[2]

PREVALENCE OF MULTINATIONAL ORGANIZATIONS IN THE WORLD

Three of the main sources that shape organizational culture are the leader, the locale, and the values (Fisher-Yoshida & Geller, 2009; Kane-Urrabazo, 2006; Weese, 1996). They are juxtaposed against each other and influence each other. The strength of each will determine the organizational culture. A strong leader will have a significant influence shaping the organizational culture more than the local culture or industry norms and practices. This leader may be influenced by his/her own cultural orientation. In other instances, the organization can be a subsidiary of a company and the local culture may have noticeably different work practices. This will influence the organizational culture, especially because so many of the staff are local and will have an effect on the communication between headquarters and the subsidiary.

Geert Hofstede, one of the earlier leaders in the field of researching organizations with multicultural workforces operating in cross-cultural settings, defines culture as "the collective programming of the mind which distinguishes the members of one human group from another" (1984, p. 21). He also states "Culture, in this sense, includes systems of values; and values are among the building blocks of culture" (1984, p. 21). This is important in an organizational context because when values are not clearly communicated to staff members, they are uncertain about how to live the values, or when they see examples of the values not being lived, it causes dissonance.[3]

People seek understanding of their environments and look for explanations for the phenomena they are experiencing. They seek coherence in themselves and understanding of their environments; they seek coordination in how they are able to communicate and work with others; and they have differing levels of dealing with the unknown or mystery inherent in any situation, especially one that is changing (Pearce, 2007).

CULTURAL DIMENSIONS IN THE WORKPLACE

Hall (1981) named context as one dimension to identify cultural norms and practices. Cultural characteristics of *low context* include a stronger rule-orientation, dependency on verbal communication, knowledge as being transferable, shorter-term relationships. At the other end are cultural characteristics of *high context* known for having longer-term relationships, stronger sense of inside knowledge learned by being part of the group and knowledge having a stronger situational influence. Combining high and low context orientations in the same organization can give pause as to how rule-oriented their practices are and how knowledge is shared and transferred.

Hofstede (1984) conducted research working with a multinational organization, IBM, in 1967 and 1973. He distributed over 116,000 surveys and when analyzed the results were developed into five dimensions of culture. They are: individualism-collectivism, which measures how independently or interdependently people function in groups; power distance, into low and high that relates to how power is shared; masculinity-femininity and how gendered roles are classified; uncertainty avoidance and how well ambiguity is tolerated; and short- or long-term orientation reflecting planning for the future or learning from the past. In more recent years, a sixth dimension was added, indulgence, and that is how much freedom or constraints there are to indulge.

The cultural paradigm of dealing with ambiguity (Hofstede, 1984) or how specific or diffuse communication is (Hampden-Turner & Trompenaars, 2000) addresses cultural comfort levels in managing the unknown. This cultural paradigm on a continuum has at one end a lot of flexibility and ability to continue onward even if the direction is not clear. On the other end is a high level of stress with ambiguity. At this end people like to know where they are headed with as much detail and specificity as possible. The anxiety can be so great it may render them incapable of performing well. "You need to specify what those in your environment care about, what they require, and then match each specific request with your own response" (Hampden-Turner & Trompenaars, 2000, p. 132).

LEADERSHIP CHARACTERISTICS

The literature on leadership stretches far and wide with universal frameworks about what constitutes good leadership.

> *Leadership scholars agree on one thing: They can't come up with*
> *a common definition for leadership. Because of such factors as*
> *growing global influences and generational differences, leadership*

will continue to have different meanings for different people. The bottom line is that leadership is a complex concept for which a determined definition may long be in flux. (Northouse, 2016, p. 5)

The common thread is that it is a process of influence to move a group of individuals toward achieving a common goal. How this is accomplished varies on the type of leader and leadership style, as well as, the context, the goals to be achieved, and the individuals being influenced.

Kouzes and Posner (2002) identified five practices "exemplary leaders" have when they are at their best: model the way, inspire a shared vision, challenge the process, enable others to act, and encourage the heart. Resonant leadership as defined by Boyatzis and McKee (2005) identify three elements to foster renewal and sustained resonance: mindfulness, hope and compassion. Hames (2007) a futurist has identified five literacies of global leadership as: networked intelligence, futuring, strategic navigation, deep design and brand resonance. Bolman and Deal (2003) leadership scholars, state that

Leadership is thus a subtle process of mutual influences fusing thought, feeling, and action to produce cooperative effort in the service of purposes and values embraced by both the leader and the led. (p. 339)

The two points most accepted about leadership is that good leaders need to have the "right stuff" and that good leadership is situational. Framed from a cultural lens, the behaviors of what looks like compassion, for example, in one culture may not translate the same in another.

From the late 1990s, the interest in global leadership has become more of its own field of study because of the prevalence of leaders working in cross-cultural environments (Dickson et al., 2003). There is an ongoing debate about whether characteristics of effective leadership are universal, or whether they are localized, and some argue there is a combination of both qualities (Javidan et al., 2006).

In spite of the rise of MNEs and an increase in cross-cultural working environments, up until the early 1990s there were few studies conducted to ascertain the perceptions and practices of leadership in diverse cultural settings. Gerstner and Day (1994) conducted a study across eight countries and rated 59 attributes to compare their leadership prototypes. They found "that there are reliable differences in the leadership perceptions of members from the various countries" they sampled in their study (p. 130). One implication is that in order to be influential people need to be perceived as leaders before they can influence and lead. Since there are differences in perceptions of leadership across cultures, it is challenging to be an effective leader across this diversity.

LEADERSHIP AND ORGANIZATIONAL CULTURE

Organizations are open systems and there is influence from leaders in setting organizational values. Liden and Antonakis (2009) have studied the role of context in behavioral research and find that "Consistent with evidence supporting both the influence of culture on leadership and leadership on culture, it may be best to portray leadership and culture as being reciprocally related" (p. 1592). Leaders require cultural sensitivity or acumen and appropriate communication to be effective in the context of their organization.

An example of this is how performance-oriented a culture is. For those cultures high in performance-orientation, such as Singapore or the United States, "They prefer a direct and explicit style of communication and tend to have a sense of urgency" (House et al., 1999, p. 300). Whereas cultures that scored low in performance-orientation, such as Argentina and Greece, prefer more indirect style of speaking without commitment. Some cultural orientations prefer a dialogue to foster better relationship-building in process of increasing overall performance and productivity. It can cause conflict in the workplace and be demoralizing if you perceive the leader as being abrasive on one hand or indecisive on the other.

In *Transnational Leadership Development*, Kathy Geller and I identified five paradoxes of effective intercultural leadership (Fisher-Yoshida & Geller, 2009). They are framed as paradoxes because the context of cross-cultural situations determines the location on the continuum of where the leader should be operating. There is no cookie-cutter advice suggesting one absolute way of behaving. The paradoxes are: knowing, which is self-awareness and honoring other; focus, which is "I" centric and "we" centric; communication, determining level of directness when communicating across difference; action, doing and reflecting; and response, short-term or long-term focus.

In the GLOBE (Global Leadership and Organizational Behavior Effectiveness Research Program) Project (1999) the research

> *identified six global leadership dimensions of culturally endorsed implicit theories of leadership (CLTs) ... These findings are consistent with the hypothesis that selected cultural differences strongly influence important ways in which people think about leaders and norms concerning, status, influence, and privileges granted to leaders. (p. 2)*

Some of these attributes are universally accepted characteristics of effective leadership and include charismatic/value-based leadership and team-oriented leadership, and to some degree humane and participative qualities of leadership. Other characteristics attributed to leaders have different connotations depending on the cultural interpretation of that behavior. One example is about alignment with a leader's public behavior versus the leader's internal intentions. If there are behavioral changes in public and private situations there is no issue for some and the leader may be viewed as adaptable or socially savvy. For others it may appear the leader is not authentic because of these behavioral changes and authenticity is a strong value.

ROLE OF NARRATIVE ON LEADERSHIP

Leaders are known for setting the vision and direction of the organization (Kouzes & Posner, 2002). Management operationalizes this vision through policies, procedures, and structures. The values and beliefs of the organizational culture are realized in the everyday practices of the organization and upheld through policies that reward those who demonstrate these core beliefs (Hofstede, 1984). One effective way of communicating the overarching vision and strategy is through storytelling.

People are storytellers and learn and live through stories. When you work with others you expect to have shared stories because you are working in the same environment. Gardner (2004) who has done research on multiple intelligences comments on how stories are central to fostering change.

> *Optimally, a new story has to have enough familiar elements so that it is not instantly rejected yet be distinctive enough that it compels attention and engages the mind. The audience has to be prepared, in one sense, and yet surprised, in another. (p. 74)*

He differentiates stories and counter stories, which are stories in opposition. An implication here is that if a leader is trying to set the tone of the organization and does this through storytelling, in order for this to take hold the dominant story must be stronger than any counter stories.

Cultures communicate through stories about membership, and they are infused with references to cultural values, implicitly and explicitly. There are cultural expectations about the meaning of work and how one is a constructively contributing member. This influences how to participate in a team and whether individual or team goals are prioritized.

Cultural values determine moral codes, what is right and wrong. You learn this when you are young, in your homes and schools, and bring this conditioned way of seeing the world with you to the workplace. You place these moral judgments on leaders, management and your peers and expect them to live up to the same ideals you have in the same way with the same behaviors. However, with the multiplicity of cultural influences, it is difficult to determine which practices are acceptable and which cross boundaries.

Pearce (2007) identified *logical forces* that are present in situations, represent these moral codes, and lead you to behave in certain predictable ways. There is a sense of *oughtness* you have due to your cultural conditioning to behave in predictable ways. "In general, whatever the logical force of a situation impels you to do will perpetuate whatever pattern is occurring" (p. 120). The more diversity in the workplace, the more variety in moral codes and logical forces compelling people to behave in ways that align with their moral codes, perpetuating the same patterns, regardless of whether there is movement or the same *unwanted repetitive patterns* (URPs) of behavior. These same moral codes guide how leaders are judged and deemed effective with opinions varying across diversity.

There are cultural norms about what it means to be an effective leader and behaviors and practices associated with those norms. Gelfand (2018) in her studies on culture, identified characteristics in categories of *tightness* and *looseness*.

> *Tight organizations boast great order, precision, and stability, but have less openness to change. Loose organizations have less discipline and reliability, but compensate with greater innovation and appetite for risk. (p. 149)*

CULTURAL NARRATIVES ON LEADERSHIP

In today's ever changing and increasingly diverse world, a flexible style of leadership is critical. However, when the repertoire of leadership skills is limited to a particular style or the leader reads the members of the organization and what is needed incorrectly there can be challenges.

If leaders think of themselves as being fair and democratic, with a more laissez-faire approach, they may resist implementing more controls because they frame it as violating their values. For leaders who believe it is necessary to exert more control in the organization it is difficult for them to share the control more broadly. These leaders have challenges changing because this is what they have done in the past, how they are known, the behavior for which they have been rewarded, and how they believe they must continue to lead.

Referring back to Gelfand's cultural tightness-looseness scale, she promotes variation when needed. There are parts of organizations that need tight structures and practices, such as accounting and sections dealing with safety, while R&D and innovation can be looser. She identifies *structured looseness* for loose organizations needing to embrace tightness into their operations and *flexible tightness* for tight organizations that need to integrate looseness into some of their functions.

People are creatures of habit and behave in predictable patterns even if these behaviors are not bringing desired results. When under stress you tend to dig deeper into the same patterns because they are familiar. You react according to the already formed brain maps in your mind (Hanson, 2013). In the neurosciences, it is said that *neurons that fire together, wire together* and these habits are culturally influenced. Each interaction can be thought of as a *speech act* and, when we string a series of these speech acts together, we form episodes (Wasserman & Fisher-Yoshida, 2017). These patterns formed by speech acts and episodes play out every day in the workplace.

An example of this is how leaders behave and communicate in the organization. They may want to have tight controls over what gets communicated, how, and be more rule driven. This can be considered along a number of dimensions: tight culture, low context, high-power distance, and direct communication. People from cultures where these values resonate will think they are good leaders and doing what leaders are supposed to do. The logical force and moral code are that the leader is mature, knows how to read the organization and can be trusted because he/she is guiding us correctly.

However, followers with different values and moral codes will disagree. They may think this leader is controlling and does not take their opinions into consideration in a shared decision-making model. As a result, they may seek more freedom and looser controls and prefer to be less rule driven. With a high-power distance, they will accept what the leader is doing as long as they feel they are being taken care of by him/her. With a lower power distance, they may more openly resist. Patterns are formed with these speech acts and episodes.

CULTURAL CONFLICT IN THE WORKPLACE

Competing dominant and counter narratives can cause confusion. Values may be called into question when practices and behaviors contradict what you believe are the espoused values of the organization and the leader espousing them. This is even more poignant for those with less tolerance for ambiguity.

Raines (2020) cites common causes of conflict in the intercultural workplace as relating to hiring and promotion practices, directness of communication, sense of personal space and physical contact, dress codes and visible expressions of identity. The degree to which these are disturbing and how much can be tolerated is related to their frequency, duration, and intensity. If the value and purpose of being a contributing member of the organization outweighs the negative drawbacks, then there is an interest in working it out. If the purpose and values become muddy and there is a decline in the cost-benefit analysis, there will be conflict, resulting in poor quality of life in the organization, lower productivity, and loss of good talent.

Just as stories can be useful to increase engagement, communicate values and culture, and inform about vision and future direction, they can also reveal underlying conflicts. Cloke and Goldsmith (2000) have been studying conflict in the workplace and the costs to the organizations and people working within them. They identify what is being voiced and the underlying meaning –

An example of the layers of meaning that are hidden in every conflict story can be found by taking any insult or accusation and examining its external, internal, and core forms. The external form is an accusation or insult, but beneath that lies a confession, and beneath that lies a request. (p. 50)

If we think of this from an intercultural perspective, we may see that some-one who states "He does not know how to lead" may be accusing or insult-ing the leader's leadership style and actually be confessing that they need more direction or looser controls, and the request is to fulfill in practice what they need to be more comfortable and successful at work.

As we have seen from different measures on Hofstede's uncertainty avoid-ance dimension, people deal with ambiguity differently and the need for a shared narrative is even more in demand than ever before. This situation is going to become more pronounced as there are increases in internet connec-tivity, MNEs, mobility, and the diversity in our immediate surroundings. This is not a phenomenon that is going to go away, in fact, it is becoming more the norm than the exception. We need to create narratives to live by that we can all follow. Gardner (2004) posits as a "general rule, when one is addressing a diverse or heterogeneous audience, the story must be simple, easy to identify with, emotionally resonant, and evocative of positive experiences" (p. 82). Leaders who tell stories to engage diverse populations in their organizations will do well to follow this advice.

CREATING A SHARED NARRATIVE

Diversity in organizations is on the rise as borders become more blurred through the increase in use of technology, virtual work teams, and MNEs. Leaders will be from more diverse backgrounds leading increasingly diverse workforces that vary on multiple levels, such as age, gender, national culture, and professional or industry culture. Therefore, there needs to be a conscious effort for leaders to figure out ways in which to create a shared narrative about leadership if they are going to be effective in their organizational con-text. There needs to be a better alignment between the expectations of the members of the organization about how they are being led and the way the assigned leaders are actually leading.

Here are a few suggestions of how to foster the creation of this shared narrative for stronger organizational alignment and cohesion. The effort to create these dynamics needs to be shared as well, so that all of the onus is not on the leader alone.

It is good practice to check assumptions about what it means to be a leader. As a leader, you have your own narrative and sense of who you are, and others need to be aware of their assumptions that guide their judgment on evaluating leaders. These assumptions will implicitly drive behavior and attitude, and if you are not self-aware there could be unintended consequences. Ignorance is not bliss; it is just ignorance.

Find out how to increase your cultural intelligence and acumen. There will always be diversity in the workforce, so it is important to increase your knowledge of these similarities and differences in order to develop your sensitivity. It does not mean you need to know all of the nuances of every culture, but you do need to know how to find out about these nuances, how they manifest, and how to address them. In general, people are more willing to give you the benefit of the doubt when they see there is a genuine effort.

As a member of the organization, you need to figure out ways to inform the leader about what you expect from someone in the leadership position. It does not mean everything will be acted on and fulfilled, but it can lead to a dialogue and mutual understanding. Information is power.

Use multiple ways to communicate to appeal to different types of audiences. The cultural diversity in the workplace brings with it different ideas and practices of how followers want to connect and communicate with their leaders. Some will want to have their voices more noticeably heard and want to have a say in policies that affect them. Others may be concerned, but do not feel comfortable speaking up and will want more indirect pathways of communication. In times of change and increased uncertainty, it is better to communicate more than less as there cannot be over communication. Communication takes many forms: with more variety, more chances of increasing dialogue, and having an informed workplace.

Increase the amount of work experience leaders have in different cultural contexts. You can have as much book learning as possible and that is good for conceptual understanding. For really understanding cultural nuances at a deeper, more visceral level, you need to experience them firsthand. It is the everyday practices that you notice in different work cultures that in a more diverse situation may be overlooked.

Recognize talent for future leaders. It is easier to continue identifying high performing potential when it is familiar. As the global work environment changes and demands placed on organizations grow, it is increasingly critical to recognize talent from diverse sources. Short- and long-term expectations for leaders need to be considered in order to thrive and even survive.

NOTES

1. This increase in diversity includes gender with multiple generations working together (Forbes, 2012).

2. There is a rich, layered and complex cultural mixture present in organizations today. Even as far back as 1959, Edward T. Hall, an anthropologist and cross-cultural researcher has been observing and commenting on this phenomenon. In his 1981 publication, *Beyond Culture*, he exclaimed, "In less complex and fast-moving times, the problems of mutual understanding were not as difficult, because most transactions were conducted with people well known to the speaker or writer, people with similar backgrounds" (p. 90). That was nearly 40 years ago when the world was a simpler place, less mobility, fewer MNEs and less diversity in the workplace.

3. The Oxford Economics study commissioned by Forbes Insights (2012) conducted a global study with the "ranking of employee diversity across 50 global economies, 14 industrial sectors and nine occupations. Additionally, the study includes data on gender and ethnic diversity across more than 500 occupations and 300 sectors in the U.S. and the U.K." (p. 12). They gathered information on best practices for diversity in the workplace to use as a benchmark to see how this relates to better business practices, opportunities, and higher productivity. It was agreed that in order to sustain economic growth, diversity was a critical strategic component. Therefore, the demand for increasing effectiveness of how diversity is addressed within and between organizations is only increasing.

REFERENCES

Auto Tech Review. (2018, January). https://autotechreview.com/technology/new-trends-in-mobility-and-implications-for-oems

Bolman, L. G., & Deal, T. E. (2003). *Reframing organizations: Artistry, choice, and leadership*. Jossey-Bass.

Boyatzis, R., & McKee, A. (2005). *Resonant leadership*. Harvard Business School Press.

Cloke, K., & Goldsmith, J. (2000). *Resolving personal and organizational conflict: Stories of transformation and forgiveness*. Jossey-Bass.

Dickson, M. W., Den Hartog, D. N., & Mitchelson, J. K. (2003). Research on leadership in a cross-cultural context: Making progress, and raising new questions. *The Leadership Quarterly*, 14(2003), 729–768.

Fisher-Yoshida, B., & Geller, K. D. (2009). *Transnational leadership development: Preparing the next generation for the borderless business world*. AMACOM.

Forbes. (2012). *Diversity & inclusion: Unlocking global potential: Global diversity rankings by country, sector and occupation*. Forbes Insights.

García-Canal, E., & Guilleén, M. F. (2015). The rise of the new multinationals. In *Reinventing the company in the digital age.* BBVA Open Mind.

Gardner, H. (2004). *Changing minds: The art and science of changing our own and other people's minds.* Harvard Business Review Press.

Gelfand, M. (2018). *Rule makers, rule breakers: How tight and loose cultures wire our world.* Scribner.

Gerstner, C. R., & Day, D. V. (1994). Cross-cultural comparison of leadership prototypes. *Leadership Quarterly, 5*(2), 121–134.

Global Workplace Analytics. (2017). https://globalworkplaceanalytics.com

Hall, E. T. (1959). *The silent language.* Doubleday.

Hall, E. T. (1981). *Beyond culture.* Doubleday.

Hames, R. D. (2007). *The five literacies of global leadership: What authentic leaders know and you need to find out.* Jossey-Bass.

Hampden-Turner, C., & Trompenaars, F. (2000). *Building cross-cultural competency: How to create wealth from conflicting values.* Yale University Press.

Hanson, R. (2013). *Hardwiring happiness: The new brain science of contentment, calm, and confidence.* Harmony Books.

Hofstede, G. (1984). *Culture's consequences: International differences in work-related values.* Sage.

House, R. J., Hanges, P. J., Ruiz-Quintanilla, S. A., Dorfman, P. W., Javidan, M., Dickson, M., Gupta, V., & Koopman, P. L. (1999). *Cultural influences on leadership and organizations: Project GLOBE.* Advances in Global Leadership.

Javidan, M., Dorfman, P. W., Sully de Luque, M., & House, R. J. (2006, February). In the eye of the beholder: Cross cultural lessons in leadership from project GLOBE. *Academy of Management Perspectives, 67*–90.

Kane-Urrabazo, C. (2006). Management's role in shaping organizational culture. *Journal of Nursing Management, 14,* 188–194.

Kouzes, J. M., & Posner, B. Z. (2002). *The leadership challenge: How to keep getting extraordinary things done in organizations* (3rd ed.). Jossey-Bass.

Liden, R. C., & Antonakis, J. (2009). Considering context in psychological leadership research. *Human Relations, 62*(11), 1587–1605.

Marques, J. (2010). Awakened leaders: Born or made? *Leadership & Organization Development Journal, 31*(4), 307–323.

Northouse, P. G. (2016). *Leadership: Theory and practice* (7th ed.). Sage.

Pearce, W. B. (2007). *Making social worlds: A communication perspective.* Blackwell.

Raines, S. S. (2020). *Conflict management for managers: Resolving workplace, client, and policy disputes* (2nd ed.). Rowman & Littlefield.

Smart Insights. (2019, February). https://www.smartinsights.com/social-media-marketing/social-media-strategy/new-global-social-media-research/

UN.org. (2018, May). https://www.un.org/development/desa/publications/2018-revision-of-world-urbanization-prospects.html

Wasserman, I. C., & Fisher-Yoshida, B. (2017). *Communicating possibilities: An introduction into the coordinated management of meaning (CMM)*. Taos Institute.

Weese, W. J. (1996). Do leadership and organizational culture really matter? *Journal of Sports Management, 10*, 197–206.

3

GLOBAL LEADERSHIP IS SHARED LEADERSHIP: HOW SMART GLOBAL LEADERS BUILD CULTURES OF COLLABORATION TO DRIVE RESULTS AND GET THINGS DONE

AMBER A. JOHNSON, TINA HUESING,
JAMES D. LUDEMA AND BRETT HINDS

Technology and globalization have transformed organizations and the lives of individuals in dramatic ways. Between 2000 and 2015, American multinationals hired more people overseas than they did in the United States (Furhmans, 2018). New communication technologies have made information transfer between low-cost labor markets, headquarters countries, and centers of commerce easy, fast, and affordable. Relationships among regions and countries opened up profitable markets for multinationals, requiring domestic leadership to manage the complexity encountered by different legal jurisdictions, languages, stakeholder groups, and cultures (Lane et al., 2004).

Along with the new markets, new forms of global leadership emerged and new definitions evolved. We define global leadership as influencing a range of internal and external constituents from multiple national cultures and jurisdictions in a context characterized by significant levels of task and relationship complexity (Reiche et al., 2017, p. 556).

Complexity is the hallmark of global leadership. To illustrate, we offer an example of a pharmaceutical company's effort to change its organizational structure, which required the tracking of 12,000 separate items across more than 100 countries and in 70 languages (Osland et al., 2017). In the face of such complex change, it is impossible to imagine that any single individual leader could alone possess the skills and capacity needed to lead. Increasingly, leadership is a collective activity, enacted across geographic boundaries. We propose that globalization is changing the nature of leadership such that effective leaders must rely heavily on personal and relational versus structural sources of power, thereby engaging others in the process of shared leadership.

In this chapter, we support our proposal with findings from three empirical studies. In the first study, we offer an inside look at the nature of global leaders' work. We spent a week each with five global leaders and conducted interviews and semi-structured observations (Huesing & Ludema, 2017; Mintzberg, 1973) to gain insight into what they do and how they lead on a daily basis. Our second study draws from interviews with leaders in the global auto industry to compare the bases of power used by global leaders versus those used by domestic leaders. In the final study, we provide a case study of a major change initiative in a global organization, demonstrating how contextual complexity, unique local knowledge and expertise, and the requirements of organizational structure contributed to the emergence of shared leadership on a highly-diverse global team.

SHARED LEADERSHIP AND BASES OF POWER IN GLOBAL LEADERSHIP

Shared Leadership

In a 2016 bibliometric analysis of published studies between 1965 and 2014, researchers found that shared leadership and collective leadership are the second and third most researched leadership models, respectively (Tal & Gordon, 2016). The authors argue this shift is a byproduct of the Knowledge Era, with its focus on democracy, globalization, and complexity. In other words, the forces that are currently shaping the global economy require new forms of leadership that are shared.

Shared leadership is defined as "a dynamic, interactive influence process among individuals in groups for which the objective is to lead one another to the achievement of group or organizational goals" (Pearce & Conger, 2003, p. 1). In contrast to traditional downward theories of leadership, shared leadership proposes that group members can "actively and intentionally shift the role of leader to one another as needed by the environment or circumstances in which the group operates" (Wassenaar & Pearce, 2018, p. 168). Shared leadership places an emphasis on the role and behavior of leadership rather than on a specific person (Lord et al., 2017).

Shared leadership is applicable where there is a high level of interdependence between group members (Wassenaar & Pearce, 2018). In the presence of shared leadership, we can expect to see leadership behaviors such as giving direction, removing obstacles, or providing support and motivation to other teammates to be practiced by more than just the positional authority (D'Innocenzo et al., 2016).

Four forms of shared leadership can emerge (Pearce & Manz, 2014). The first is *rotated* shared leadership, where the role of the leader is determined at different points in time based on expertise. Second, *integrated* shared leadership is a more dynamic form in which leadership roles shift fluidly and rapidly within a single meeting or incident as topics change or the focus on different aspects of an initiative emerge. Third, *distributed* shared leadership reflects organizational structures that allow for autonomy and decision-making across the organization. Finally, the fourth form of shared leadership is *comprehensive* shared leadership, which is reserved for organizational cultures where shared approaches are infused throughout. In all of the four styles, it is important to note that hierarchical leadership structures often still exist, but leadership roles and behaviors shift as needed by the environment or circumstances (Pearce & Manz, 2014).

In a meta-analysis of the shared leadership literature, shared leadership was found to have a greater effect in complex environments (Wang et al., 2014), making it especially suitable for global teams. Sharing leadership has been shown to increase dispersed global team performance and thus help to overcome the challenges of virtual team collaboration (Hoegl & Muethel, 2016). Researchers suggest this is true because shared leadership pushes decision-making to the local level, allowing for more culturally-relevant and efficient processes (Pearce & Wassenaar, 2014).

Bases of Power

To explore shared leadership in a global context, it is important to understand the ways in which leaders exercise power. The concept of power was introduced into leadership studies by Robert Dahl in 1957. Power is defined as, "A has power over B to the extent that [A] can get B to do something that B would not otherwise do" (Dahl, 1957, pp. 202–203). This definition was expanded by French and Raven (1959) by outlining five bases of power: (a) reward power, (b) coercive power, (c) legitimate power, (d) referent power, and (e) expert power. By 1998, the list was expanded to 11 and subdivided into structured and personal bases of power (Raven et al., 1998). The consolidated list is shown in Table 3.1.

For global leaders, six bases of power are particularly important to understand. Two of them are relatively weak when compared with domestic leaders, which makes the other four essential and moves global leaders in the direction of shared forms of leadership. *Impersonal reward power* is the power a leader has to provide financial reward to followers. This base of power is weak for global leaders because it is typically diminished or unavailable. Survey results show that only 40% of global leaders have direct responsibility for a follower's annual compensation assessment (Hinds, 2020). *Legitimate power of position* is also weak for global leaders because they often have no direct line of authority over the members of the global teams they lead.

In contrast, four other bases of power are more evident in the work of global leaders. *Legitimate power of dependence* refers to the reciprocal interdependence between leaders and followers and among team members on the same project (Castañer & Ketokivi, 2018). It is essential for global leaders because they rely on the unique cultural, technical, and relational expertise of each team member to accomplish shared goals. *Referent power*, described

Table 3.1. Leader Power Bases.

Structured Bases	Personal Bases
Impersonal Reward Power	Referent Power
Impersonal Coercive Power	Expert Power
Personal Coercive Power	Informational Power
Legitimate Power of Position	Legitimate Power of Dependence
Legitimate Power of Equity	Personal Reward Power
Legitimate Power of Reciprocity	

Source: Adapted from Raven et al. (1998).

as a feeling of membership between individuals, is also essential for global leaders because their team members are often geographically and culturally dispersed. A strong sense of connection and membership supports trust, collaboration, and investment in the success of the team as a whole. *Expert power* and *information power* are the most important bases of power in a global environment because they incorporate local knowledge, including policies, practices, and cultural understandings, which may not be available to all team members and could significantly affect the outcome of a project. Global leaders depend on global team members to exercise their context-specific expert and information power on behalf of the whole, promoting shared leadership.

THE EMPIRICAL EVIDENCE OF SHARED LEADERSHIP

To further illuminate the idea of shared leadership as an essential ingredient in global leadership, we provide in this section empirical evidence from three original studies of global leaders. The first study shows how the task, culture, and relationship complexity of global leaders' work makes traditional hierarchical forms of leadership inadequate and requires collaborative approaches. The second study goes a step further and shows how the complexities of global leadership constrain bases of power that support hierarchical leadership and enable bases of power that favor shared leadership. The third study provides a case of shared leadership in action in a global change initiative characterized by high levels of task, culture, and relationship complexity. It shows how shared leadership can be put into practice through shared decision-making and organizational structure to drive successful global change.

Study 1: The Nature of Global Leaders' Work

Similar to Mintzberg (1973), we observed five global leaders at their workplace for a week each. Our study participants came from the telecom industry, aerospace and energy, software development, tracking technologies, and for-profit higher education. Three worked in the United States (two on the West Coast and one in the Midwest), two worked in Europe (Belgium and Spain). All five were global leaders whose responsibilities crossed multiple boundaries and who worked with others from multiple national cultures and jurisdictions. During our study, we took extensive field notes, complemented our observations with informal interviews and archival documents, and analyzed our data using the conventions of grounded theory (Charmaz, 2014).

We identified 10 characteristics of global leaders' work:

1. Working continuously across multiple time zones and geographical distances;

2. Working extremely long hours to accommodate the needs and calendars of the corporate offices along with those of team members scattered around the globe;

3. Navigating flexible schedules and fluid time to be available at all times to meet the immediate resource requirements of others;

4. Depending primarily on various forms of electronic technology for communication, none of which are as rich as face-to-face interaction;

5. Spending long periods of time alone connected only electronically to others;

6. Traveling extensively to establish and maintain relationships and negotiate complex deals;

7. Serving dual roles as functional experts (like Chief Financial Officer or Vice President of Global Services) with the added responsibilities of global leadership;

8. Facilitating vast amounts of information, advice, and action among global team members and up and down the chain of command;

9. Managing the complexities of multiple and often conflicting political regimes, legal systems, labor laws, ethical standards, Human Resources practices, financial requirements, currencies, exchange rates, cultures, customs, and languages; and

10. Confronting risk, including financial, legal, ethical, and reputational risk and the risk of corporate espionage, kidnapping, extortion, and global terrorism (Huesing & Ludema, 2017).

These 10 factors illustrate the task, culture, and relationship complexity of global leadership and establish the need for shared forms of leadership.

Since their territories spanned multiple time zones, it was not uncommon for the global leaders in our study to work from early in the morning to late at night. The participant located in Barcelona, Spain, often worked from his home office when he was not traveling. This made it easier for him to be at work early in the morning when he would communicate with his team members in Singapore, where it was afternoon already. He would respond to email that had come in during the night and be in phone conversations. The global leader used a sticky note attached to his computer screen to remind him of the various time zones he was dealing with. Around lunchtime, the VP would take a longer break, perhaps to go for a walk with his wife, before he returned to his desk in the afternoon when his colleagues in Chicago would come online. He would often stay at his desk until 10 p.m. (local time) or later. His schedule was very flexible with work and other aspects of his life intermingled.

Global leaders travel regularly to meet with their dispersed team members in person. All five participants of our study stated that face-to-face meetings were still the best way to lead and an absolute necessity because they strengthened relationships and facilitated collaborative problem solving and innovation. Since they were not always able to have face-to-face meetings, they had to rely heavily on communication technology to remain in touch with their teams. A global leader located in San Francisco, the CEO of a software company with business units in multiple South American countries, used technology that his software developers preferred and was connected to his teams via various tools (SMS, Skype, Slack, email) throughout the day.

We observed a constant interaction between the global leader with individual team members or groups of team members. All of the global leaders we studied adjusted their time and the means of communication to what their team members preferred, even when this meant long work hours or multiple tools and channels of communication for them. They also worked hard to handle multiple time zones, national holidays, and cultural differences in work habits, making sure that arrangements were convenient for their team members rather than imposing their schedules on others.

The work of our global leaders was made increasingly complex because multiple national entities were often involved. In one example, team members based in Argentina working for an American company did not want to receive their pay in Argentine pesos or have it deposited in Argentine banks because of chronic currency devaluations. To accommodate the team members, the global leader explored various alternatives such as depositing the money in US dollars in US banks, depositing the money in US dollars or Uruguayan pesos in Uruguayan banks, paying in cash in Uruguay with either US dollars or Uruguayan pesos, and other offshore options. Each alternative had legal, ethical, and financial implications that needed to be considered and required a complex blend of local and global knowledge and understandings.

In another example, a global leader explained how changes to tax law in one legal entity needed to be addressed at the corporate level:

> When the UK tax law changed, it was not material to our financial statements. Yet, I had to write a seven-page memo to show it doesn't apply to us. There are just too many things. We spend a tremendous amount of time trying to understand the rules.

These examples provide a small glimpse into the complexities facing global leaders. Such complexities cannot be managed with traditional hierarchical forms of leadership. They require local expertise, and the global leader relies on local leaders' insights into what is important and how it should be handled. Research, understanding, problem solving, and decision-making need to be conducted jointly, requiring shared forms of leadership.

Study 2: Global Leadership and Bases of Power

To gain additional insight into the emergence of shared global leadership, we interviewed 18 global leaders in the automotive manufacturing industry using the Critical Incident Interview technique (Flanagan, 1954). The interviews explored global leadership through the lens of bases of power. We asked the interviewees to share two stories of leading a change in a follower's work practices, one involving a global follower and the other involving a domestic follower. As the global leaders told their stories, we looked for similarities and differences in the way the global leader used bases of power with global followers versus domestic followers. The interviews were recorded, transcribed, and analyzed using the conventions of Grounded Theory (Charmaz, 2014).

Of the twenty-three interviewees, eleven were US citizens, six were Chinese citizens, four were Japanese citizens, one was a citizen of Great Britain, and one a German citizen. Seventeen worked within the engineering function and six worked within the purchasing function. Seventeen interviewees were men, and six were women. All global leaders were in a structured supervisor role versus a team leader role, which meant that legitimate power of position was always present. The leader–follower relation also had high levels of reciprocal interdependence (Castañer & Ketokivi, 2018), which meant the success of both the leader and follower were dependent on one another.

Our results showed that the application of expert power or information power was the primary basis for shared leadership. When a global follower possessed information or knowledge that was important for the global leader and the success of the project, the roles of leader and follower became less defined and shared leadership emerged. Bases of power such as legitimate power of position, forms of reward and coercive power, and referent power did not have the same fluidity of transfer within a leader–follower relationship and did not contribute significantly to shared leadership.

During the interviews, there were two general cases in which shared leadership emerged. The first case was where the global leader and global follower were from the same functional domain (e.g., engineering) and working in different regions of the world. In this case, the follower could possess regional knowledge that was not available to the global leader. This regional knowledge introduced both strong and weak shared leadership examples. When the regional knowledge, such as regional market conditions, regional customer wants, or regional government regulations were critical to the decision-making, the regional knowledge gave the global follower regional expert power and a strong shared leadership role. If the global follower possessed regional knowledge that was valuable but not critical, the global follower demonstrated regional information power (as opposed to regional expert power) and established a weak form of shared leadership in which he or she provided information but was not responsible for decision-making. During the interviews with global leaders, EG, a senior executive interviewee working in the United States, described how her experience in the United States and close proximity to US customers was a benefit to her global leader who was South Korean and based in South Korea.

> *Now, I got their attention because I'm living here. I know what's happening a lot more than they could ever know by reading the snip-its. [I] provide additional information that may not be on the internet through web searches because of the relationship I may have with the various members of the different companies here.*

After a visit to EG's US office, her South Korea manager acknowledged EG's regional expert power with the statement, "They're all very close to the tech center, less than an hour away. You will always have better information than we have being 7,000 [miles away]." This is an example of rotated shared leadership (Pearce & Manz, 2014) where the role of the leader is determined at different points in time based on expertise.

The second general case where shared leadership emerged was where the global leader and global follower worked in different functional domains (e.g., one in engineering and the other in purchasing). If the global leader and global follower work on the same project but in different functional domains, there is a clear separation of expert power and information power within the project team. As tasks progressed through the life of a project, different functional domains were called upon to provide input and make decisions. This ebb and flow of domain expert power and domain information power is an example of integrated shared leadership (Pearce & Manz, 2014) in which leadership roles shift fluidly and rapidly within a single meeting or project as topics change or the focus on different aspects of an initiative emerge.

Study 3: Global Leadership Is Shared Leadership in Action

In Study 3, we use a single-case example to explore the emergence of shared leadership across a global executive leadership team. This demonstrates how complexity (as established in Study 1), the presence of expert and information power (as established in Study 2), and organizational structure create the conditions for the emergence of shared leadership. The example provided here is one case from a larger comparative-case study of the success factors in leading global change projects (Johnson, 2020).

WaterOrg is a multinational non-governmental organization based in Houston, Texas, and working throughout Africa, Latin America, and Asia. The organization began when oil industry executives decided to use their technical drilling expertise to help bring clean water to developing communities. They turned to local non-profits to create connections and develop relationships in these areas, and the US-based leaders provided funding and drilling expertise. As the organization grew, this division of labor led to quality control issues and a lack of accountability. WaterOrg decided to restructure to address these concerns. A new role of Regional Vice President (RVP) was created to provide executive-level leadership to large territories, such as all of Latin America or West Africa. This is an example of distributed shared leadership in which structures are created that allow for autonomy and decision-making across the organization (Pearce & Manz, 2014).

RVPs provide an important boundary-spanning role for managing complexity (Butler et al., 2012), as they draw on their connections to different levels of the organization and the cultures in which the organization works. In this boundary-spanning context, one RVP explains how organization-wide decision-making works: each leader is expected to contribute their expert knowledge (a form of expert power) to identify ways in which a decision may challenge national or local cultures or may require consideration of professional functions such as HR or finance policy. When included in the decision-making, the RVPs are then better able to support new policies as they are implemented in the field:

> If I'm part of the development process, then I'll make noise during that time. I'll make sure I'm representing my constituents so that I can say [to the field], "What we decided." I can speak of "we," not what Houston decided.

Mutual decision-making, a component of shared leadership, is particularly important on global leadership teams as representatives from different regions bring local knowledge (expert and information power) that impacts the outcomes of change initiatives. For example, during a recent restructuring at WaterOrg, headquarters-based staff questioned the need for employees in the field to manage purchasing of office and cleaning supplies. In headquarters, this function is easily managed through online shopping. An RVP explained that purchasing supplies in developing communities cannot rely on online shopping or delivery and can be time consuming. In this, the RVP advocated for the field; likewise, leaders at headquarters received the expert knowledge of the RVP and adapted decisions to accommodate it. This cycle of *advocacy* using expert power and *adaptation* illustrates a simple process of shared leadership.

In more complex work, an example of expert power contributing to shared leadership can be seen as leaders from different functions at Water-Org worked as equals to create a new set of global project standards. Historically, processes and standards were set by headquarters. In the new structure, however, the CEO tasked two RVPs and a global operations director with creating a new set of standards for the organization's program area model. To design the model, the global operations director spent two months in Africa, working with the continent's RVP. They began by talking about what they wanted to happen, shaping a vision of what a program area might look like and then working to define the terms and create measurements and formal objectives. Their design was sent to the RVP of Latin America for revision before the final design was submitted to the CEO. This mutual process of *visioning, defining, advising,* and *revising* is another model of shared leadership that again relies on reciprocal contributions of expert knowledge.

Taken as a whole, this case study provides an example of comprehensive shared leadership in which an organizational culture is created that infuses shared approaches throughout (Pearce & Manz, 2014). The creation of RVPs elevated non-US leaders into positions where the emergence of shared leadership became more probable. More recently, RVPs were made members of the global executive team. One executive team member explains:

> *When we initially established the regions, RVPs were not part of the [global executive] team. I think that created some tension because they felt like it was a* them and us *kind of culture. But in the more recent reorganization, we're bringing them to the table as part of the senior team, in a much more collegial, collaborative environment. And I think they see that they're part of the solution.*

Members of the global executive team report this shift has led to more consistent information sharing and shared decision-making, and that it has allowed team members to rely on one another. One executive of a functional area notes RVPs now say, "You're the technical expert. I'll trust you on this one," where previously they might have said, "It's my region, I'll make the decision. You're just the advisor." This significant structural change, coupled with the creation of processes for mutual decision-making and collaborative visioning, defining, revising, and refining on key initiatives created a culture in which shared leadership was institutionalized, supported, and leveraged throughout the organization.

Study 3 provides an illustration of the central points of Studies 1 and 2: Within global leadership teams, complexity created by the multiplicity of languages, cultures, time zones, legal jurisdictions, etc., necessitates reliance on other leaders who hold expert and information power, creating conditions where shared leadership can emerge. If attention is paid to creating structures and processes that support rotated, integrated, and distributed forms of shared leadership, a comprehensive culture of shared leadership can be developed, leading to regular rhythm of cooperative acts such as advising, adapting, visioning, defining, revising, and relying.

SHARED LEADERSHIP FOR A GLOBAL FUTURE: IMPLICATIONS

This chapter connects the literature on global leadership with that of shared leadership and bases of power. The chapter then illustrates the changing nature of shared leadership in the global context with findings from three empirical studies. In the first study, we observed that complexity of the global context necessitated a shared approach. In the second study, we researched the bases of power that global leaders utilize when leading global and domestic followers in the global auto industry, finding that shared leadership was more likely to emerge in the presence of expert and information power.

In the third study, our case illustrated how the presence of global complexity and expert and information power, along with organizational structure, contribute to the emergence of a culture of comprehensive shared leadership as demonstrated by a regular rhythm of cooperative acts such as shared decision-making and advising, adapting, visioning, defining, revising, and relying. Together, these studies argue that the future of global leadership is one of shared leadership, which allows global leadership teams to navigate complexity, rely on regional and functional expertise, and contribute to cooperative acts.

Our chapter has both academic and practitioner implications. Fruitful channels of future research can be envisioned; for brevity, we will identify just three. First, Mintzberg's (1973) seminal study could again be replicated, this time with an intentional focus of identifying the nature of shared leadership among global executive teams. While recent uses of Mintzberg's methods revealed the nature of global leaders work (Huesing & Ludema, 2017), the finding of shared leadership was an unexpected discovery. Repeating this study in a shared global leadership context could extend our understanding of how and why shared leadership emerges on global leadership teams.

Second, enacting a shared leadership approach allows global leaders to call on the team's expert knowledge: intellectual, psychological, and social capital that can navigate the complexity of global work. Further consideration of the role of expert and information power in global teams is needed, in contrast with their use in domestic teams. Are expert and information power used differently among global teams, and under what conditions do they contribute to the emergence of shared leadership? Our study focused on the auto industry; can the findings be extended to other industries? And finally, a third research question arising from this chapter considers the role of organizational structure in the emergence of shared leadership on global teams. What structures allow for shared leadership and cooperative acts to emerge across regions and functions, and what structures or practices inhibit shared leadership emergence?

Additionally, this chapter suggests important implications for practitioners who want to engage shared leadership in a global context. First, we propose that in light of increasing globalization, leaders must turn their attention to the creation of shared leadership among their global executive teams, especially in areas in which the work is interdependent (Wassenaar & Pearce, 2018), as seen in Study 1, and reliant on expert knowledge and information, as seen in Study 2. Study 3's findings encourage leaders to consider whether the organization's structure might inhibit or enable the emergence of shared leadership. If leaders are not seeing the shared decision-making they desire, for example, they could consider whether team members with the relevant expert knowledge also have the organizational position needed for their voice to be heard. Practitioners may also find benefit in revisiting the models of shared leadership (Pearce & Manz, 2014) to assess what, if any, model their team is enacting; the absence of shared leadership may be instructive for global leaders. Where it is not present, is the organization too reliant on more coercive forms of power? Can those forms of power be exercised effectively across geographic boundaries? If not, it may be a warning sign to invest in the creation of a shared leadership culture.

Globalization has changed the way we work. The nature of leadership must adapt as our organizations grow to encompass more geographies, cultures, languages, and ways of working. Shared leadership emerges in these complex environments as a means of managing the interdependency of boundary-spanning work; but enacting shared leadership means shifting the bases of power on which leaders historically relied. It may also require shifting organizational structure to accommodate more voices. Scholars and executives alike must adapt quickly to keep pace with the changes of our ever more global world.

REFERENCES

Butler, C. L., Zander, L., Mockaitis, A. I., & Sutton, C. (2012). The global leader as boundary spanner, bridge maker, and blender. *Industrial and Organizational Psychology, 5*(2), 240–243. https://doi.org/10.1111/j.1754-9434.2012.01439.x

Castañer, X., & Ketokivi, M. (2018). Toward a theory of organizational integration. *Advances in Strategic Management, 40*, 53–80. https://doi.org/10.1108/S0742-332220180000040002

Charmaz, K. (2014). *Constructing grounded theory* (2nd ed.). Sage.

D'Innocenzo, L., Mathieu, J. E., & Kukenberger, M. R. (2016). A meta-analysis of different forms of shared leadership–team performance relations. *Journal of Management, 42*(7), 1964–1991. https://doi.org/10.1177/0149206314525205

Dahl, R. (1957). The concept of power. *Behavioral Science, 2*(3), 201–215. https://doi.org/10.1002/bs.3830020303

Flanagan, J. C. (1954). The critical incident technique. *Psychological Bulletin, 51*(4), 327–358. https://www.apa.org/pubs/databases/psycinfo/cit-article.pdf

French, J. R., & Raven, B. H. (1959). The bases of social power. In D. Cartwright (Ed.), *Studies in social power* (pp. 150–167). University of Michigan, Oxford University Press.

Furhmans, V. (2018). Big U.S. companies reveal how much they rely on overseas workers. Retrieved April 10, 2019, from https://www.wsj.com/articles/big-u-s-companies-reveal-how-much-they-rely-on-overseas-workers-1523448000

Hinds, B. (2020). *The nature of global leaders' power.* (Publication No. 28023874) [Doctoral dissertation, Benedictine University]. ProQuest Dissertations & Theses Global.

Hoegl, M., & Muethel, M. (2016). Enabling shared leadership in virtual project teams: A practitioners' guide. *Project Management Journal, 47*(1), 7–12. https://doi.org/10.1002/pmj.21564

Huesing, T., & Ludema, J. D. (2017). The nature of global leaders work. *Advances in Global Leadership* (Vol. 10). https://doi.org/10.1108/S1535-1203(2009)0000005017

Johnson, A. A. (2020). *Closing the global change gap: Success factors for leading change through task, relationship, and cultural complexity* (Publication No. 28085866). [Doctoral dissertation, Benedictine University]. ProQuest Dissertations & Theses Global.

Lane, H. W., Maznevski, M. L., & Mendenhall, M. E. (2004). Globalization: Hercules meets Buddha. In *The Blackwell handbook of global management: A guide to managing complexity* (pp. 3–25). https://doi.org/10.1111/b.9780631231936.2004.00003.x

Lord, R. G., Day, D. V, Zaccaro, S. J., Avolio, B. J., & Eagly, A. H. (2017). Leadership in applied psychology: Three waves of theory and research. *Journal of Applied Psychology, 102*(3), 434–451. https://doi.org/10.1037/apl0000089.supp

Mintzberg, H. (1973). *The nature of managerial work*. Harper & Row.

Osland, J. S., Ehret, M., & Ruiz, L. (2017). Case studies of global leadership: Expert cognition in the domain of large-scale global change. *Advances in Global Leadership* (Vol. 10). https://doi.org/10.1108/S1535-120320170000010002

Pearce, C. L., & Conger, J. A. (2003). *Shared leadership: Reframing the hows and whys of leadership*. Thousand Oaks, CA: Sage.

Pearce, C. L., & Manz, C. C. (2014). Introduction to shared leadership. In C. L. Pearce, C. C. Manz, & H. P. Sims (Eds.), *Share, don't take the lead: Leadership lessons from 21 vanguard organizations* (p. xi). Information Age Publishing.

Pearce, C. L., & Wassenaar, C. L. (2014). Leadership is like fine wine: It is meant to be shared, globally. *Organizational Dynamics, 43*(1), 9–16. https://doi.org/10.1016/j.orgdyn.2013.10.002

Raven, B. H., Schwarzwald, J., & Koslowsky, M. (1998). Conceptualizing and measuring a power/interaction model of interpersonal influence. *Journal of Applied Psychology, 28*(4), 307–332. https://doi.org/10.1111/j.1559-1816.1998.tb01708.x

Reiche, B. S., Bird, A., Mendenhall, M. E., & Osland, J. S. (2017). Contextualizing leadership: A typology of global leadership roles. *Journal of International Business Studies, 48*(5), 552–572. https://doi.org/10.1057/s41267-016-0030-3

Tal, D., & Gordon, A. (2016). Leadership of the present, current theories of multiple involvements: A bibliometric analysis. *Scientometrics, 107*(1), 259–269. https://doi.org/10.1007/s11192-016-1880-y

Wang, D., Waldman, D. A., & Zhang, Z. (2014). A meta-analysis of shared leadership and team effectiveness. *Journal of Applied Psychology, 99*(2), 181–198. https://doi.org/10.1037/a0034531

Wassenaar, C. L., & Pearce, C. L. (2018). Shared leadership. In J. Antonakis & D. V. Day (Eds.), *The nature of leadership* (3rd ed., pp. 167–188). Sage.

4

HOMO UBUNTU LEADERSHIP FOR THE TWENTY-FIRST CENTURY

ELIANE UBALIJORO AND SEAN LEE

INTRODUCTION

Since at least the Axial Age of 700–200 BCE, civilizations of Eurasia, and now the dominant global cultures, have cultivated an ideal of the individual seeking personal fulfillment. Individual goals, entrained with the possibilities offered by continuous technological advancement have driven civilization from the Iron Age to the Information Age. But the singular emphasis on the individual also feeds a cultural narrative that neglects one of the most salient facts of human biology: that we evolved as a profoundly *social* species. The basic architecture of the human brain developed for over 300,000 years for life in small, closely knit social groups. Living conditions, language and technology led to the development of critical anatomical, physiological and neurological traits evolved specifically for social interactions.

Neurologically, human brains are *social brains;* entrained, entangled and mutually dependent to a degree otherwise unknown in nature. Ontologically, the human mental universe can thus be understood at least as much as a social creation as an individual one. While this perspective is largely missing in cultures with Eurasian Axial Age origins, it is well embodied in the African philosophy of *Ubuntu,* often characterized by statements such as "I am who I am through all of us." We believe this view of humans first and foremost as social "*homo ubuntu*" offers a unique framing and important new light on leadership. This is well beyond "social soft skills" critical to building forward stronger as we navigate the reset that the COVID-19 pandemic is forcing upon us. According to António Guterres, Secretary General of the United Nations (2020),

> we cannot go back to the old normal of inequality, injustice and heedless dominion over the Earth. Instead, we must step towards a safer, more sustainable and equitable path. We have a blueprint: the 2030 Agenda, the Sustainable Development Goals and the Paris Agreement on climate change. The door is open; the solutions are there. Now is the time to transform our relationship with the natural world – and with each other. And we must do so together. Solidarity is humanity. Solidarity is survival.

It is time to reclaim our interconnectedness as social beings and as part of the web of life.

Peace Nobel Laureate Wangari Maathai in her memoire *Unbowed* wrote:

> I profoundly appreciated the wisdom of my people, and how generations of women had passed on to their daughters the cultural tradition of leaving the fig trees in place…People in that region had been spared landslides, as the strong roots of the fig trees held the soil together in the steep mountains. They also had abundant, clean water. But by the early 1970s, landslides were becoming common and sources of clean water for drinking were becoming scarce. (2006, p. 122)

Maathai in her autobiography mourns the relationship she had with nature as a child. She leads us to reflect on the legacy current generations are inheriting of a disconnected relationship to nature as biodiversity extinction rates accelerate and natural ecosystems disappear, creating havoc. In her follow up book, *Replenishing the Earth: Spiritual Values for Healing Ourselves and the World* (2010, pp. 16–17), she wrote:

> Through experience and observations, I have come to realize that the physical destruction of the earth extends to humanity, too. If we live in an environment that's wounded – where the water is polluted, the air is filled with soot and fumes, the food is contaminated with heavy metals and plastic residues, or the soil is practically dust – it hurts us, chipping away at our health and creating injuries at a physical, psychological, and spiritual level. In degrading the environment, therefore, we degrade ourselves and all of humankind.

The pandemic has revealed this starkly. As biodiversity loss accelerates, zoonosis is also accelerating. Our disconnection from nature continues to grow. This jump from diseases of wildlife to emerging diseases affecting humanity is a symptom of the degradation we need to stop. How we honor the wisdom of our ancestors as we relate to each other and to the earth are embodied in Ubuntu and Ukama, which can be harnessed for twenty-first-century leadership. These concepts honor both planet and humanity.

> *Ubuntu (humanness) is a concrete expression of ukama, that is, humanness needs to be understood relationally. In other words, humanness is an expression of interconnectness [sic.] between people themselves, and between people and the biophysical world.... The sense of wholeness and interconnectedness of self with the social and natural by implication means that caring for others also involves a duty to care for nature...Cultivating ubuntu by definition involves healing of self, society and nature. (Le Grange, 2012, p. 63)*

It is noteworthy that hunter-gatherer societies have practiced for millennia situational and inclusive leadership only relatively recently (re)discovered in modern leadership theories such as servant leadership, transformational leadership and holocracy (decentralized management and organizational governance). In this chapter, we will first explore the leadership skills most desired in the twenty-first century before reviewing the neurobiology of our extreme social nature, particular in the context of our Paleolithic past, and in contrast to today's dominant individualistic culture. Finally, we explore why moving toward a Homo Ubuntu mindset could prove critical to sustainably addressing the current challenges we face.

OUR INTERCONNECTEDNESS AND THE FOURTH INDUSTRIAL REVOLUTION

According to Mamphela Ramphele (2020), Ubuntu *"is the capacity in African culture to express compassion, reciprocity, dignity, harmony, and humanity in the interests of building and maintaining community."* Homo sapiens originated in Africa over 300,000 years ago (Science Magazine, 2017) and has since spread all over the planet. From the "one who knows" that sapiens represents, it is time to expand us to the ones who relate to all that Ubuntu offers. We are today at a time of peril in terms of our connection to each other, to the planet and the overexploitation of the resources available to us. We propose to reconnect to the wisdom of Africa, as we navigate these turbulent times.

According to Klaus Schwab, the Founder and Executive Chairman of the World Economic Forum, (2016)

> *The First Industrial Revolution used water and steam power to mechanize production. The Second used electric power to create mass production. The Third used electronics and information technology to automate production. Now a Fourth Industrial Revolution is building on the Third, the digital revolution that has been occurring since the middle of the last century. It is characterized by a fusion of technologies that is blurring the lines between the physical, digital, and biological spheres.*

What does this mean for leadership in the twenty-first century? The accelerated rate of disruption creates "a time of great promise and great peril" (Schaub, 2017). Currently, a few companies globally have capitalized on the big data age in ways that have shifted economic power away from third industrial revolution tycoons to digital game changers. These fourth industrial revolution game changes are able to organize, analyze and mobilize information from large sets of data computationally in ways that create immense value. As this value continues to grow, there are also 2.7 billion people on the planet who live in constant food insecurity and 800 million who go to bed hungry. At the same time, one third of all global food production goes to waste. This represents the exact amount of food that could feed the needs of the food insecure in the world. Being able to capture the nutrition locked in the food that is currently wasted but could be instead mobilized to feed the hungry would have a transformational value for society. It is time to connect the value of knowing to the value of caring for all.

Food, climate, environmental and political inequities weigh heavily on the bottom of the pyramid, representing the billions of poor people in the world that have the least access to financial digital transactions. According to McKinsey Institute (2015), 700 billion dollars could be added to Sub Saharan Africa's GDP by 2025 if gender parity could be reached in financial access alone. As Schaub (2017) notes, humanity grounded in care

> *has the potential to connect billions more people to digital networks, dramatically improve the efficiency of organizations and even manage assets in ways that can help regenerate the natural environment, potentially undoing the damage of previous industrial revolutions.*

What is needed is to sail through the turbulence we face by flipping the VUCA world from Volatile, Uncertain, Complex and Ambiguous to Visionary, Understanding, Clear and Agile. This requires a worldview and a capacity to relate to each other and to the planet that we feel are embodied by *Homo Ubuntu*.

HARNESSING UBUNTU IN A FUTURE OF GREAT DISRUPTION AND DISTRIBUTED EVERYTHING

Weaving African proverbs collected by the late Malawian Organizational Development Chiku Malunga in his work, we explore how to harness Ubuntu in our current VUCA world.

> *There is nothing more important than relationships. It is better to be surrounded by people than to be surrounded by things.*
> African Proverb

How we relate to self, others and the earth with care are central to the Ubuntu worldview (Elkington, 2019). As Malunga notes,

> *All living systems are interconnected and interrelated. They are all interconnected and interrelated to form the one grand system called the universe. Any positive or negative impact on one system sends ripple effects to the entire universe. This is the basis of the saying; one can do no evil but to oneself. For the good of humanity and all forms of life a key word in all the systems is "relationships."* (2014, p. 85)

The famous quote, "If you want to go fast, go alone. If you want to go far, go together," is often mentioned as an African proverb, most likely because it expresses a stance that seems uniquely at home in the Ubuntu philosophy. It is the essence of oral traditions that they, like the concept of Ubuntu itself, cannot be clearly sourced, but that does not diminish their moving power. In his book, *Understanding Organizational Leadership Through Ubuntu*, Malunga (2009) uses the above proverb and others to illustrate how African wisdom can help transform organizations in the twenty-first century. Malunga shares how harnessing the following five people-centered Ubuntu principles can help humanity reconnect to its origins as we journey into a more and more complex world that demands we cultivate the wisdom of our ancestors:

1. Reciprocity, inclusivity and shared destiny through collective responsibility

2. Importance of people and relationships over things

3. Participatory leadership and decision making

4. Loyalty and openness to change for the greater good, grounded in trust and fairness

5. Reconciliation as a goal of conflict management.

Ubuntu leadership requires letting go of blame and ego, to open to our interdependence, shared responsibility and interconnectedness. Ubuntu leadership harnesses the energy of relating, so that in our doing, our being shines bright – I see you and I welcome you so we can all fully live whole heartedness. "I am because we are" links us to our ancestors and to our hyper-connected twenty-first century world.

Our hyper-connectedness allows some using sophisticated algorithms to predict our wants and desires before we know them. Others use big data to invest more profitability. Power outages are catastrophic now not only because we are caught off from electricity but more importantly because the machines that run our lives use up energy we do not sustain anymore from our human relating. According to futurist Barbara Marx Hubbard (2008), the internet has become the human nervous system.

Our technologically sophisticated world requires leadership skills that harness emotional intelligence. What is needed for our mindsets to match our exponential technological growth goes back to the tacit knowledge that was kept by wise men and women the world over. Plants signaled to them their uses. These healers possessed what we would call today supernatural capacities to connect with nature, to sail at night guided only by stars and to listen to the animal world for signs of danger (e.g., the arrival of a tsunami or toxic plants to avoid eating). They lived our interconnectedness with everything. They held polarities we can no longer tolerate and transmitted this wisdom to next generations through metaphors, proverbs and storytelling. They had reverence for all forms of life and the elements. Their wonder opened them to discovery, where our fears and disconnect from relatedness have led us to want to master the wildness of nature.

We live today in a world where 96% of mammals are represented by humans and domesticated animals for livestock or as companions to remind us of the wildness we are pushing to extinction (Bar-On et al., 2018; Rosane, 2018). We anxiously walk through urban jungles desperate to commune with nature. We grow houseplants and spend exorbitant amounts of money to buy purebred pets with precise characteristics that fit our lifestyles. Our desire to eliminate uncertainty has led us to avoid all that is foreign and unpredictable in general. Our respect, even tolerance of what is different is eroded.

THE VOLUNTARY ENGAGEMENT WITH FEAR

With Ubuntu leadership, we can regain a compassionate curiosity to navigate the turbulence of the twenty-first century. We can journey ahead, listen deeply and dialogue with greater empathy and presence through uncertainty. We can flow with nature, harness the brilliance of biological ecosystems to see diversity as sources of resilience and innovation rather than something to eliminate. We can collaborate across disciplines beyond hierarchy while acknowledging the grace of each unique contribution to benefit the whole. To paraphrase Audre Lorde (1997, p. 13), "When [we] dare to be powerful, to use [our] strength in the service of [our] vision, then it becomes less and less important whether [we are] afraid."

Ubuntu leadership can relieve the anxiety in the world that comes from isolation. This disregards our dreams. The power of community can acknowledge our unique individual strengths and vulnerabilities. Where one's vulnerabilities encounter another's strengths, we can work collectively to address the three wicked issues of the twenty-first century (Harari, 2018):

1. Climate change

2. Replacement of human jobs by machines with the advance of artificial intelligence

3. The possibilities of nuclear warfare with more and more countries accessing these capabilities.

Our ancestors sat in dream circles, danced rhythmically until exhaustion and explored various ways to connect to the metaphysical. How do we engage in twenty-first-century practices that elevate "Homo ubuntu" in all of us to be here in this space while also being in the future and in the past to retrieve information we need to journey sustainably?

Leadership will require transparency, honesty, and curiosity to encourage ideas and initiative more than criticism. We need to see each other instead of tearing each other down. This will require leaders who do not confuse clarity with certainty. The need for simplicity will have to override the urge for the simplistic but dangerous. Complexity must be accepted and integrated. We can reconnect to the wisdom held by our elders. We can value common sense, often lost when trauma settles in and heal from the destructive materialistic path that is fueling climate change. This can be encouraged through embracing our ancestors' use of storytelling versus our modern desire for rigid rules. Engaging people requires encouraging lucid and coherent vision that has space for agility and holds the complex with clarity.

> *When the lion is running and stops to look back, it is not that the lion is afraid but is rather trying to see the distance he has covered.*
> African Proverb

BEYOND *HOMO SAPIENS* – TOWARD "HOMO UBUNTU"

Homo, nosce te ipsum. (Human, know yourself) Carl Linnaeus (1707–1778)

Aristotle wrote that man at his best is the "noblest of creatures." For Hamlet, man was "the paragon of all animals," and, according to Charles Darwin humans are with "almost unlimited intellectual capacity." Within this long cultural tradition, it is unsurprising that the first scientific classification of our species by the eighteenth century naturalist Carl Linnaeus in his *Systema Naturae* was as *homo sapiens* – "wise man" (Barry Jones 2018, p. 518).

Over the last several years, neurological and psychological research has been forming a view of the human mind rather different than that of the traditional "wise man." For one, it is becoming clear that our long and growing list of cognitive biases reflects the mind's *modus operandi* more than its aberrant behavior. Indeed, most of our cognitive biases tend to be universal across socioeconomic classes and quite resistant to correction. It is revealing, for example, that in a random group of professionals, including academic fields, over two thirds to three fourths of people consider themselves above average in their professional abilities (Cross, 1977) – and above average in their abilities to resist biased assessments (Scopelliti, 2015).

Key to understanding the workings of the human mind is the evolutionary purpose of the brain. Like all brains in the animal kingdom, the human brain's operational purpose is essentially what engineers refer to as a *model-predictive controller*. As a general principle, the brain must create predictive computational models of its sensory states and employ these models to control behavior. Models are updated to enhance their predictive value, based on internal and external feedback data via neurochemical reward systems (Barrett, 2017; Pinker, 1997).

With this image of the brain as a model-predictive controller, we can begin to gain important insights into actual human behavior. To begin with, cognitive biases are a natural outcome of models designed for limited time and resources; models typically need to be only "good enough" in the moment. More generally in this view, cognitive beliefs are active constructions of the brain resulting from predictive models that are not optimized for truth, wisdom or other abstract high-order goals, but for their efficacy in supporting the body's physiological balance, a process referred to as allostasis (Barrett, 2017; Kleckner, 2017). For example, confirmation bias can be particularly understood in this light as the cognitive pathway that preferentially selects confirmatory information to reduce physiological stress – a process one experiences as "feeling better" about one's prior beliefs and decisions.

From the model-predictive controller perspective, we can also understand why humans are a uniquely social species. Social feedback, particularly turbo-charged through language, provides a virtually unlimited supply of feedback data with which to update predictive models that are crucial for the desired outcomes of survival and procreation. However, lack of diversity in these social interactions, can not only entrench our biases but unconsciously transmit these through technology as artificial intelligence gains more and more power in our world.

Humans are indeed profoundly social animals. Measured by the number and cognitive depth of our connections, we are immeasurably more social than any other species. The fact that we have by far the largest encephalization quotient (weighted ratio of brain to body size) in the animal kingdom is, according to the "Social Brain" hypothesis, a direct result of the enormous computational demands on our brains for human social living (Dunbar, 1998).

One well-known factor connected with that extra demand is that the human brain is apparently built for a very large Dunbar number – the number of intimate social relationships we can cognitively maintain at one time. For other primates, that number maxes out at around 50; for humans, it is at least three times that. The company Gore and Associates has famously used this limit to structure its workforce into units of 150 (Delany, 2016).

How deeply we are embedded in each other's thoughts can already be seen, for example, in basic two-person conversation. Invariantly across cultures, the average gap between two people taking turns at speaking is only a few hundred milliseconds. That is far too short for conscious processing if each speaker waits until the other is finished before formulating a response. What happens instead is that both speakers are subconsciously predicting the other, while modeling and formulating their own responses well ahead of exchanging sound waves and other physical cues. Studies have also shown this mechanism begins as early as infancy, for example, as mother and baby mutually regulate each other's facial expressions (Barrett, 2017).

For humans, especially since the appearance of language, the most relevant sensory data and modeling by far comes from other humans who are, of course, also executing similar models. As a result, human brains are wired to live in recursive cognitive loops with each other, rather something like an infinite hall of (curved and imperfect) mirrors. It turns out that convening around Stone Age campsites for cooking, eating, discussing, scheming, planning and wondering did not just begin our culture; it defined much of our biology.

In short, the human mental universe – intellectual, emotional and spiritual – is a direct product of the innate mental entrainment we evolved to have with each other. As counter-intuitive as it may feel to each of us, living our own conscious experience: no thought or feeling that any individual has is "their own" as much as it is "our own." The importance of this point, we believe, cannot be overstated. Just as nothing in biology makes sense without the theory of evolution, nothing about how humans *actually think and act* makes sense without a framework that recognizes the core Ubuntu tenet: "I am who I am through all of us."

We remark here only briefly that such a view introduces an ontology of being that is in stark contrast to the dominant cultural traditions of Eurasia. These traditions, developed during the Axial Age of 700–200 BCE by canonical sages from the Israeli prophets to the Greek rationalists, Eastern spiritualists, and many others, anchored their analyses of the human condition within the individual. This "individualist" perspective, often reflected in today's dominant global culture as near universal reverence for values such as *self*-fulfillment, *self*-improvement, *self*-sufficiency,

Our sociality has been offered as a possible explanation for why we emerged from the last ice age, but Neanderthals did not. Neanderthals were not only stronger, but had slightly larger brains than modern humans. They controlled fire to make sophisticated multi-component tools, created artworks, cared for the elderly and the sick, buried the dead, and possibly sailed the Mediterranean. Finally, Neanderthal sites show a clear trajectory of increasing cultural sophistication over the millennia.

Yet anthropologist Stanley Ambrose (2015) has argued that there are several direct and indirect indications that Neanderthals were *less social* than their *sapiens* contemporaries were. Excavated Neanderthal stone tools, for example, are almost never further away than 25 km from their quarry sources. This corresponds approximately to the maximum daily range of movement of a single group. In later sapiens, in stark contrast, large quantities of stone tools are often found hundreds of kilometers from the nearest quarry source. This strongly indicates widespread peaceful contact and exchange with other groups outside their own (raids on foot without pack animals are hardly practical over longer distances).

Neanderthals lived in harsh conditions during the ice age that made it difficult to sustain groups of more than 25 individuals. As conditions changed with the end of the ice age, Homo sapiens was able to thrive more and take advantage of their larger population and communities. Genetically, Neanderthals were also less diverse, even though they were active in Eurasia for hundreds of thousands of years before sapiens arrived, which also suggests that there was less exchange between different populations.

Among the early humans, peaceful-coexisting can be observed over several millennia. A graceful, "feminization" of sapiens skull and skeleton took place particularly in South and East Africa as early as 60–50,000 years ago, just as refined art, sophisticated tool making, and spread to new living ranges emerged. It was precisely these new groups of people – physically less robust, initially not necessarily "cleverer" than their contemporaries, but certainly more *social* – who migrated from Africa over the next 10–20,000 years and eventually replaced all other homo populations worldwide.

It is worth noting that, according to Ambrose (2015), today's hunter-gatherers in open savannah areas are much more social than in other cultures, easily exchanging openly and peacefully with strangers. Unfortunately, this social trust cultivated by our hunter-gatherer ancestors became the great exception among later humans. During the Neolithic period – when personal wealth became culturally established and every stranger posed a potential threat to land, property and livelihood – this social trust was eroded.

SUSTAINABLY ADDRESSING THE CURRENT CHALLENGES WE FACE

In the process of helping the earth to heal, we help ourselves.
Wangari Maathai

The challenges facing humankind this century are truly unprecedented and existential. A changing climate, frequent dangerous weather events and rising ocean levels, a loss of natural habitat and biodiversity as well as disruptive population demographics are creating an uncertain and unsustainable future. With hundreds of millions facing long-term disruptions to food, water, healthcare and basic infrastructure, our current trajectory threatens to render large areas of the planet economically and physically uninhabitable. Concurrently, rapidly advancing technologies in the fields of IT, biotech, the Fourth Industrial Revolution and artificial intelligence, while providing great opportunities, are poised to remake the global economy faster than human societies can adjust. Indeed, many signs of these strained adjustments are already visible. Societies around the globe are facing rising tides of inequality, polarization, and resurgent authoritarian politics. Individually, rates of depression, burnout and sleep loss are also rising, along with their health consequences like diabetes, obesity, and cardiovascular disease.

The fact that these problems are all of our own making should give some measure of hope that they can be addressed in time before the worst of the damage becomes unrecoverable. But that, in our view, will require visionary leadership of a very different kind than that nurtured so far by the individualist cultural traditions that have brought us to this point. Such a new type of leadership would need to go beyond learned soft management skills, even beyond what is now commonly taken as environmental and social consciousness. It would begin first and foremost with a courageous look at where we are as a species and how we got here; a fearless reassessment of our own nature, beyond the cultural myths wrapped up in the designation *homo sapiens*.

It has become almost conventional wisdom to say the problems we modern humans face with our technologically advanced civilization are ultimately due to the legacy of our Paleolithic brains – what Astronomer Carl Sagan famously called our "evolutionary baggage" (Sagan, 1980). Our tendency for aggression, hostility to strangers and submissiveness to leaders are all legacies of our earliest existence, in this popular view. But in fact, the archeological and anthropological evidence tells a very different story.

> *If we stand tall today it is because we stand on the shoulders of those who have gone before us.* African Proverb

In truth, many of the political and societal problems of behavior that are commonly branded as "human nature" are rooted in the periods long after we had become biologically modern. Oppressive social hierarchy and patriarchy, excessive wealth accumulation and pursuit of individual desires at the expense of the community needs, depletion of resources and irreversible degradation of the environment – are all behaviors that appeared later in human history. That implies that they are not as encoded in our basic neural architecture as in the operating systems of our cultures.

One need not romanticize our Paleolithic legacy, or suggest that twenty-first century humans become hunter-gatherers, to point out that their cultures offer much to learn from and emulate. As we have already pointed out, much of recent modern leadership theory is in many ways a rediscovery of the practices of hunter-gatherer who generally practice situational and "horizontal leadership" rather than the "vertical leadership" paradigm of post-Neolithic societies.

Overall, they also tend to be significantly more social, egalitarian and mutually supportive in their relationships. Eurocentric cultural traditions that lionize individual achievement, duality and fulfillment have also brought our species and the planet to the brink of unrecoverable damage. Now more than ever, leadership needs to transform worldviews focused on being right, fragmentation or achievement of the few, to a load we all carry equally, regardless of position or status. Here again, Ubuntu is a perspective that makes clear that we all are leaders and all carry the responsibility that entails. As Richard Leider writes of the Hadzabe people, a hunter-gatherer people in the Lake Eyasi basin of Tanzania, "It is considered bad to hoard or accumulate more than what one needs. Everyone shares. Everyone serves. Everyone leads."

As far as understanding the transformative role that an Ubuntu approach could play, we believe it is worth taking a special look at Africa itself, home to this singular philosophy. Africa has the paradoxical status of being the birthplace of humankind and human technology while being commodified through slavery and natural resource exploitation during the centuries in which the planet first became dominated by humans and technology. Yet, the now converging global trends of climate change, biodiversity loss, demographic disruption and the fourth industrial revolution could make the continent key for the global future and survival.

To begin with, Africa is on the front lines of all of these disruptive trends. The failure to address adequately these trends in time risks an unprecedented humanitarian crisis on an unprecedented scale. But at the same time, Africans have been navigating for decades if not centuries, social stressors which in the developed world are generally considered inconceivable: poverty and migrations at the scale of whole populations; failing infrastructure and basic services; and polarized, arbitrary and authoritarian politics. The sheer resilience of Africans to move forward under these continuing circumstances could well be a seminal lesson of our species into the future.

One crucial way Africans are moving forward is in technology-enabled innovation. Moore's Law is breaking through to even the remotest areas and poised to transform the global economy and culture in unprecedented ways. Mobile tech, renewable energy, 3D printing, smart manufacturing, the internet of things, transportation, remote sensing, artificial intelligence, virtual reality, and many other disruptive technologies are just beginning to transform the global economy. Less well known in this context is the fact that Africa is in many ways at the cutting edge of these technology-enabled disruptions. Already a leader in mobile banking, mobile health and off-grid solar energy, Africa is showing the way toward a new model of innovation itself; one that from the initial design phase and through all stages is inherently inclusive. From R&D, product performance and pricing to logistics, investment and growth strategies, innovation in Africa differs starkly from canonical models developed in industrial countries that were developed under starkly different market conditions.

Within this new paradigm of innovation are vital lessons for a planet constrained by resources, environmental stress and social disruptions. Institutions like the African Academy of Sciences, the African Institutes for Mathematical Sciences, Ashesi University, the African Leadership Group, the African Design Centre and the Next Einstein Forum are exciting examples of institutions harnessing Africa's capacity for technological leapfrogging. They are doing this while also elevating our capacity to relate to each other, to the forces we face and the caring we can bring to healing ourselves and the planet.

REFERENCES

Ambrose, S. (2015). *Volcanic winter, population bottlenecks and human evolution.* Lecture at Peabody Museum. https://www.youtube.com/watch?v=Nj1ds5JsyGE

Bar-On, Y., Phillips, R., & Milo, R. (2018). The biomass distribution on Earth. *PNAS, 115*(25), 6506–6511. https://doi.org/10.1073/pnas.1711842115

Barrett, L. (2017). *How emotions are made.* Houghton Mifflin Harcourt.

Cross, K. P. (1977, Spring). Not can but will college teachers be improved? *New Directions for Higher Education, 1977*(17), 1–15.

Delany, K. (2016). In Quartz Magazine Online. Something weird happens to companies when they hit 150 people. https://qz.com/846530/something-weird-happens-to-companies-when-they-hit-150-people/

Elkington, R. (2019). Ubuntu as ancient wisdom for modern ethics: A systems thinking ecosophy for the 21st century denudation of integrated world capitalism. *Journal of Leadership Studies Symposium on Ancient Wisdom for Modern Leadership Ethics.*

Feely, D. (2017). 5 Critical Factors of Emotional Intelligence That Can Change Your Life. Retrieved October 13, 2019, from http://transforming.com/2017/08/09/5-critical-factors-emotional-intelligence/

Goleman, D., & Bennis, W. (2011). The power of truth: A conversation between Daniel Goleman and Warren Bennis. https://www.audible.com/pd/The-Power-of-Truth-Audiobook/B004SCCWV6

Harari, Y. (2018). *21 lessons for the 21st century.* Penguin Random House.

Hari, R., Henriksson, L., Malinen, S., & Parkkonen, L. (2015). Centrality of social interaction in human brain function neuron. *Neuron, 88*(1), 181–193.

Jones, B. (2018). *Dictionary of world biography: Fifth edition.* ANU Press.

Kleckner, I. et al. (2017). Evidence for a large-scale brain system supporting allostasis and interoception in humans. *Nature Human Behavior.*

Le Grange, L. (2012). Ubuntu, Ukama and the healing of nature, self and society. *Educational Philosophy and Theory*, 44(SUPPL.2), 56–67. https://doi.org/10.1111/j.1469-5812.2011.00795.x

Leider, R. (2014). What can hunter-gatherers teach us about servant-leadership? https://richardleider.com/what-can-hunter-gatherers-teach-us-about-servant-leadership/

Lorde, A. (1997). *The cancer journals, special edition*. Aunt Lute Books.

Maathai, W. (2006). *Unbowed: A memoir*. Knopf Publishing Group.

Maathai, W. (2010). *Replenishing the earth: Spiritual values for healing ourselves and the world*. Random House.

Malunga, C. (2009). *Understanding organizational leadership through Ubuntu*. Adonis & Abbey Publishers Ltd.

Malunga, C. (2014). *Organizational wisdom in 100 African proverbs: An introduction to organizational paremiology*. Adonis & Abbey Publishers Ltd.

McKinsey Institute. (2015). The Power of Parity: How advancing women's equality can add $12 trillion to global growth. https://www.mckinsey.com/~/media/McKinsey/Featured%20Insights/Employment%20and%20Growth/How%20advancing%20womens%20equality%20can%20add%2012%20trillion%20to%20global%20growth/MGI%20Power%20of%20parity_Full%20report_September%202015.ashx

Pinker, S. (1997). *How the mind works*. W.W. Norton and Company.

Ramphele, M. (2020). Ubuntu: The Dream of a Planetary Community. In P. Clayton, K. M. Archie, J. Sachs, & E. Steiner (Eds.), *The New Possible: Visions of Our World beyond Crisis* (Ch. 5, p. 45). Cascade Books, an Imprint of Wipf and Stock Publishers. Kindle Edition. f

Rosane, O. (2018). In Ecowatch online. Humans and Big Ag livestock now account for 96 percent of mammal biomass. https://www.ecowatch.com/biomass-humans-animals-2571413930.html

Sagan, C. (1980). *Cosmos*. Random House.

Schwab, K. (2016). The Fourth Industrial Revolution: What it means, how to respond. https://www.weforum.org/agenda/2016/01/the-fourth-industrial-revolution-what-it-means-and-how-to-respond/

Scopelliti, I. (2015). Bias blind spot: Structure, measurement, and consequences. *Management Science*, 61(10), 2468–2486.

Sveiby, K. E. (2009). The first leadership? Shared leadership in indigenous hunter-gátherer bands. https://www.sveiby.com/article/The-First-Leadership-Shared-Leadership-in-Indigenous-Hunter-Gatherer-Bands.

Wikipedia Entry. (2019, October). "*Encephalization Quotient*."

World Economic Forum. (2017). The Fourth Industrial Revolution. https://www.weforum.org/about/the-fourth-industrial-revolution-by-klaus-schwab

5

GLOBAL RESONANCE AND GLOBAL LEADER IDENTITY: COMPLETING THE CYCLE OF KNOWING, DOING, AND BECOMING

KATHLEEN A. CURRAN

Undeniably, globalization has brought increased contact among cultures, which concomitantly has increased cultural complexities and interdependencies among myriad evolving and reimagined elements. COVID-19 has "complexponentially" added increased unpredictability to the phenomenon. In this context of hybridity, cultural blending, and border disregard, leadership has necessarily shifted from the notion of *leading globally*, which simply applied traditional methods and models in new geographies, to *global* leadership, defined by

> *the processes and actions through which an individual influences a range of internal and external constituents from multiple national cultures and jurisdictions in a context characterized by significant levels of task and relationship complexity. (Reiche et al., 2016, p. 6)*

This comprehensive definition shines light on the requisite capacity and capabilities of the individual leader to learn, inspire, facilitate and integrate diverse people, priorities and pulls in the context of complexity. It also directs attention to the implicit need to view global identity and global leadership developmentally in the context of a fluid environment rather than to search for key traits, competencies, and traditional metrics for success.

This chapter speaks to this suggested shift in perspective and advances a new lens and model for cultivating a global leader identity, which iteratively serves as the mediating variable for effective global leadership in practice. Firstly, rooted in contemporary and post-modern views of identity development, globalization-induced sources of global identity tensions trigger an expanded conceptualization based on a developmental paradigm, crucial to the "ability and willingness of leaders to think, act, and transcend boundaries of values and goals on a global scale" (Ananthram & Nankervis, 2014, p. 201). Secondly, the simultaneous process of cultivating global leadership through Global Resonance generated from a global identity will be advanced (Curran, 2018). Together, the praxis offered addresses the call for a developmental process that is sensitive to "cultural interchange, the complexities of social positions, and the dynamics of global interconnectedness" (Hermans & Kempen, 1998, p. 1112), underscored by the assuredness of an ever-changing world.

GLOBALIZATION: CHANGES IN RESPONSIBILITY

Globalization is clearly recognized as an impetus of change, but "not often enough do we emphasize the globalization of responsibility" to challenge privilege and a taken-for granted social order (Rosenmann et al., 2016, p. 202). The social order referenced has tended to describe a dynamic environment that evolved in mushroom-like, unanticipated ways and demanded different methods of leading that exceeded traditional management practices. Marquardt and Berger (2000), now almost two decades ago, laid out key contrasts between traditional versus global leadership, intuitively highlighting the broad distinctions crucial to challenging the status quo and stepping up to the new order. Table 5.1 highlights the contrasts in knowing, doing, and becoming of a traditional manager and a global leader.

The features identified in Table 5.1 summarize the global leader's underpinning attitudes and beliefs, and related practices that facilitate more inclusivity and integration among interdependent elements both internal to the organization and across communities in which organizations operate and serve. The evolution from the traditional manager to the global leader also underscores *responsibility* as a core shift in both the delineation of activities as responsibilities and embracing the sense of responsibility within a broader and more complex global scope. The phenomenon of globalization has thus obliged a shift in focus *from* understanding global leaders in the context of a fixed core of a culture, assumed to be a stable and homogenous entity comprised of values, beliefs, and behaviors that should be protected, *to* the transnational edges or

Table 5.1.   Traditional Versus Global Leadership.

Traditional Manager	Global Leader
Functional definition of role; delineated responsibilities; metrics results focused	Role spans function, cultural, geographic boundaries. Fluidly defined responsibilities. Metrics inclusive of process, diversity
Control over resources seen as scarce and needing protection	Continual reinventing of resources seen as infinite
Cautious approach to dynamic environment; Change = threat	Open approach to dynamic environment; Change = opportunity
Eliminate or avoid conflict by using structured way to operate and communicate	Paradox expected; conflict is source of learning and new opportunities
Goal is to avoid surprises	Not surprised by surprises; goal is to be flexibly prepared for surprises, agile
Development limited to mastery of specific knowledge and skills	Lifelong learning – breadth, depth and scope
Reactive, protective, centralized focus: behind the curve	Proactive, "heat-seeking," multi-perspective focus: continually looking for the next curve

Source: Adapted from *Global Leaders for the 21st Century*, Marquardt and Berger (2000).

cultural contact zones characterized by continually shifting cultural hybridity thus surprise (Hermans & Kempen, 1998; Pratt, 1991).

Strikingly, the common denominator of globalization for the global leader is the resulting intensification of competing demands, multiple tensions, and paradox, the "contradictory yet interrelated elements that exist simultaneously and persist over time" (Smith & Lewis, 2011, p. 382). Serving multiple stakeholders; maintaining harmonious homogeneity on a diverse team or workgroup; taking short- or long-term views; role and communication style differences; and, taken together, the continual calculating to determines the behavioral priority at any given time present recognizable dilemmas. For example, the COVID-19 global pandemic laid bare worldwide socioeconomic inequities as well as dysfunctional supply chains; climate change has increased in urgency, awareness and relevance than ever before. Clearly, due to the multiple pandemics with no clear, there is a heightened need for global leaders to reach decisions rapidly with fluid and incomplete data. Profoundly relevant for global leaders, therefore, is the capacity to simultaneously thrive in the dynamic *culture contact zones*, rife with shifting tensions, while accessing learning from experiences from multiple sources, including the relatively more established and comfortable cultural core, where values, attitudes, and behaviors were assumed relatively familiar, understood and predictable.

Clearly, the phenomenon of globalization has stimulated both a *state* of interconnectedness (Roudometof, 2005) and a multidimensional, transformational *process*. Elden (2005) has argued that "globalization is a reconfiguration of existing understandings" (p. 8). In addition to the physical and virtual sense of geographical space, time, and borders, the deterritorialization of cultures has also brought disruption (Appadurai, 1990; Hermans & Kempen, 1998; Papastergiadis, 2005). Place, space, and territorial elements traditionally demarcated a bounded cultural group; psychologically, cultural borders lent identity and asserted terms of belonging, relational expectations, loyalties and rules to abide by for membership. Arnett (2002) asserts that "globalization has had a primary psychological influence on issues of identity" (p. 774). Globalization and exposed socioeconomic fissures have therefore redefined traditional links among certainty, security, and shared understanding across social units, raising new identity tensions along the way.

Crucial capacities of the global leader have also been reframed. Often used synonymously with capability, the term capacity in this chapter is used intentionally. Etymologically, capacity refers to the potential to hold knowledge and skills that can be consciously selected and deployed; capacity, therefore, is an internal source possessed by every individual. Using developmental lenses, the global leader identity is thus considered in the hybrid culture contact zones in order to show how it unfolds to reflect a self that has the capacity to be receptive to transformation and a continual process of becoming. Adult development and intercultural sensitivity models provide the theoretical underpinning to the deepening and broadening capacity that influences leaders' patterns of thinking, ways of differentiating stimuli, and integrating coherent sense of their experiences to their worldviews – in fact, to their whole person (Bennett, 2004; Cook-Greuter, 2004; Kegan, 1983, 1994; McCauley et al., 2006).

A brief look at the contemporary and post-modern approaches to identity and identity development suggests perspectives that parallel the traditional manager's personal epistemologies. Early contemporary literature tended toward perspectives on identity that asserted a proclivity for stability at an individual's culture core; that is, an identity that relied on a sense of secure boundaries and affiliations comprised of values, beliefs, shared norms and behaviors (Erikson, 1968). Social constructivists emphasized the salience of context in the formulation of identity (Adams & Marshall, 1996; Gergen, 1991), fundamental to intercultural studies. The effects of social interaction on identity development; group affiliation and social categorization were seen as the basis for one's social identity (Ferrari et al., 2010; Mead, 1934; Tajfel, 1978).

Contemporary literature also tended toward culture core contrasts as sources of relative cultural identity (Geertz, 1979; Markus & Kitiyama, 1991; Triandis, 1989). For example, many anthropologically oriented contrasts identified relative orientations in individualism and collectivism, attitudes toward risk, and internal and external locus of control differences (Hofstede, 1983; Hui & Triandis, 1983; Trompenaars, 1993). Vertically rooted belonging was reinforced through identification with familiar geographies, and sociocultural norms and groups, and supported and defended by maintaining and assimilating to traditional power structures. In contrast to later identity perspectives, relational views were very much based on polarized dualities. Unfortunately, such dichotomous perspectives tended to overgeneralize divergence among conceptualizations of identity differences among large populations, sometimes unintentionally perpetuating taken-for-granted views on culture cores as homogenous groups with like beliefs and values. Illustratively, the protective view, as pointed out in Table 5.1, encouraged traditional managers, for example, to cling to stable self-defining indicators which may emphasize preference for control and avoidance of conflict.

Post-modern theoretical perspectives made valuable contributions to moving the construct of identity away from the traditional view as an abstract source of protection – fixed, stable, homogenous – to something more dynamic, fluid, and responsive to a new kind of hybrid environment. Building on the work of social constructivists, post-modern scholars concur with the notion that identity is formed, not in a monologue, but in dialogue with a larger cultural system – "It is in transformations of social processes that discourses and identities can shift to accommodate new ways of being" (Hammack, 2008, p. 235). Hybridity literature, in particular, highlighted the reflexive relationship between global and local perspectives, with fluid identity shifting as the self moved from space to space and relationship to relationship (Bauman, 2011; Urry, 2003; Yeoh et al., 2003). As Gergen (1991) notes,

> Under postmodern conditions, persons exist in a state of continuous construction and reconstruction; it is a world where anything goes that can be negotiated...each reality of self gives way to reflexive question, irony, and ultimately, playful probing of yet another reality. (p. 67)

Despite the support for fluidity in identity construction, however, the postmodern view tended toward narrow unidirectionality in intent and purpose, that is, of acculturation and fitting in, and instrumentally targeting aims for achieving strategic objectives, respectively. A sense of home and belonging tests global leaders as their activity in the deterritorialized space challenges the reality of metaphorically sequentially dropping anchor in selected ports, which offers minimal security, stability, or the distinctiveness that generally drives group membership. Furthermore, the fluidity of continuously dropping and lifting anchor contests the need for commitment or loyalty to any port, as well as challenges the extent of the sense of marginality.

In contrast to contemporary writing, post-modern literature has extended identity development as a fluid ongoing dialogic renegotiating process, creating and deploying a configuration of multiple identities as needed, a sense of horizontal rootedness and multiple loyalties. Provocatively, global identity has been briefly explored in the leadership literature as the possible antecedent to a global mindset and global competence or as the mediating factor between the two (Ananthram & Nankervis, 2014). Therefore, a new conceptualization of global identity that holds capacity for resonant connection among turbulence in the deterritorialized culture contact zones is needed.

TOWARD AN EXPANDED CONCEPTUALIZATION OF GLOBAL IDENTITY

Tensions for the global leader's global identity stem from the complexity of identity construction variables, the shifting constellation among those interdependent variables, and the often-competing priorities for allegiance and responsibility, ubiquitous in the global environment. Tension and reconciliation are part of the process of global identity development; global leaders influence and are influenced by continuously evolving myriad stimuli. Challenging the traditional construct of identity, Fig. 5.1 shows how global leaders' experience an identity-reconstruction-and-development-in-context process that uses three main elements to reconcile tensions and cultivate a global identity salient to the environment: multidimensionality, interdependency, and advocacy that nurtures the global identity.

Multidimensionality

Qualitatively different from the common construct of simultaneously held multiple identities, such as, father, tennis player and musician, the dimension of multidimensionality refers to a constellation of multiple identities. Similar to the guidance that constellations of symbols and signs provide to Polynesian

Fig. 5.1. Sources of Global Leader Tensions and Global Identity Dimensions.

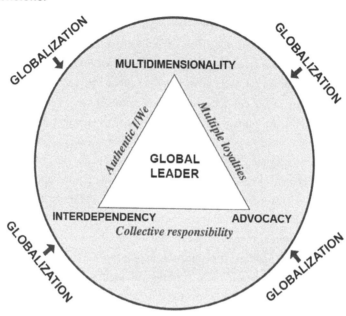

navigators, constellations of identities provide the global leader a kind of internal compass, or "na'au, the knowledge of the heart" (Polynesian Voyaging Society, 2019), that facilitates Global Resonance (Curran, 2018). A cultural composite enables affiliation with others at the human level and deprioritizes any specific cultural self, which prevents reverting to a polarized view of self and other. Multidimensionality of a global identity "emphasizes personal active relationships rather than group belonging" (De Rivera & Carson, 2015, p. 310) and gives leaders the focus for where they are going as well as where they are at the present moment, crucial for navigating the global environment and reconciling the tension of adaptive authenticity without traditional identification sources. This multidimensional relationality also sustains multiple loyalties that nurtures the global identity.

Interdependency

Interdependency, an element of a global leader's global identity, refers to an integrated, purpose-driven vertical and network-based horizontal rootedness among a dispersed collective. The sense of belonging becomes less externally labeled, more internally generated, and spans increasingly blurred boundaries. Relations are not just interconnected; they inextricably and interdependently intertwined. The matrix structure of a corporation operationally reflects this notion as does the effects of multiple pandemics at the individual, social, and international levels; the global identity of the global leader therefore intentionally invites and constructs interdependent relations in the context of hybridity in the deterritorialized environment.

Inclusion and communal reciprocity, related to belonging and loyalty to others, is common in non-Western paradigms. For example, Confucian cosmopolitanism (Ivanhoe, 2014) portrays membership and responsibility in a series of concentric circles, the center of which is the immediate family, with outwards circles incorporating other close relations and the world. Ujamaa na kujitegemea offers a Tanzanian process of interdependency in which implicit efforts and benefits are reciprocally shared, while Ubuntu, a Xhosa and Zulu term encompasses feelings of connection and compassion. All aptly illustrate the dimension of interdependency. Leading with agility, navigating uncertainty, and inspiring others, a global identity holds the capacity for interdependent, relational views of self and others, and sees and synergistically connects the inherent value among an expansive and diverse collective. Importantly, accountability and shared outcomes become collective responsibility, no longer tethered to a command and control or problem-solver mentality.

Advocacy

Understanding the self as a citizen of the world anchors a sense of membership in the world as a collective. Not dependent on boundaries that make in-group and out-group distinctions, a global identity is grounded in interdependent belonging based on a network of shared and mutual responsibility (De Rivera & Carson, 2015). The implication of that responsibility, expanded view of self, and relational place in the world illuminates the dimension of advocacy. Adding to a global identity's capacity for multidimensionality and interdependency, global self-identification is a "higher level of self-identification with the world than with a particular nation-state" (Zhou, 2016, p. 155) which shifts intent to finding integrated goals, albeit an especially challenging intent in the increasingly turbulent environment. Identification with a global collective therefore translates to the conscious effort devoted to increased accountability and responsibility to advocate for collective, global interests.

Conflicting concerns and tensions between local and global responsiveness and responsibility are abundant for a global leader; the three dimensions of the conceptualization of global identity facilitates a leader's capacity to build extensive networks of trusting relationships, connect with diverse constituencies, and create space for the voice of the interdependent collective. Conclusively, the expanding reach and touch of globalization has prompted the construct of global identity that reimagines how global leaders make sense of their world and experiences in it.

GLOBAL RESONANCE AND GLOBAL IDENTITY

Resonance, a principle drawn from the natural sciences, provides a metaphorical base for the process of Global Resonance. The concept describes predictable patterns of vibration, in contrast to turbulence found in an environment of interfering waves impinging from many unexpected sources. Travelers frequently experience unpredictable air patterns; luckily, airplanes are built with flexibility that enables them to withstand the conflicting pushes and pulls of turbulent winds. Similarly, a global leader's capacity for resonance provides a source of equilibrium among myriad unpredictable tensions, operationalized by creating a sense of safety, acceptance, welcome and inclusion, crucial to both authenticity and agility in the hybrid context in which global leaders live and work. Profoundly, resonance requires two; whether in music or relations, one cannot resonate alone.

Tensions for global leaders in the deterritorialized global environment contributed to the advancement of a conceptualization of global identity, based on developmental paradigms and inclusive of multidimensionality, interdependency and advocacy, all salient to current and future global leadership. Global Resonance, a developmental process generated by the *intent to connect*, symbiotically cultivates global identity while inspiring application of attitudes and behaviors crucial to the development of global leaders. Fig. 5.2 illustrates a symbiotic process of knowing, doing, and becoming by using arrows that point two directions: outside to inside and inside to outside.

Intercultural competence, cultural intelligence, global mindset are well established constructs that have been shown to act as antecedents that expand an

Fig. 5.2.   Outside-In and Inside-Out: The Symbiotic Cycle of Knowing-Doing-Becoming.

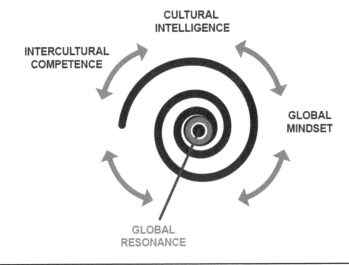

individual's cognitive complexity (Ananthram & Nankervis, 2014; Beechler & Javidan, 2007; Clapp-Smith & Lester, 2014; Early & Ang, 2003; Levy et al., 2016). Intercultural exposure engenders the potential for increased intercultural sensitivity, which in turn increases a global leader's intercultural competence and global mindset and creates an ever broadening and deepening space for Global Resonance. Shown by inward pointing arrows, the transformative developmental process of *becoming* thus generates the capacity for global resonance.

Arrows pointing from the inside-out depict the capacity for Global Resonance, inspired by intent, and synonymous with global leader identity; this becomes the source from which tensions are resolved, perspectives shift, and the process of co-creation flows. Developed from inside-out, Global Resonance influences the difference in practice of the knowing and doing capabilities, that is, global mindset that lends greater systemic lens, cultural intelligence that converts motivation to behavior, and intercultural competence that puts knowledge into cultural specific context.

Intent, a part of the nature of consciousness, creates a relationship among consciousness and the external world; "all thought is directed toward something" (Powers & Knapp, 2011, p. 90). While not completing a linear causal transaction, the power of intent has been shown to influence matching behaviors and collective performance as well as contribute to positive agency (Martins, 2018; Reddish et al., 2013; Turner, 2017). Intent, therefore, provides the internal source from which embodiment and practice of Global Resonance flows, and from which global mindset, cultural intelligence, and intercultural competence are put into practice; each creates space for and begets the other in an expanding and qualitatively distinctive flow. "In order for a holistic transformation to take place, it requires the involvement of the whole person, that is addressing all mind, body and spirit," as well as in relation to others (Papastamatis & Panitsides, 2014).

Clearly, global leadership is not an individual, independent activity; it is, notably, an interdependent and facilitative one, regardless of context; multiplier effects of interdependence, ambiguity and flux increase the magnitude of importance of the dynamic process of connection (Mendenhall et al., 2012). While globalization may greatly impact economic, political and technological interdependence, it also transforms the experience, behavior and identity of a global leader (Rosenmann et al., 2016). The global leader, therefore, becomes the catalytic element within the broader resonant system.

Similar to the expanded conceptualization of global identity, Global Resonance stands on the foundation firmly built by previous research and models of cross-cultural and intercultural competence (Hall, 1959; Hammerich & Lewis, 2013; Hofstede, 1991; Meyer, 2014; Trompenaars, 1993), cultural intelligence (Early & Ang, 2003), and global mindset (Javidan & Bowen, 2013). These and many more have focused on applied knowledge and skills for specific cultural contexts and functions. Yet, complex, socially constructed systems such as cultures and interactions in the hybrid contact zones cannot be reduced to predictable patterns, as contemporary literature sought and post-modern literature revealed. Kedia and Mukherji (1999) assert that global leaders need "to have openness that allows a global mindset to form, evolve and develop" (p. 232), which suggests an identity and "activity of being" (Kegan, 1982).

Developed and generated from the inside-out and outside-in simultaneously, Global Resonance as a process completes a global leader's *knowing-doing-becoming cycle*. Fig. 5.3 depicts this cycle within the construct of global identity; the components are briefly described with feelings and actions, in order to create the deeper sense of the cycle beyond cognitive explanations.

Fig. 5.3. Global Resonance: A Global Leader's Knowing-Doing-Becoming Cycle.

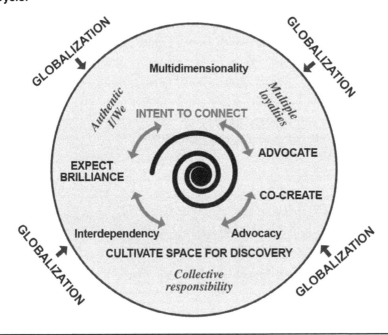

Intent to connect: Conscious Receptivity

Global Resonance begins from a place of conscious receptivity, not only accept-ing, but expecting and inviting the possibility to be changed by the interaction with another. The will to connect, also part of intent, provides impetus for the following emergent invitation to discovery, co-creation and advocacy to unfold. It is not a pre-planned place but a state of being of openness to possibilities, referred to as open will (Scharmer, 2013); a sense of readiness that sets the stage for connection to happen (Keller & Brown, 1968); and an empathic, other-centered praxis state, based on unconditional positive regard (Rogers, 1961). "Unconditionality implies a total openness, of house, of being, of culture, to the other" (Peters, 2012, p. 43). Surpassing the *hope* that connection will be made, *intent* establishes the sincere will and conscious decision to catalyze relations with and among others. To experience this phase of Global Resonance, consider this question: *I WILL connect, therefore, what kind of person do I want/need to be in this relationship? What impact might my conscious WILL to what follows?*

Expect Brilliance

Global Resonance assumes that a certain level of cross-cultural and intercultural competence, cultural intelligence and global mindset exists. Experiences have raised cultural awareness and increased the sensitivity to cultural differences, even if the perspectives may range in terms of understanding motivations. Within the emergent process of Global Resonance, honor and respect for the expected brilliance of the other is held in order to open the door to acceptance and suspended judgments. Cultural differences are acknowledged, but allowed to move off center stage, as individuals connect without distraction and bring whole selves to the dynamic and evolving interaction. In fact, only by consciously acknowledging culturally influenced perspectives and expectations can an individual allow them to move aside to become resources to draw on, not filters that can distort. Inherent in the context of a global leader's responsibilities, cultural complexity is expected; in this stage, however *not knowing* is embraced and sparks a challenge to preconceptions. Prior judgments of good and bad/right and wrong are suspended. Iteratively, increased awareness and compassion for another springs from within, facilitating the intent to connect. Practicing this stage, reflect on this question: *How can I allow my truth and my knowledge to inform, not distort, what I expect and experience?*

Cultivate Space for Discovery

Cultivating transformative space for discovery begins co-creation possibilities; unfolding and emergent meaning is allowed for and uninterrupted. This dialogic space is where "I" is transformed to "We." The multidimensionality and interdependency of a leader's global identity facilitates collective and meaningful shape of the "We." Again, the *knowing* and *doing*; that is, behavioral skills of intercultural competence, cultural intelligence and global mindset are not undeveloped; they are now being engaged differently in *becoming*.

Facilitating diversity of thinking and recognizing diversity in development are fundamental to co-creating Global Resonance. Critical in the global context of complexity, the process of transformative dialogue (Gergen et al., 2001), an asking-orientation that is based on curiosity, openness, respect and full expression of thought and feeling, contribute to Global Resonance.

There is also a consciousness in operationalizing *intent*. For example, if a leader is intent on connecting, then *how* she or he engages in dialogue is influenced. There are no universal rules for transformative dialogue; dialogue itself will alter the character of transformative utility (p. 686).

The basis of co-creating is exploration and discovery. The power of questions has been frequently underscored and reframing of issues and questions unlocks infinite possibilities (Gregersen, 2018). Cultivating space for discovery is not new, but the catalytic intent enables the capacity and capability to flourish within global complexity. To explore your capacity to open space, think about this: *How can I invite transformative dialogue, which inspires emergent and shared learning, and balances power?*

Co-Create

Wicked problem solving is rife with complexity and change. Global Resonance enables reframing and recognizing individual's contributions to the shared vision, and away from potentially adversarial blame or responsibility. Power differentials become more balanced and diverse influences leveraged in a partnership, which enriches the connection and shared outcome, and promotes commitment to action. "Collaborative construction of new realities emerges. Collectively knowing, moving and doing together, [resonant partners] are co-creating the change, solution or direction from within their connected state of being" (Gergen et al., 2001). The outcome is greater than one could have created alone, iteratively nourishing the continually *becoming* global leader. Reflecting on how you can co-create, consider this: *How can WE realize our common purpose and construct OUR new realities?*

Advocacy: Courageous Consciousness

Consciousness of what is and has been discovered increases awareness of influences, differences and possibilities that can no longer be ignored; courage to give voice to them is part of the global leader's responsibility. In helical fashion, therefore, advocacy re-fuels the cycle and redraws on *intent*, the element of global identity that is

> *childlike in simplicity…walking into each day and each moment*
> *with an open heart, active imagination and desire to connect, while*
> *holding the capacity for risk, passion for story, love of possibility.*
> *(Poulos, 2008)*

Actioning from your experience, consider this question: *How can I use my conscious courage to give voice to our discovery?*

SUMMARY AND NEXT STEPS

The emergent process of global resonance brings the inherent and somewhat overlooked attention to the dynamism of global leaders' global identity and practice. Nonproportionally, efforts and experiences of global leaders provide outside-in cultural data, for example, individual mindset shifts, and adaptation skills which symbiotically stretch capacity for inside-out growth and iteratively increase cognitive complexity and flexibility. Just as the nautilus shell expands as the creature grows, the leader's capacity, or container of data and experience, increases to accommodate more, creating the global identity and means of connecting with resonance in the global environment, the relevance for which has never been greater.

The comprehensive model proposed is theoretically based yet would benefit from further research into nascent claims. Previous research threads were pulled to develop the conceptualization of global identity; empirically examining the meaningfulness of the global identity dimensions, especially as they relate to global leader experience and development, would contribute to increasing clarity and coherence to the definition. Developing ways to measure the three elements of global identity would also help to improve the research rigor in this important area.

Comparative research is also needed to test the practicality of Global Resonance as a contributing factor for global leader effectiveness in the complex and dynamic global environment. Mendenhall et al. (2017) suggest that developmental readiness may play a role in explaining varying responses to tensions by individuals when in new cultural contexts. Intentionality as a key feature of Global Resonance and global identity may similarly be explored to help elucidate the value suggested in the model. Further, compelled by pandemic-induced political conditions around the world, the emergent nature of the global leader identity and practice proposed should be tested in the context of formal leadership voids, where emergent leaders have stepped forward. Finally, Global Resonance is offered as a replicable developmental process. How executive coaching and other formal learning and development initiatives facilitate the development of Global Resonance would support advancing the praxis of global leadership.

In conclusion, as presented, global identity and Global Resonance may appear elusive in the complexity of the global context; the feeling is strong, however, that the emphases on responsibility and intent that this chapter carries can offer hope to global leaders who hold immense power to make the world a better place for their teams, organizations, and the communities they serve.

REFERENCES

Adams, G. R., & Marshall, S. K. (1996). A developmental social psychology of identity: Understanding the person-in-context. *Journal of Adolescence*, *19*, 429–442.

Ananthram, S., & Nankervis, A. R. (2014). Outcomes and benefits of a managerial global mind-set: An exploratory study with senior executives in North America and India. *Thunderbird International Business Review*, *56*(2), 193–209.

Appadurai, A. (1990). Disjuncture and difference in the global cultural economy. *Theory, Culture & Society*, *7*(2–3), 295–310. https://doi.org/10.1177/02632769 0007002017

Arnett, J. J. (2002). The psychology of globalization. *American Psychologist*, *57*(10), 774–783. https://doi.org/10.1037//0003-66X.57.10.774

Bauman, Z. (2011). Migration and identities in the globalized world. *Philosophy and Social Criticism*, *37*(4), 425–435. https://doi.org/10.1177/0191453710396809

Beechler, S., & Javidan, M. (2007). Leading with a global mindset. In M. Javidan, R. Steers, & M. Hitt (Eds.), *Advances in international management* (Vol. 19, pp. 131–169). Elsevier.

Clapp-Smith, R., & Lester, G. V. (2014). Defining the "mindset" in global mindset: Modeling the dualities of global leadership. *Advances in Global Leadership*, *8*, 205–228.

Cook-Greuter, S. R. (2004). Making the case for a developmental perspective. *Industrial and Commercial Training*, *36*(6/7), 275–281. https://doi.org/10.1108/00197850410563902

Curran, K. (2018). Developing global resonance for global leadership. In R. J. Thompson & J. Storberg-Walker (Eds.), *Leadership and power in international development: Navigating the intersections of gender, culture, context, and sustainability* (pp. 311–329). Emerald Publishing.

De Rivera, J., & Carson, H. A. (2015). Cultivating a global identity. *Journal of Social and Political Psychology*, *3*(2), 310–330.

Dyer, J., Christensen, C. M., & Gregersen, H. B. (2011). *The innovator's DNA*. Harvard Business Review Press.

Early, P. C., & Ang, S. (2003). *Cultural intelligence: Individual interactions across cultures*. Stanford University Press.

Elden, S. (2005). Missing the point: Globalization, deterritorialization and the space of the world. *Transactions of the Institute of British Geographers*, *30*, 8–19. https://doi.org/10.1111/j.1475-5661.2005.00148.x

Erickson, E. H. (1968). *Identity, youth, and crisis*. Norton.

Ferrari, M., Robinson, D. K., & Yasnitsky, A. (2010). Wundt, Vygotsky, and Bandura: A cultural-historical science of consciousness in three acts. *History of the Human Sciences*, *23*(95), 95–118.

Geertz, C. (1979). From the native's point of view: On the nature of anthropological understanding. In P. Rabinow & W. M. Sullivan (Eds.), *Interpretive social science* (pp. 225–241). University of California Press.

Gergen, K. J. (1991). *The saturated self*. Basic Books.

Gergen, K. J., McNamee, S., & Barrett, F. J. (2001). Toward transformative dialogue. *International Journal of Public Administration*, *24*(7–8), 679–707.

Gregersen, H. (2018). *Questions are the answer: A breakthrough approach to your most vexing problems and work and in life*. Harper Collins.

Hall, E. T. (1959). *The silent language*. Doubleday.

Hammack, P. L. (2008). Narrative and the cultural psychology of identity. *Society for Personality and Social Psychology*, *12*(3), 222–247. https://doi.org/10.1177/1088868308316892

Hammerich, K., & Lewis, R. D. (2013). *Fish can't see water: How national culture can make or break your corporate strategy*. John Wiley & Sons.

Hermans, H. J. M., & Kempen, H. J. G. (1998). Moving cultures: The perilous problems of cultural dichotomies in a globalizing society. *American Psychologist*, *53*(10), 1111–1120.

Hofstede, G. (1983). National cultures revisited. *Behavior Science Research*, *18*(4), 285–305. https://doi.org/10.1177/106939718301800403

Hofstede, G. (1991). *Culture's consequences: Software of the mind*. McGrawHill.

Hui, C. H., & Triandis, H. C. (1983). Multistrategy approach to cross-cultural research: The case of locus of control. *Journal of Cross-Cultural Psychology*, *14*(1), 65–83. https://doi.org/10.1177/0022002183014001005

Ivanhoe, P. J. (2014). Confucian cosmopolitanism. *Journal of Religious Ethics*, *42*(1), 22–44.

Javidan, M., & Bowen, D. (2013). The 'global mindset' of managers. *Organizational Dynamics*, *42*(2), 145–155. https://doi.org/10.1016/j.orgdyn.2013.03.008

Jokinen, T. (2005). Global leadership competencies: A review and discussion. *Journal of European Industrial Training*, *29*(3), 199–216.

Kedia, B. L., & Mukheriji, A. (1999). Global managers: Developing a mindset for global competitiveness. *Journal of World Business*, *34*(3), 230–251. https://doi.org/10.1016/S1090-9516(99)00017-6

Kegan, R. (1982). *The evolving self: Problem and process in human development.* Harvard University Press.

Keller, P. W., & Brown, C. T. (1968). An interpersonal ethic for communication. *Journal of Communication*, *18*, 73–81.

Kluckhohn, F. R., & Strodtbeck, F. L. (1961). *Variations in value orientations.* Row, Peterson.

Levy, O., Peiperl, M. A., & Jonsen, K. (2016). Cosmopolitanism in a globalized world: An interdisciplinary perspective. *Advances in Global Leadership*, *9*, 281–323.

Markus, H., & Kitiyama, S. (1991). Culture and the self: Implications for cognition, emotion and motivation. *Psychological Review*, *98*, 224–253.

Marquardt, M. J., & Berger, N. O. (2000). *Global leaders for the 21st century.* State University of New York Press.

Martins, N. O. (2018). An ontology of power and leadership. *Journal for the Theory of Social Behaviour*, *48*(1), 83–97. https://doi.org/10.1111/jtsb.12155

McCauley, C. D., Drath, W. H., Palus, C. J., O'Connor, P. M. G., & Baker, B. A. (2006). The use of constructive-developmental theory to advance the understanding of leadership. *The Leadership Quarterly*, *17*(6), 634.

Mead, G. (1934). *Mind, self, and society.* University of Chicago.

Mendenhall, M. E., Reiche, B. S., Bird, A., & Osland, J. S. (2012). Defining the "global" in global leadership. *Journal of World Business*, *47*, 493–503. https://doi.org/10.1016/j.jwb.2012.01.003

Mendenhall, M. E., Weber, T. J., Arnardottir, A. A., & Oddou, G. R. (2017). Developing global leadership competencies: A process model. In J. Osland, M. Li, & M. Mendenhall (Eds.), *Advances in global leadership* (Vol. 10, pp. 117–148). Emerald Publishing.

Meyer, E. (2014). *The culture map: Breaking through the invisible boundaries of global business.* Public Affairs.

Papastamatis, A., & Panitsides, E. (2014). Transformative learning: Advocating for a holistic approach. *Review of European Studies*, *6*(4), 74–81. https://doi.org/10.5539/res.v6n4p74

Papastergiadis, N. (2005). Hybridity and ambivalence: Places and flows in contemporary art and culture. *Theory, Culture & Society, 22*(4), 39–64. https://doi.org/10.1177/0263276405054990

Peters, M. A. (2012). Western models of intercultural philosophy. *Analysis and Metaphysics, 11*, 30–53.

Polynesian Voyaging Society. (2019). https://www.pbs.org/wayfinders/polynesian8.html

Poulos, C. N. (2008). Accidental dialogue. *Communication Theory, 18*(1), 117–138.

Powers, B. A., & Knapp, T. R. (2011). *Dictionary of nursing, theory and research* (4th ed.). Springer Publishing Company.

Pratt, M. L. (1991). Arts of the contact zone. In J. M. Wolff (Ed.), *Professing in the contact zone* (pp. 1–20). NCTE.

Reddish, P., Fischer, R., & Bulbulia, J. (2013). Let's dance together: Synchrony, shared intentionality and cooperation. *PLoS ONE, 8*(8), e71182. https://doi.org/10.1371/journal.pone.0071182

Reiche, B. S., Bird, A., Mendenhall, M. E., & Osland, J. S. (2016). Contextualizing leadership: A typology of global leadership roles. *Journal of International Business Studies, 48*(5), 1–22. https://doi.org/10.1057/s41267-016-0030-3

Rogers, C. R. (1961). *On becoming a person.* Houghton Mifflin.

Rogers, P., & Tan, J. S. (2008). Fifty years of intercultural studies: A continuum of perspectives for research and teaching. *University of Michigan, Ross School of Business Working Paper Series, Working Paper No. 1104.* http://ssrn.com/abstract=1132328

Rosenmann, A., Reese, G., & Cameron, J. E. (2016). Social identities in a globalized world: Challenges and opportunities for collective action. *Perspectives on Psychological Science, 11*(2), 202–221. https://doi.org/10.1177/1745691615621272

Roudometof, V. (2005). Transnationalism, cosmopolitanism, and globalization. *Current Sociology, 53*(1), 113–135. https://doi.org/10.1177/0011392105048291

Scharmer, C. O. (2013). Addressing the blind spot of our time: An executive summary of the new book by Otto Scharmer. Theory U: leading from the future as it emerges. *Social Technology of Presencing, 1–20.* https://www.presencing.org/assets/images/theory-u/Theory_U_Exec_Summary.pdf

Smith, W. K., & Lewis, M. W. (2011). Toward a theory of paradox: A dynamic equilibrium model of organizing. *Academy of Management Review, 36*(2), 381–403.

Tajfel, H. (1978). The achievement of group differentiation. In H. Tajfel (Ed.), *Differentiation between social groups: Studies in the social psychology of intergroup relations* (pp. 77–98). Academic Press.

Triandis, H. C. (1989). The self and social behavior in different cultural contexts. *Psychological Review, 96*, 269–289.

Trompenaars, F. (1993). *Riding the waves of culture*. The Economist Books.

Turner, C. K. (2017). A principle of intentionality. *Frontiers in Psychology*, 8(137), 1–10. https://doi.org/10.3389/fpsyg.2017.00137

Urry, J. (2003). *Global complexity*. Blackwell Publishing.

Yeoh, B. S. A., Willis, K. D., & Fakhri, S. M. A. K. (2003). Transnational edges. *Ethnic and Racial Studies*, 26(2), 207–217. https://doi.org/10.1080/01419870 32000054394

Zhou, M. (2016). Social and individual sources of self-identification as global citizens: Evidence from the interactive multilevel model. *Sociological Perspectives*, 59(1), 153–176. https://doi.org/10.1177/0731121415579281

PART II

THE STUDY OF GLOBAL LEADERSHIP

6

UNIVERSITY-BASED LEADERSHIP EDUCATION FOR PROFESSIONALS WORKING IN THE GLOBALIZED CONTEXT

WENDY E. ROWE AND WANDA KRAUSE

Addressing the question of leadership education for professionals working in the globalized context requires clarifying what it means to be a leader and, therefore, what competencies are required for people navigating the existing and growing forces of globalization in their teams, workplaces, organizations or communities. Various definitions of globalization exist (Knight, 2003, 2004; Scholte, 2002). However, in this chapter, we choose to work with a definition that aptly embraces an understanding that prepares leaders for working on the micro and macro levels in the global world. Scholte (2002) conceptualizes globalization as forces that reduce barriers to connections and relationships between people. Globalization as a process of "building connections between people across a one world," as Scholte (2002, p. 14) defines it, offers a process for the global leader who wants to actively engage in practices that increase cross-cultural awareness and communication, as well as actions that build and lead collaborative solutions to address complex global problems.

This chapter will address broader questions pertaining to globalization forces that impact on the leadership demands of professionals engaged in global activism or work in the international or multi-cultural context. Next, it will look more specifically at the leadership competencies required of these individuals and provide a comprehensive review of a university-based program, the Global Leadership Program at Royal Roads University: its learning principles, curriculum content, and pedagogical practices that enhance the learning of global leadership competencies. Finally, this chapter will delineate how the program seeks to develop the global leader to meet contemporary challenges related to globalization and global issues.

GLOBALIZATION DEPENDS ON
CONNECTIONS AND RELATIONSHIPS

Globalization is a term that has been burdened with conceptualizations that first require discussion. Scholte (2002) provides a critique of localized and ethnocentric conceptualizations of globalization, such as internalization, liberalization, universalism and westernization. According to Scholte, arguments that build on these conceptions fail to open insights that are not available through preexistent vocabulary (2002, p. 8). She argues for a definition based on connections and relationships across a one world:

> *globalization as the spread of transplanetary – and in recent times more particularly supraterritorial – connections between people. From this perspective, globalization involves reductions in barriers to transworld contacts. People become more able – physically, legally, culturally, and psychologically – to engage with each other in "one world." (p. 14)*

Hence, for Scholte (2002), people may live together not only in local, provincial, national, regional realms, and built environments, but also in *transplanetary* spaces; that is, where the world is a single place. *Supraterritorial* relations are social connections that transcend territorial geography. They are relatively delinked from territory; that is, domains mapped on the land surface of the earth (p. 17). Globality, as such, refers to "social links between people located at points anywhere on earth, within a whole-world context. The global sphere is then a social space in its own right" (p. 15). By viewing globalization as a process of *building connections between people across a one world*, possibilities exist for change in global conditions and events, for example, leading to increased trade and economic growth, management of environmental resources, elevating human quality of life, preventing the spread of world diseases, and depletion of resources, reducing pollution and other threats to climate change, adoption of standards promoting human dignity and rights, and prevention of war and conflict, plus many more globally significant issues.

FORCES OF GLOBALIZATION THAT HINDER OR FACILITATE CONNECTION BUILDING

Numerous factors may hinder or facilitate globalized connection building. There is a tendency of those who work in the global world to refer only to the macro and external factors of politics that generate competition for resources and power challenges discounting other processes because these are relegated to the private sphere and thought to have no political import (Krause, 2012, p. 52). However, forces of globalization that may hinder or facilitate connection building are also at the micro level. These are the personal or individual factors, which includes (a) one's subjectivity, the inner and personal dimensions of the whole self level (physical, emotional, mental, spiritual), and one's consciousness level (Krause, 2013, pp. 59–68); and (b) one's outer or external and more easily observable behaviors and actions (i.e., performance, choices, skills).

In discussion on the influencers and drivers to connection building, it is critical to acknowledge personal leadership work. The forces that hinder connection building at this level include lack of self-awareness and bias (Krause, 2019a, p. 251). Shifting larger political, social and economic structures and systems toward balance, justice, and equality will be a futile attempt without "the transformation of consciousness that occurs through everyday practice and transformation exercising agency towards the transformation of the self and of power relations" (Krause, 2019b, p. 94). Who we are matters profoundly to being able to create the changes we want to see. To become a global leader means moving past these limiting beliefs and transforming mental models that are holding us back (Krause, 2013, p. 70). Hence, personal capacities comprise the cornerstone to the learning and growth that the global leadership program at Royal Roads University enables.

Cultural competencies in a globalized world form another cornerstone to the Royal Roads program. Understanding oneself in relation to others, understanding different cultures, acquiring cultural sensitivity, and acquiring intercultural communication skills becomes important to the endeavor of building cultural competencies in a globalized context. However, when enhancing global cultural competency, it is critical to recognize the power dynamics of different collectives differentiated largely on cultural identity which has led to exclusion and marginalization of some groups of people as well as erosion of cultural markets in some instances. The erosion of culture includes the fast disappearance of native languages and Indigenous peoples' heritages which have been undercut or erased across the world (Scholte, 2002, p. 29). Global cultural competency must include cultural sensitivity, awareness of cultural exclusions and more diverse cultural knowledge that is less Eurocentric. As Henderson notes, when most professors describe the "world," they describe artificial Eurocentric contexts (2000, p. 58). Many parts of the existing Eurocentric academy have not fully accepted diversity of knowledge as embedded in cultures different to western thought (Battiste, 2000, p. xix).

Scholte (2002) points out, connection building will be facilitated through using methods of study that go beyond territorial geography, enabling access of technology to all and in particular the marginalized, or the growth of transplanetary and supraterritorial interconnections between marginalized and repressed groups.

One of the shifts that globalization forces have created is an opening for a higher order of leader. This era of globality as transplanetary and supraterritorial is seeing connectivity, climate change, and technological advances, as examples, occurring at much faster rates than ever before. Given these rapid shifts and the positive and destructive globalization forces, as elaborated above, we are at a time when we require global leaders most critically. In this chapter, we will refer to the importance of leadership – more specifically leadership capabilities and behaviors – that facilitate positive and sustainable connections between different nation-state leaders and aid in addressing the global forces.

RELATIONSHIP BUILDING COMPETENCIES REQUIRED OF GLOBAL LEADERS

The world is complex with significant differences geographically, economically, culturally, politically, and culturally. For leaders to comprehend and have the capacity to build relationships across diverse groups and across regional geo-political and cultural boundaries, it requires competencies that include what they know about the world and who are its citizens, having systems thinking capabilities so as to comprehend the complexity and macro/micro interactions of multiple global drivers, are self-aware and culturally sensitive to the differing perspectives of others, and finally have the skills to work collaboratively with diverse others to influence action and progress for the betterment of the world.

This conceptualization of the global leader as a person who is building relationships in the global context can be seen in the following definition of global leadership:

> *Global leadership is the capacity to lead and support oneself, others, organizations, communities, and complex systems in ways that enhance the well-being of communities and the planet, both today and in the future. An orientation to diversity and global citizenship is fundamental to our understanding of global leadership and allows us to recognize and value the multiple and evolving ways of being, doing, and knowing. Global leadership acknowledges that all communities are global communities and that we are fundamentally interconnected. Global leaders are guided by principles of mindfulness and compassion and work to promote dignity, humanity, prosperity, and justice for all. (Rowe et al., 2015, p. 193)*

Characteristics and competencies for global leaders have been well articulated by many scholars and practitioners (Mendenhall et al., 2018). Joyce Osland (2018) describes a five-level structure to represent universal global leadership characteristics: (1) global knowledge; (2) threshold traits of integrity, humility, inquisitiveness and self-resilience; (3) attitudes and orientations (the global mindset) toward a global context; (4) interpersonal skills for working cross-culturally in teams; and (5) systems thinking skills. At a more micro level, we find intercultural competency (Cushner & Chang, 2015; Elola & Oskoz, 2008), emotional intelligence (Holtbrugge & Engelhard, 2016), moral and ethical reasoning (Luo & Jamieson-Drake, 2015), altruism and ability to appreciate cultural differences (Yang et al., 2016), perception of self and worldview in relation to culturally diverse others (Bell et al., 2016), and global citizenship awareness (Coers et al., 2012). All these competencies support efforts of globalization to build connections with people in a "one world."

Life experiences also significantly contribute to the development of global leaders – experiences of multi-culturalism, global travels and living, and multiple language proficiency. Building global competencies for professionals who work in a domestic company that is impacted by global forces or must deal with the complexity of multi-cultural employees, clients or work colleagues requires educational programs in high schools, in universities and in the work place.

The personal leadership competencies relate to globalizing forces on the micro level – the individual consciousness and behavior. Here, learning how to embed and practice values of trust and tolerance, for example, must be learned before leadership competencies of being in service to others. The cultural competencies in a diverse global context relate to those competencies that are critical to addressing global challenges that are rooted in culture and a collective's consciousness. One needs to go beyond inclusion to plurality and diversity, where diversity is not simply about color, race, ethnicity, gender, sexual orientation, religion, age or educational level, but includes disabilities and various challenges; it includes approaches and ways of learning information; it encompasses the logic a person holds to make sense of the world and process information (Krause, 2019a, p. 255).

The competencies that are required to lead change in complex environments involve understanding of the larger systems forces. While we refer to the micro and macro level changes, it is important that the global leader understand their role in the micro influencing the macro larger forces and how the larger forces intersect. It is the work of the global leader to move from an ego-centric perspective to an ethnocentric, a worldcentric to even a kosmocentric (Wilber et al., 2008, pp. 80, 122). In other words, one learns they are not the center of the universe and grows to understand their role in it as being in service of the larger whole. The global leader knows and embodies the higher levels of being and acting and knows that the competencies related to the basics of survival often take precedence, such as in how to deliver the basics of life, how to ensure access to energy, or security of person and property. As Hamilton articulates it,

> *[t]hey also need to know how to feed the babies and the families. They also need to know how to educate people who are most disconnected and disadvantaged about key leverage values of life. (p. 117)*

GLOBAL LEADERSHIP EDUCATION

The next question concerns: How are global leaders created? Do they come with innate abilities and traits, or are they developed through experiences, training and education? The answer appears to be yes to both questions. Many of the characteristics associated with global leaders are thought to be innate or pre-dispositional traits – intelligence, integrity, humility, inquisitiveness, resiliency, optimism, tolerance of ambiguity, self-confidence, and self-awareness (Bird et al., 2010; Bird & Osland, 2008; Black, 2006; McCall & Hollenbeck, 2002; Osland, 2018). However, these traits are not enough. Becoming a global leader requires knowledge of the geo-political world and its people (Bird & Oddou, 2018), skills for interacting with diverse people (Bird et al., 2010), and real-life strategies for creative problem solving and adaptability in the global world (Deal et al., 2003; Osland & Bird, 2018; Zaccaro et al., 2006).

There are many who argue that real-life international assignments (Kohonen, 2005; McCall & Hollebeck, 2002; Zaccaro et al., 2006), cross-cultural experiences (Osland, 1995) and "hard knocks" on-the job training (Collins, 2001; Iacocco, 2008) are required for global leaders to strengthen pre-dispositional traits and develop cross-cultural competencies and adaptability. This is consistent with a theory that global leaders learn best in the context in which they will practice and from other leaders that they trust (Ready, 2002). Here one sees senior managers provided with coaching and mentoring (Oliver et al., 2009; Osland et al., 2012), given expatriate international work assignments (McCall & Hollebeck, 2002) and exposed to leader story telling (Ready, 2002). More intentional are the skill-based programs that focus on foreign language training (Caligiuri, 2006), conflict management, negotiation, and customs and norms of other countries.

There is no doubt that international work-based assignments present valuable opportunities to learn many global leadership skills (Osland et al., 2006). Therefore, we argue higher education institutions must play a role in bringing relevant theory to practice – theories of human behavior, communication, social systems, cultural influence, political dynamics, conflict and peace, and aid in the development of the global leader. We argue university education programs must contribute to changes in mental models and uncover unconscious biases through critical analysis of social, political, and economic systems. We, further, argue university leadership programs must seek to expose assumptions about the intersectionality of race, age, gender, class, and other characteristics to develop leaders with better awareness and therefore ability to navigate environments of diversity and conflict (Deal & Prince, 2003).

Finally, we consider those university programs that teach theory within the context of practice application, incorporating many elements found in corporate training programs (Crawford et al., 2002). This is not found in the formalized university classroom but in university programs that provide education in the context of practical experience, augmented and supported by coaching, training, and mentoring (Gosling & Mintzberg, 2006, 2004). According to Malcolm Knowles (1984), there are four principles that are applied to adult learning: (1) adults need to be involved in the planning and evaluation of their instruction; (2) experience (including mistakes) provides the basis for learning activities; (3) adults are most interested in learning subjects that have immediate relevance to their job or personal life; and (4) adult learning is problem-centered rather than content-oriented (Kearsley, 2010). These principles of learning are incorporated into the MA in Global Leadership (MAGL) program at Royal Roads University, Canada, across nine key competencies areas for the development of the global leader.

COMPETENCIES UNDERLYING THE ROYAL ROADS UNIVERSITY MA IN GLOBAL LEADERSHIP PROGRAM (MAGL)

The competencies chosen as learning goals for the MAGL program were developed through a consultative process with over 60 scholars, practitioners and educators (Rowe et al., 2015).

A. Personal Leadership Working in a Global Context

Personal Leadership Working in a Global Context entails understanding one's values, beliefs and behaviors in the context of other people, being aware of one's orientation in the world, being accountable for one's behavior, and being open to learning. It includes being able to manage one's emotional reactions and being adaptive and resilient in complex changing environments.

1. *Self-Reflective Practice* entails orienting toward personal mastery and developing a supportive, self-reflexive practice. This inward focus entails continual self-reflection and approaching internal and external challenges through the lens of lifelong learning. Cultivating one's mental, physical, and spiritual health through regular inward-focused practices provides the foundation needed to serve others and to engage in global leadership from a healthy, professional, respectful position.

2. *Resilience and Personal Adaptability* refers to the ability to adapt, learn and change in response to complex, challenging and stressful environments through exercise of self-awareness and management of feeling and emotions, development of supportive and productive relationships and through implementation of action plans that enhance self-management capabilities, resilience and the ability to thrive in complex environments.

3. *Self-in-Systems Management Capability* refers to awareness of self in relation to others in a global context (e.g., how one's actions affect others +/–), and in relation to broader social-ecological systems. Exercises responsibility and accountability in interactions with self and others. Looks for leverage points for positive change of self, regardless of position in a system.

B. Leading in a Diverse Global Context

Leading in a Diverse Global Context is the ability to engage in effective and appropriate interaction with others in a variety of cultural contexts (both globally and locally), and to honor differences in values, beliefs, and behaviors. Diversity reflects multiple ways of being, doing, and knowing across and within diverse contexts, populations, groups, and systems. Leading in diversity is grounded in an understanding of one's own cultural identity, being aware that other cultural values, beliefs, and behaviors exist, using appropriate communication practices, managing inevitable contact with others, working together and engaging collaborative learning across real or perceived cultural divides.

1. *Culture – General and Specific Knowledge* is defined as knowledge of the societal-level values and norms on which most cultures vary. This

general understanding moves beyond cultural stereotypes and mono-
cultural models toward fluid, emergent, and dynamic intercultural and
intersectional understandings of the diversity and ever-changing nature
of human experience. Culture-specific knowledge includes understanding one's own values, norms, beliefs, rites, rituals and behaviors
which result from having grown up within specific countries, cultures,
and contexts (e.g., generation, socio-economic background, historical
conditions), in comparison with the values, norms, beliefs, rituals, and
behaviors of those from other cultures and contexts - recognizing both
similarities and differences.

2. *Intercultural Interaction and Communication* refers to the ability to
interact with and communicate in a variety of mediums with people of
different cultures, ages/generations, and other dimensions of difference,
demonstrating awareness of communication methods, protocols, and
norms appropriate to the setting.

3. *Intercultural Group Facilitation* refers to the ability to work effectively with groups and teams taking into account generational,
gendered, cultural, and other differences, to include skills in forming
working groups/teams, facilitating group performance, managing
tension and negotiating conflict situations, and exercising hosting and
fellowship behaviors.

C. Leading Sustained Change in Complex Environments

Leading Sustainable Change in Complex Environments refers to the ability of a leader to understand the complex political, social, and economic
issues in the world and how they impact communities and organizations.
Such leaders can work within and mobilize the resources of the international
organizations as well as community-based organizations to affect change in
organizations or in communities.

1. *Knowledge of Global Political, Social and Economic Issues* includes
knowledge of the complex political, social, and economic drivers
impacting communities (e.g., national borders, indigenous communities,
environmental ecosystems, and generations), and their interrelationships across a variety of international and global systems. Drivers of

change might include climate change and natural disasters, wars, conflict and forced migration, globalization and immigration patterns, new technologies, global conventions, treaties, agreements, and policies.

2. *Knowledge of International Organization Systems and Change Strategies* includes knowledge of organizational mandates, policies, structures and performance systems of the United Nations (and its affiliates), international and local non-government organizations (NGOs), governments, and civil society, in terms of how they deliver support for communities in need (e.g., humanitarian aid), support global markets, facilitate social/educational capacity development, and implement other change initiatives.

3. *Capability to Lead Change in Complex Environments* refers to the abilities to create vision, and to organize and facilitate processes of change through collaboration with others and across multiple cultural, social, and political boundaries, exercising creativity and innovative thinking, and making use of collaborative and dialogic processes.

PRINCIPLES OF LEARNING FOR THE MAGL PROGRAM

Andragogy learning principles incorporated in the MAGL Program are articled in the *Royal Roads University Learning and Teaching Model*, Revised Version (Hamilton et al., 2013), which was adopted from UNESCO's Commission on Education for the Twenty-First Century (Delors, 1996) and subsequent work by UNESCO'S Education for Sustainable Development Initiative (2012). This model organizes learning into the following five pillars:

a) Learning to Know – the development of skills and knowledge needed to function in this world, e.g., formal acquisition of literacy, numeracy, critical thinking and general knowledge (the mastery of learning tools).

b) Learning to Do – the acquisition of applied skills linked to professional success.

c) Learning to Live Together – the development of social skills and values such as respect and concern for others, of social and interpersonal skills; and the appreciation of cultural diversity. These are fundamental building blocks for social cohesion, as they foster mutual trust and support and strengthen our communities and society as a whole.

d) Learning to Be – the learning that contributes to a person's mind, body and spirit. Skills include creativity and personal discovery, acquired through reading, the Internet, and activities such as sports and arts.

e) Learning to Transform Oneself and Society – when individuals and groups gain knowledge, develop skills, and acquire new values as a result of learning, they are equipped with tools and mindsets for creating lasting change in organizations, communities, and societies.

In addition, there are a number of key learning principles and pedagogical features that underlie student experiences in the MAGL program, including emphasis on authentic collaboration, a competency framework that guides learning outcomes, blended online courses and intensive residencies, a flexible curriculum, intensive learning, feedback and coaching during intensive residencies, and competency assessment of student progress.

1. Authentic collaboration

The MAGL program strongly emphasizes collaborative, experiential and dialogue-based learning. Piggot-Irvine (2012) encourages the use of "authentic collaboration" which is characterized by holding empathy for the perception of others, and coming to genuine acceptance of the validity of another's way of being/thinking, as well as seeing the world through others' eyes. It also involves suspending one's own known perceptions and opening up to unknown other perceptions. It is associated with co-generation: achieving new levels of awareness of both our own and others' perspectives. A high degree of skill development is required for such collaboration and such skill is intricately associated initially with our individual ability to overcome very common defensive tendencies followed by the development of dialogue and inquiry-based values and strategies that are associated with openness (p. 87).

2. A Competency Framework Guides the Learning Outcomes

The program framework links theory to practice. Learning outcomes for each competency domain are organized into areas of knowledge learning (the head), new attitudes and perspectives (the heart) and new skills or behaviors (the hands). Courses include learning at the level of the head, heart, and hands through case studies, inquiry projects, exercises, and applied projects in which students will connect "ideas to practice" in their workplaces and their communities.

3. Blended Online Courses and Intensive Residencies

Courses in the MAGL program are offered in a blended learning model so as to permit working professionals to engage in study while also living and working in their own communities (Hamilton et al., 2017). Blended learning programs usually consist of short residencies of intensive face-to-face study with on line courses in between the face-to-face residencies. Fleck (2012) observed intensive learning periods,

> can be designed to maximize interactions between student peers with relevant experience to share, and to facilitate the development of real world business relationships that can offer considerable value beyond the merely didactic benefits of transmission teaching. (p. 403)

4. Flexible Curriculum with Consistent Critical Features

The MAGL curriculum has a consistent format and key features of the courses that are offered across all offerings (e.g., three assignments of which one is always a team assignment), while at the same time is sufficiently flexible that it can be adapted to different specialized groups of learners and programs. This is done by combining required readings, sessions, and course practices (identified as "foundational sessions" and "foundational learning structures") on one hand, with supplementary readings and complementary sessions on the other. Additionally, some on line courses are offered as electives, to facilitate the transferring in of credits earned from certificate programs that address learning outcomes similar to those emphasized in the MA Leadership program.

5. Intensive Learning, Feedback and Coaching During Intensive Residencies

During the face-to-face residency, students engage in intensive self-exploration, develop new relationships across many cultural boundaries, and learn new personal and interpersonal skills. Every knowledge plenary on theories and concepts is integrated with exercises to apply the concepts to oneself or working world. The residencies are highly intensive and experiential. To support learning in this environment, faculty advisors provide students comprehensive feedback, coaching, and academic assessment.

6. Competency Assessment of Student Progress

Students are assessed not only on their capabilities to write or talk about leadership but on their capabilities to demonstrate it in practice. Experiential learning requires not only experiencing, but also reflecting on that experience, conceptualizing and applying relevant theories and concepts, and then applying new understandings to practical applications. A goal of the MAGL program is to integrate professional practice and theory to help students more closely assess the quality of their own behaviors, thinking, and interactions both in the cohort and in their workplaces.

STUDENTS IN THE MAGL PROGRAM

The MAGL program deliberately seeks students who have prior professional experiences (or have worked in the past) in international non-government organizations (INGOs), international governments, indigenous organizations, or globally focused social-purpose organizations and have a minimum of five years of experience in leadership roles at a community or organizational level, with responsibility for implementing programs or influencing change or improvements in socio-economic conditions within international or indigenous communities.

SPONSORSHIP REQUIREMENTS AND OTHER PARTNERSHIPS

Organizational sponsors and partners are critical to the success of the MA Global Leadership program. Each student is encouraged to establish a relationship with an organizational or community sponsor who will be able to provide mentorship and organizational supports, especially in regards to the student's culminating program capstone project. Case examples and project ideas are sought from these partners and are used in the classroom, often as leadership challenges.

THE MAGL CURRICULUM

There are four domains of curriculum content.

Domain One comprises courses primarily related to A and B competencies (described above) addressing development of personal awareness, resiliency, systems thinking, and cross-cultural communication and interaction skills. These courses are foundational.

Domain Two courses address knowledge creation and transfer specific to international community development. These courses are offered as electives and covers topics such as community development in a global context, conflict and tensions and socio-political dynamics of the global world.

Domain Three courses address knowledge creation and transfer specific to organizational leadership. These courses include the organizational dynamics of social purposes organizations and strategic analysis, decision-making and evaluation.

Domain Four courses are specific to real world experiences. These include an international study abroad trip (two-to-four weeks), an eight-month capstone project for a sponsoring organization, and/or an internship in a globally oriented organization.

Fig. 6.1 shows the courses offered in the MAGL Program for the 24-month program.

Fig. 6.1.   MA Global Leadership Program.

MA GLOBAL LEADERSHIP (24 month option)
Leadership to Build Capacity & Sustainability for Individuals, Organizations and Communities in a Global Context

> **GBLD 501: Personal Capacities for Working in Complex Global Systems**
> (prerequisite to continue) *(3 credits online)*

> **GBLD 505: Personal Capacities for Working in Complex Global Systems**
> (prerequisite to continue) *(9 credits)*
> *3 weeks online, 2 weeks on campus, 5 weeks online*
> • Cultural competency
> • Resilience & adaptability
> • Teamwork skills
> • Systems thinking

> **REQUIRED 12 elective credits from Modules A and B or D or 3 credits from any elective in Module A or B or D**
> **and 9 credits from an area of specialization.**
> (Note: Modules A, B and D run simultaneously, giving multiple choice points for students)

A. Module Electives: Global Organizational Leadership
1. GBLD 510: Social Structures and Dynamics within Social-Purpose Organizations *(3 credits online)*
2. GBLD 511: Strategic Analysis, Decision Making and Evaluation *(3 credits online)*

B. Module Electives: Community Capacity Development
1. GBLD 520: Navigating Geo-Political Dynamics of Global Communities *(3 credits online)*
2. GBLD 521: Community-Development Models *(3 credits online)*
3. GBLD 522: Managing Difficult Relationships Within and Across Community Dynamics *(3 credits online)*

C. Module: Specialization
Up to 9 credits (three courses) may be transferred from another program at RRU or outside recognized institution (with permission of instructor)

D. Module: International Leadership Field Trip
GBLD 535: International Cultural Leadership Field Trip: Strategic Partnerships *(3 credits)*
2 weeks online, 2 weeks abroad, 3 weeks online

> **GBLD 610: Project Planning and Partnership Building**
> * Must have prerequisites and 2 MAGL electives
> to proceed to GBLD 610
> *3 weeks online, 1 week on campus, 3 weeks online (3 credits)*
> • Stakeholder development
> • Project management skill building and planning

> **GBLD 640 Capstone Project** *(9 credits)*
> • Independent work over 9 months
> • Project implementation

Curriculum content is delivery in delivered through a structured schedule that builds on knowledge domains from personal competencies to group interaction competencies and final competencies related to system change.

First, there are the foundational and required courses, an on-line overview course on global leadership (Personal and Theoretical Foundations to Global Leadership) followed by the two-week intensive residency term (Personal Capacities for Working in Complex Global Systems). Each of these courses are 10 weeks in duration, and represent 12 credits (25% of total program credits). Students may elect to complete the foundation courses for a Certificate in Global Leadership.

As shown in Fig. 6.1, students are required to complete four three-credit courses, choosing from six electives offered in the MAGL program or by taking courses elsewhere in the University. One of the electives is an international student trip that includes several weeks of online study to learn about their host country and a two-week trip to a middle economy country.

In the past five years, student trips were to Ecuador (see Rowe, Krause, Hayes et al. for a description of this experience). In the final year of the program, students take a required course on planning a leadership capstone project, to include topics such as project management, engaging stakeholders in a collaborative initiative and action inquiry methods. This is offered through an intensive residency with additional weeks of on-line discussion.

Students complete the MAGL program with an eight-month long capstone project which must require leadership engagement, benefit an organization or community and involve stakeholders in an inquiry process. Projects may vary greatly and have in past years included needs assessment studies, development of educational curriculum, strategic plans for an international business or non-profit organization, documentary videos on a global issue, etc.

Plans are underway to add an internship with a global organization in lieu of the capstone project. Also, an on-campus program is being developed so that all courses can be delivered on campus, taking into consideration international students who need a two-year residency in Canada to establish immigration eligibility.

Students have the option to double up on courses and to take the second residency immediately following the first residency so as to complete the MAGL program in 13 months.

The focus of the MAGL curriculum and its delivery structure is to develop student leadership competencies that will equip them to navigate the globalized world. Development requires self-awareness. When students become aware of their strengths and areas for improvement, they become more intentional in their learning goals. Self-assessment also contributes to greater cultural self-awareness of how one's own attitudes and behaviors impact on others (Oddou & Mendenhall, 2018; Rabin, 2017).

For this reason, all students entering the program take the Global Competency Inventory (Bird et al., 2010). While there are numerous assessment tools available, applicable to both expatriate, and educational environments, the GCI is most aligned with the competencies built into the MAGL program.

CREATING THE STUDENT LEARNING COMMUNITY

Student learning is facilitated through a number of mechanisms. Firstly, the MAGL program makes use of a cohort learning model. A group of students enters the program at the same time and completes all required courses together, in addition to many elective courses. This creates opportunities for culturally and experientially diverse individuals to come together to interact in both classroom team assignments as well as social settings. Competency and cross-cultural communication are practiced, especially when completing team assignments.

Secondly, the diversity of students who have years of professional and often international experiences across multiple industry and social-purpose sectors intensifies the learning opportunities far beyond what the instructors can provide. In a learning community, students learn from each other.

Thirdly, students in a learning community develop networks of professional associations as well as strong personal friendships that motivate them to stay engaged and to take advantage of every learning opportunity. These relationships tend to last far beyond the duration of the course, contributing to new jobs, job advancement, further educational study and a more enriched life.

Experiential activities complete the learning environment in the classroom and on-line learning environment. Experiential activities may range from exercises to illustrate a concept, case studies that provide opportunity to apply critical thinking, inquiry and problem-solving skills to field study experiences that real the full glory of issues in the real world.

Simulation exercises also create opportunity for students to solve real leadership challenges as a class group. Typically, a real problem is presented to the class, often with presenters from an organization experiencing the problem or needing to address the issue. An example of a global leadership learning exercise is illustrated well by the Barnga Game: When Cultures Play by Different Rules (Thiagarian & Thiagarajan, 2011). Participants play a card game but unbeknownst to each other, each player has different rules. Without using verbal communication, the participants have to deal with the confusion, frustration, and undercurrent of communication since usually there are several teams/tables playing the card game.

According to Oddou and Mendenall (2018), travel abroad or international internships should be incorporated into University degree programs wherever possible. The MAGL program offers an elective course for students consisting of both on-line study and discussion and a field study experience in an international developing nation location. The purpose of the trip is to have real-life experiences in a developing (middle income) country, experience thriving international cultural communities, see "first hand" and develop better understanding of the global issues that are affecting people and the country, engage in dialogue with locals in different cultural contexts, build global networks to support life-long learning and development in the global context and promote strategic partnerships between University and host country.

During the international study-abroad trip, the students must learn to cope with different people, different customs, different sleeping arrangements, different foods, etc., all while learning how to interact appropriately and respectfully with people who may speak a different language and have different ways of being and seeing the world. The potential for culture shock is great but students have a whole year to prepare, through learning about the host country, asking questions and mentally coming to terms with the fact there will be many differences to adapt to.

MAGL INSTRUCTORS AS SCHOLAR PRACTITIONERS

A final key ingredient in the successful creation of a university program for global leaders is working with instructors who are scholar practitioners in leadership, with extensive experience living and/working in globalized settings. Global leadership educators should be expected to have knowledge of relevant concepts and theories that explain the global world – the economic and political forces of globalization, norms and customs, conflicts and tensions, international governance bodies, and strategies to address global issues. They should have a global mindset, be adaptable and culturally sensitive, and possess the personal cross-cultural communication skills that make it possible for them to interact with students across diverse cultures and learning styles (Blaess et al., 2012). In many ways, the global leadership educator provides the "magic sauce" for students to absorb the new information and experiences that have been designed for them to grow into global leaders.

DISCUSSION

University programs, such as the MAGL, offer unique environments where students can learn more about themselves in a safe place, engage in critical thinking, and come to understand the forces and elements of larger global systems. When university programs are places where knowledge and experiences are transferred into action and practice, there is a potential for transformational growth (Mezirow, 2018). When university programs are aligned with and sensitive to the global market of contemporary and future challenges, they are well suited to support those wanting to create transformation in the world. In this chapter, we argue that there is a growing and critical need for these programs, and provide an example for how students can be supported to move theory to practice and create change in ways that address critical global issues.

REFERENCES

Battiste, M. (2000). Introduction. In M. Battiste (Ed.), *Reclaiming indigenous voice and vision* (pp. xvi–xxx). UBC Press.

Bell, H. L., Gibson, H. J., Tarrant, M. A., Perry, L. G., III, & Stoner, L. (2016). Transformational learning through study abroad: US students' reflections on learning about sustainability in the South Pacific. *Leisure Studies*, 35(4), 389–405.

Bird, A., Mendenhall, M. E., Stevens, M., & Oddou, G. (2010). Defining the content domain of intercultural competence for global leaders. *Journal of Managerial Psychology*, 25(8), 810–828.

Bird and Oddou. (2018). Global leadership knowledge creation and transfer. In M. E. Mendenhall, J. S. Osland, A. Bird, G. R., Oddou, M. J. Stevens, M. L. Maznevski, & G. Stahl (Eds.), *Global leadership: Research, practice, and development* (3rd ed., pp. 302–324). Routledge.

Bird, A., & Osland, J. (2004). Global competencies: An introduction. In H. Lane, M. Mendenhall, M. Maznevski, & J. McNett (Eds.), *Handbook of global management: A guide to managing complexity* (pp. 57–80). Oxford.

Blaess, D. A., Hollywood, K. G., & Grant, C. (2012). Preparing the professoriate to prepare globally competent leaders. *Journal of Leadership Studies*, 6(2), 88–94. https://doi.org/10.1002/jls.21240

Caligiuri, P. (2006). Developing global leaders. *Human Resource Management Review*, 16, 219–228.

Coers, N., Rodriguez, M. T., Roberts, T. G., Emerson, H. C., & Barrick, R. K. (2012). Examining the student impacts of three international capstone experiences. *North American Colleges and Teachers of Agriculture Journal*, 56(2), 55–62.

Crawford, C. B., & Strohkirch, C. S. (2002). Leadership education for knowledge organizations: A Primer. *Journal of Leadership Education*, 1(2), 18–33.

Cushner, K., & Chang, S. (2015). Developing intercultural competence through overseas student teaching: Checking our assumptions. *Intercultural Education*, 26(3), 165–178.

Deal, J. J., Leslie, J., Dalton, M., & Ernst, C. (2003). Cultural adaptability and leading across cultures. In W. H. Mobley & P. W. Dorfman (Eds.), *Advances in global leadership* (pp. 149–166). JAI Press.

Deal, J. J., & Prince, D. W. (2003). *Developing cultural adaptability: How to work across differences.* Center for Creative Leadership.

Delors, J. (1996). *Learning: The treasure within. Report to UNESCO of the International Commission on Education for the Twenty-First Century.* http://unesdoc.unesco.org/images/0010/001095/109590eo.pdf

Elola, I., & Oskoz, A. (2008). Blogging: Fostering intercultural competence development in foreign language and study abroad contexts. *Foreign Language Annals, 41*(3), 454–477.

Fleck, J. (2012). Blended learning and learning communities: Opportunities and challenges. *Journal of Management Development, 31*(4), 398–411. https://doi.org/10.1108/02621711211219059

Gosling, J., & Mintzberg, H. (2004). The education of practicing managers. *MIT Sloan Management Review, 45*(4), 19.

Gosling, J., & Mintzberg, H. (2006). Management education as if both matter. *Management Learning, 37*(4), 419–428.

Grundy, S. L., Hamilton, D., Veletsianos, G., Agger-Gupta, N., Márquez, P., Forssman, V., & Legault, M. (2017). Engaging students in life-changing learning: Royal roads university's learning and teaching model in practice – revised edition. https://viurrspace.ca/handle/10613/5357

Hamilton, M. (2008). *Integral city: Evolutionary intelligences for the human hive.* New Society Publishers.

Hamilton, D., Marquez, P., & Agger-Gupta, N. (2013). Royal Roads University learning and teaching model. http://media.royalroads.ca/media/marketing/view-books/2013/learning-model/index.html

Henderson, J. S. Y. (2000). Postcolonial ghost dancing: Diagnosing European colonialism. In M. Battiste (Ed.), *Reclaiming indigenous voice and vision* (pp. 57–76). UBC Press.

Holtbrügge, D., & Engelhard, F. (2016). Study abroad programs: Individual motivations, cultural intelligence, and the mediating role of cultural boundary spanning. *Academy of Management Learning & Education, 15*(3), 433–455.

Iacocca, L. (2008). *Where have all the leaders gone?* Simon and Schuster.

Ife, J. (2016). *Community development in an uncertain world: Vision, analysis, and practice* (2nd ed.). Cambridge University Press.

Irving, J. A. (2010). Educating global leaders: Exploring intercultural competence in leadership education. *Journal of International Business & Cultural Studies, 3*(1), 1–14.

Kearsley, G. (2010). Andragogy (M.Knowles). The theory into practice database. http://tip.psychology.org

Knight, J. (2003). Updating the definition of internationalization. *International Higher Education, 33*, 2–3.

Knight, J. (2004). Internationalization remodeled: Definition, approaches, and rationales. *Journal of Studies in International Education, 8*(1), 5–31.

Knowles, M. S. (1984). New roles for teachers – Empowerers of lifelong learners. *Journal of Children in Contemporary Society, 16*(3–4), 85–94.

Kohonen, E. (2005). Developing global leaders through international assignments: An identity construction perspective. *Personnel Review, 34*(1), 22.

Krause, W. (2012). *Civil society and women activists in the Middle East.* I.B. Tauris.

Krause, W. (2013). *Spiritual activism: Keys for personal and political success.* Turning Stone Press.

Krause, W. (2019a). Leading in times of cultural diversity: Achieving wellbeing, inclusivity, and organizational performance. In J. Marques (Ed.), *The Routledge companion to management and workplace spirituality* (pp. 250–259). Routledge.

Krause, W. (2019b). Leadership lessons from women in high-risk environments. In. S. L. Steffen, J. Rezmovits, S. Trevenna, & S. Rappaport (Eds.), *Evolving leadership for collective wellbeing: Lessons for implementing the United Nations sustainable development goals* (pp. 83–98). Emerald Publishing.

Luo, J., & Jamieson-Drake, D. (2015). Predictors of study abroad intent, participation, and college outcomes. *Research in Higher Education, 56*(1), 29–56.

McCall, M. W., & Hollenbeck, G. P. (2002). *Developing global executives: The lessons of international experience.* Harvard Business Press.

Mendenhall, M. E., Weber, T. J., Arnardottir, A. A., & Oddou, G. R. (2018). Developing global leadership competencies: A process model. In *Advances in global leadership.* Emerald Publishing Limited.

Mezirow, J. (2018). Transformative learning theory. In *Contemporary theories of learning* (pp. 114–128). Routledge.

Oliver, D., Church, A., Lewis, R., & Desrosiers, E. (2009). An integrated framework for assessing, coaching and developing global leaders. In W. Mobley, Y. Wang, & M. Li (Eds.) *Advances in global leadership (advances in global leadership* (Vol. 5, pp. 195–224). Emerald Group Publishing Limited. https://doi.org/10.1108/S1535-1203(2009)0000005012

Oddou, G. R., & Mendenhall, M. E. (2017). Global leadership development: Processes and practices. In *Global leadership* (pp. 229–269). Routledge.

Osland, J. (1995). *The adventure of living abroad: Hero tales from the global frontier.* Jossey-Bass.

Osland, J. S. (2018). An overview of the global leadership literature. In M. E. Mendenhall, J. S. Osland, A. Bird, G. R. Oddou, M. J. Stevens, M. L. Maznevski, &

G. Stahl (Eds.), *Global leadership: Research, practice, and development* (3rd ed., pp. 57–117). London: Routledge.

Osland, J. S., Bird, A., Mendenhall, M., & Osland, A. (2006). 11 Developing global leadership capabilities and global mindset: A review. In *Handbook of research in international human resource management* (p. 197).

Osland, J., & Bird, A. (2018). Process models of global leadership development. In M. E. Mendenhall, J. S. Osland, A. Bird, G. R. Oddou, M. J. Stevens, M. L. Maznevski, & G. Stahl (Eds.), *Global leadership: Research, practice, and development* (3rd ed., pp. 179–199). Routledge.

Piggot-Irvine, E. (2012). Creating authentic collaboration: A central feature of effectiveness. In O. Zuber-Skerritt (Ed.), *Action research for sustainable development in a turbulent world* (pp. 89–107). Emerald.

Ready, D. A. (2002). How storytelling builds next-generation leaders. *MIT Sloan Management Review*, 43(4), 63–69.

Rowe, W. E., Heykoop, C., & Etmanski, C. (2015). A master's degree in global leadership. In F. W. Ngunjiri & S. R. Madsen (Eds.), *Women as global leaders* (pp. 187–208). Information Age Publishing Inc.

Scholte, J. A. (2002). *What is globalization? The definitional issue – Again.* CSGR Working Paper 109/02. Centre for the Study of Globalisation and Regionalisation, University of Warwick, Warwick.

Tarique, I., & Schuler, R. (2010). Global talent management: Literature review, integrative framework, and suggestions for further research. *Journal of World Business*, 45, 122–133.

Thiagarajan, S., & Thiagarajan, R. (2011). *Barnga: A simulation game on cultural clashes*. Nicholas Brealey.

UNESCO. (n.d.). *Education for Sustainable Development 2005–2014.* Retrieved from http://menntuntilsjalfbaerni.weebly.com/uploads/6/2/6/2/6262718/unesco_5_pillars_for_esd.pdf

Wilber, K., Patten, T., Leonard, A., & Morelli, M. (2008). *Integral life practice: A 21st century blueprint for physical healthy, emotional balance, mental clarity, and spiritual awakening*. Integral Books.

Yang, M., Luk, L., Webster, B., Chau, A., & Ma, C. (2016). The role of international service-learning in facilitating undergraduate students' self-exploration. *Journal of Studies in International Education*, 20(5), 416–436

Zaccaro, S. J., Wood, G. T., & Herman, J. L. (2006). Developing the adaptive and global leader: HR strategies within a career-long perspective. In R. J. Burke & C. L. Cooper (Eds.), *The human resources revolution: Why putting people first matters* (pp. 277–302). Routledge.aaa aaa

7

YIN AND YANG: OPPOSING VIEWPOINTS ON WESTERN-BASED LEADERSHIP STUDIES PROGRAMS IN MAINLAND CHINA

JEFF BOURGEOIS AND BRETT WHITAKER

INTRODUCTION

As a dominant foundational component of Taoism and other philosophies, the Chinese concept of Yin and Yang emphasizes the harmony and dualism of the universe (Lang & Zhang, 1999; Wang, n.d.). Often presented visually with the black and white symbol of balance, Yin and Yang represents the tensions and harmony between attraction and opposition as inseparable elements of cosmic, philosophical, and cultural phenomena (Cartwright, 2018). Philosophers and historians believe the interaction of Yin and Yang originally represented naturally occurring dualities such as day and night, water and land, as well as movement and rest, dating as early as the fourteenth century BCE (Wang, n.d.). In the following chapter, the authors incorporate the tradition of Yin and Yang to present opposing viewpoints relative to establishing Leadership Studies curricula founded in Western thought as part of a transnational offering in mainland China. With evidence in support and in opposition to this practice, consideration is given to perspectives and arguments approaching both poles of the issue.

BACKGROUND

Altbach and Knight (2007) estimate a marked expansion of transnational higher education (TNE) in its many incarnations, in volume, scope and complexity since the 1980s. International branch campuses (IBCs), as one form of TNE, often provide an institution with additional sources of revenue, increased brand recognition, and a greater research presence in foreign environments (He & Wilkins, 2018). McBurnie and Ziguras (2007) map the largest expansion of TNE institutions from Western English-speaking countries to markets in Asia. Other scholars predict Asian countries – most notably China and India, will comprise the largest importers of transnational education by the year 2025 (Hsiao, 2003).

Since the Chinese government opened the door to and created guidelines for a Western higher education presence in mainland China, more than one thousand partnerships and programs from universities in dozens of countries arrived in an attempt to further institutional missions of globalization and internationalization (Iftekhar & Kayombo, 2016). According to the Ministry of Education (MOE) guidelines, transnational education initiatives in China are obligated to partner with a Chinese institution, most of which are located in eastern provinces with higher economic and educational levels (He & Wilkins, 2018). Foreign institutions with individually independent mechanisms of governance or finance (Bourgeois, 2017) are prohibited under the terms of the MOE provisions. The Chinese government, Ozturgut (2012) and Lubbers (2016) report, view these foreign partnerships as opportunities to introduce innovative, high quality educational opportunities and resources. As of 2015, over 450,000 students were enrolled in one of the many forms of TNE programs in the People's Republic (Lubbers, 2016). Business and foreign language programs paved the way for, technology, engineering, and science-based disciplines. Additionally, programs in leadership, and variations thereof, have been introduced into the curriculum.

Unlike other academic disciplines, though, Leadership Studies programs predicated on Western ideologies may conflict with Chinese culture, traditions, and values (Hofstede, 1993). Steers et al. (2012) remind us "leadership is a cultural construct... embedded in the diverse cultures where it is exercised, and changes accordingly" (p. 481). Ma and Tsui (2015) suggest leadership practices reflect the distinct cultural elements of a society, and the study of foreign concepts of leadership, therefore, may neglect or undermine the needs and goals of the host culture. Further considerations of culture and language combine to limit the transferability of leadership – as a word and as a concept, from a Western context to global settings (Steers et al., 2012).

For Western institutions considering the robust student market of China, such cultural differences may prove to be unfamiliar dilemmas or an emerging world of opportunity. It is critical to weigh benefits as well as costs – financial, ethical, or otherwise – to institutions, host communities, and most importantly, to students. As this chapter presents arguments on both sides of the debate, leaders and educators are encouraged to proceed with caution and plan with care in applying appropriate arguments to specific situations.

While Nancy Huber (2002) reminds us that leadership education arrives in many manifestations in an increasing number of institutions and organizations around the world, this chapter focuses on formalized Leadership Studies curricula offered at the university level. While the authors acknowledge the value and importance of leadership education delivered through co-curricular and student affairs programming (Jenkins, 2019), the presented arguments are made relative to classroom academic programs grounded in theoretical premises. It is the cultural tensions and opportunities between these Western premises and that of the Chinese host culture that may require specific consideration as discussed in the chapter.

YIN: IN SUPPORT OF WESTERN LEADERSHIP STUDIES PROGRAMS IN CHINA

The benefits of establishing Leadership Studies programs in mainland China reach beyond educational missions toward globalization. For institutions, increased enrollments and revenues generated by a Chinese contingency can support valuable research and scholarly investigations into leadership issues at home and abroad. Tens of thousands of students seeking Western educational experiences bring valuable perspectives on leadership challenges. While their engagement in the learning process adds to the creation of new knowledge and thought, their tuition dollars fund established researchers in pursuit of global scholarship.

In the broader realm of nurturing future leaders, preparing students for the important work of social justice and the responsibility of facilitating the

leadership education of future generations with a globally conscious curriculum affords them an opportunity to adopt multicultural perspectives.
The value of foreign-born faculty in the classroom and in faculty circles has
been researched and documented in the literature (Gahungu, 2011). Creating pathways for the development of faculty guided by Western thought
empowers Chinese learners to draw on meaningful examples from their own
cultural journeys. Considering the rise of globalization and the introduction
of international organizations in Chinese society, students in a variety of disciplines from business to education to communications can benefit in their
exposure to multicultural perspectives on leadership.

On a sociopolitical level, Leadership Studies programs have the potential
to introduce visionary and influential solutions to host communities in mainland China. With most programs facilitated in English, new cross-cultural
discoveries and exchanges are afforded to local stakeholders who might otherwise remain ignorant of international ideas and advances. Faculty serve as
caring and respectful ambassadors of culture and innovation while functioning as catalysts for adaptive change and social progress. Additionally, Western faculty may mentor students and provide valuable guidance in achieving
resolution to modern issues. At the same time, faculty gain new insights on
social dilemmas and conditions. These invaluable contributions to communities into which Leadership Studies programs expand represent the manifestation of lessons reflected in their curriculum.

Finally, the field of Leadership Studies benefits from partnerships with
Chinese institutions. The National Leadership Education Research Agenda
includes Global and Intercultural Leadership among the priorities of application and content (Andenoro, 2013). The vast cultural differences that exist
between the People's Republic and much of the Western world provide fertile
ground for robust understanding of Leadership in a global and multicultural
context.

YANG: IN OPPOSITION OF WESTERN LEADERSHIP
STUDIES PROGRAMS IN CHINA

As with any academic endeavor, there are inherent obstacles to the overall success of a Leadership Studies program in mainland China. One must
consider multiple arguments against the viability and sustainability of

these kinds of cross-border leadership education initiatives. While this is not an exhaustive accounting, several arguments arise that are worthy of consideration.

Perhaps most existential to this work is the issue of academic colonialism. Though not explicitly within the context of Leadership Studies, calls for universities to leave their foreign host communities have resulted from perceptions of imperial activity (Altbach, 2003; Ozturgut, 2012). Critics of transnational education initiatives warn against the willful or unintended omission of local stakeholders in the creation and delivery of such educational programs (Coelen, 2018; De Costa, 2018).

Neocolonialism is more specifically defined as a perpetuation of Western colonialism after the end of the colonial era as "former colonizers continue to economically, culturally, financially, militarily and ideologically dominate developing nations" (Chilisa, 2005, as cited in Siltaoja et al., 2019). Because of the strong, inherent dependence on culture of the discipline, this cautionary commentary of TNE at large is most certainly applicable more specifically to Sino-Foreign Leadership Studies curricula. The conception of Western-oriented degree programs supported by Western curriculum, built on Western scholarship, only utilizing Western pedagogy, and offered in China is pretentious. The idea that Western higher education is enlightened in some manner, and the principles upon which it is built are not only applicable to other cultures, but superior, creates a sense of academic arrogance. Authors and researchers have raised such concerns in the past. Though not explicitly within the context of Leadership Studies, calls for universities to leave their foreign host communities have resulted from perceptions of empirical activity (Altbach, 2003; Otzurgut, 2015). With regard to the student experience, the challenge for Chinese students to adapt from a traditionally teacher-centered educational culture – language not withstanding – to Western pedagogical and curricular approaches may also influence student learning and satisfaction (Van Auken et al., 2009).

Geert Hofstede (1980) reminds us that leadership is a social construct informed by shared values and cultural conditioning. In the groundbreaking GLOBE Study by Dorfman et al. (2012), research supported the notion that these shared values shape the expectations and perceptions of what leadership is and what it could be. Cultural attributes such as levels of assertiveness, collectiveness, or gender egalitarianism vary from society to society, defining unique perceptions and practices of leadership (Dorfman et al., 2012).

It could be perceived as unethical and irresponsible acting with an intentional indifference to the weight of these differences in the leadership classroom.

Changing cultural mental models is a long and difficult endeavor. Where other disciplines, such as those in the STEM fields, may benefit from the introduction of new technology and modern approaches, Leadership Studies programs may present opposing ideologies to ancient practices and ways of thought (Steers et al., 2012). Ma and Tsui (2015) estimate that traditional Chinese philosophies predate Western theories of leadership by more than 2000 years. Daoism, Confucianism, and other ancient Chinese teachings provide a cultural foundation for approaches to leadership that Western-based leadership programs in their comparative infancy have the potential present theory and behaviors which may not align with the age-old beliefs.

Beyond the concern of colonialism, another pragmatic tension lies in the relevance of student programming options. While Western scholarship may support particular curricular outcomes, there is limited evidence these outcomes serve the best interest of students in mainland China, many of whom may never live or work in another country. This concern is further exacerbated by limits inherent in accreditation standards, curricular requirements, and other forms of educational alignment. Conversely, Western course design may be negligent of the leadership ideas, observations, and involvement students bring with them to the classroom experience. Thus, the possibility to convey unintended messages may be obscured by language and cultural connotations. Concepts and behaviors such as negotiation, collaboration, and delegation may invoke images colored by students' prior knowledge that do not fully integrate with the corresponding Westernized notions. Faculty may find themselves requiring specialized expertise in the traditions and practices of China, and more specifically, the program's host community.

Finally, these academic initiatives may lack academic rigor and the institutional ability to effectively operate the program. A number of practical limitations to success and quality are often difficult to overcome in foreign environments. Language barriers, structural design of the program, infrastructure and course design, different pedagogical expectations, student readiness, and a host of other issues may limit the rigor of these programs (Ozturgut, 2008). Logistically, government regulations, trade restrictions and tariffs may render the importation of texts and other resources as cost prohibitive. Without total access to appropriate materials, programs may not have the capacity to offer a full, comprehensive rendering of the curriculum, limiting students' abilities to make critical connections or practical inferences. Furthermore, partnering institutions may be incentivized to compromise program rigor in an effort to maintain economic viability of the program. Thus, strong and transparent support from the collaborating institution is vital to the success of any programmatic endeavor. Redden (2018) presents in detail the recent case of a large Dutch university's aspirations to collaborate with a Chinese partner derailed by insufficient cooperative support.

WEIGHING THE BALANCE

Ultimately, readers will be faced with weighing the balance of these arguments for and against the viability and success of these Leadership programs. Whether a program in Leadership creates an air of educational colonialism or presents an opportunity for ambassadorship will be resolved in the finer details of the partnership and curriculum. Of course, one of the challenges of arriving at any sort of resolution in this matter is that the viability and benefit of a particular program may be vastly different depending upon the perspective and motivations of the person assessing such a program. To be sure, a Sino-Foreign academic partnership supporting a Leadership Studies curriculum requires the cultural and organizational awareness that so vitally underscore the discipline.

While financial revenues are widely recognized as the leading motivation for the establishment of IBCs, the establishment of Leadership Studies programs in mainland China must aspire to loftier goals. Equipping changemakers to shape and direct the future of the world's most populous nation is important work. The considerable risks associated with growing enrollments and expanding institutional footprints present salient threats to the sustainable quality of Leadership Education. Reflection on the departmental and institutional motivations for internationalization and expansion into mainland China must respect Chinese traditions and deep-seeded philosophies regarding success, prosperity, and respect. Here, Leadership Educators have an opportunity to educate students with what we do, as well as why and how we do it, rather than exclusively with what we present in the classroom.

As institutions develop and launch Leadership Studies programs on partnered campuses, the endeavor should be approached in the spirit of collaboration rather than colonialism. Embracing the contributions and multidimensional opportunities of the Chinese host institution and community can ensure the abundance of success that, likely, framed the initiation of the academic marriage. This cooperative dialog must occur not only in determining the presence of a Leadership program, but in making decisions regarding course content and objectives (Siltaoja et al., 2019). Attempts to merely replicate Leadership curricula and courses from the main campus could prove more harmful than helpful to students in their journey of Leadership Education. Applying the message of critics of transnational education, department and institutional must avoid a competitive or territorial stance and take appropriate measures to assure an equal exchange of knowledge and regard for lived leadership experiences (De Costa, 2018).

The objective of the chapter is not to arrive at a conclusive determination for the reader. Rather, through careful analysis, the reader will arrive at a nuanced understanding of these transnational academic endeavors. It is the hope and objective of the authors that readers develop a deep appreciation for the complexity of the circumstances surrounding leadership education in China, and the fallacy of defining these programs in the binary sense of success or failure.

THE CALL

The authors conclude this chapter with a call for readers. After careful consideration of the benefits and challenges of the establishment of Westernbased leadership curriculum in mainland China, readers are summoned to contribute to the discussion and the overall state of such programs. These contributions may come in the form of change-making action to address obstacles preventing effective leadership studies partnerships, or in the form of future study to expand the awareness of cultural and pragmatic opportunities to inform and shape future initiatives.

First, we invoke a call to action. Because these transnational education initiatives are happening right now, it is imperative that academic leaders and practitioners, as well as others tasked with decision-making for such programs, consider these arguments and reach a determination allowing for constructive progress forward. Departments and institutions must be mindful of operational details and procedures within the partnership to maintain the integrity of the field and the value of the discipline on campus.

Strategies such as hiring faculty specifically to teach at the China location, rather than re-assigning or exchange programs from the home institution may afford faculty opportunities to develop deeper connections and understandings of local traditions, assumptions, and practices regarding leadership (Feng, 2013; Salt & Wood, 2014).

In addition, the authors provide a call for scholarship. While the extant body of literature has recently seen increasing consideration and investigation of transnational education programs in China writ large, Leadership Studies programs deserve additional attention. Given the state of the literature, there is fruitful and relevant scholarship that may support informed arguments relative to these initiatives. From pedagogy to global leadership, to academic colonialism, the Leadership field has a number of research streams that may help provide the basis for confidence in the future of globalized leadership education in mainland China. Furthermore, to ensure critical and thoughtful examination of current and potential contributions of Western-based programs, future studies will approach the matter framed through Chinese and international lenses.

Like the ancient tradition of Yin and Yang, the arguments for and against the introduction of Western-based Leadership curriculum in mainland China present a unique and complex tension. While it is possible for a harmonic presence of foreign courses and programs in the Chinese higher education environment, the acknowledgement and tolerance for inherent cultural differences will ultimately determine whether they fail or flourish.

REFERENCES

Altbach, P. G. (2003). Academic colonialism: Accreditation of foreign universities. *International Higher Education, 32*(1), 5–7.

Altbach, P. G., & Knight, J. (2007). The internationalization of higher education: Motivations and realities. *Journal of Studies in International Education, 11*(3–4), 290–305. https://doi.org/10.1177/1028315307303542

Andenoro, A. C. (2013). The national leadership education research agenda: Strategic priorities and deepened perspectives. *Journal of Leadership Education, 12*(3), 1–9.

Bourgeois, J. (2017). *Neither here nor there: Transformational leadership and cultural intelligence in presidents of U.S.-Accredited Universities Located in Foreign Countries*. University of San Diego.

Cartwright, M. (2018). Yin and yang. *World History Encyclopedia*. Retrieved November 16, 2019, from https://www.ancient.eu/Yin_and_Yang/

Coelen, R. (2018). TNE in HE is about collaboration, not neo-colonialism. *University World News*, https://www.universityworldnews.com/post.php?story=2018070612240068

De Costa, P. (2018, June 29). A better way forward for transnational higher education. *University World News*, https://www.universityworldnews.com/post.php?story=20180626103409378

Dorfman, P., Javidan, M., Hanges, P., Dastmalchian, A., & House, R. (2012). GLOBE: A twenty year journey into the intriguing world of culture and leadership. *Journal of World Business*, 47(4), 504–518. https://doi.org/10.1016/j.jwb.2012.01.004

Feng, Y. (2013). University of Nottingham Ningbo China and Xi'an Jiaotong-Liverpool University: Globalization of higher education in China. *Higher Education*, 65(4), 471–485.

Gahungu, A. (2011). Integration of foreign-born faculty in academia: Foreignness as an asset. *International Journal of Educational Leadership Preparation*, 6(1), n1.

He, L., & Wilkins, S. (2018). Achieving legitimacy in cross-border higher education: Institutional influences on Chinese International Branch Campuses in South East Asia. *Journal of Studies in International Education*, 22(3), 179–197. https://doi.org/10.1177/1028315317738774

Hofstede, G. (1980). Motivation, leadership, and organization: Do American theories apply abroad? *Organizational Dynamics*, 9(1), 42–63.

Hofstede, G. (1993). Cultural constraints in management theories. *Academy of Management Perspectives*, 7(1), 81–94.

Hsiao, C.-M. (2003). Transnational Education Marketing Strategies for Postsecondary Program Success in Asia: Experiences in Singapore, Hong Kong, and Mainland China, (December).

Huber, N. S. (2002). Approaching leadership education in the new millennium. *Journal of Leadership Education*, 1(1), 25–34.

Iftekhar, S. N., & Kayombo, J. J. (2016). Chinese-Foreign cooperation in running schools (CFCRS): A policy analysis. *International Journal of Research Studies in Education*, 5(4), 73–82.

Lang, K. R., & Zhang, J. L. (1999, July). A Taoist foundation of systems modeling and thinking. In *Proceedings of the 17th international conference of the system dynamics society and the 5th Australian and New Zealand Systems Conference* (pp. 20–23).

Lubbers, J. C. (2016). The quest for capacity development in Chinese higher education: Can top foreign universities serve as 'catfish' in China? A study exploring foreign faculty members' experiences in Sino-Foreign Joint Ventures (Master's thesis).

Ma, L., & Tsui, A. S. (2015). Traditional Chinese philosophies and contemporary leadership. *The Leadership Quarterly, 26*(1), 13–24.

McBurnie, G., & Ziguras, C. (2007). Institutions, not students, get the travel bug. *Far Eastern Economic Review,* (January/February), 58–61.

Ozturgut, O. (2008). Joint venture campuses in China. *International Higher Education,* (53), 16–17.

Ozturgut, O. (2012). China's socio-economic transformation and Sino-US joint venture companies in China. *Journal of Organizational Psychology, 12*(2), 109–124.

Redden, E. (2018). Why the University of Groningen canceled plans for branch campus in China. *Inside Higher Education,* 1–6. www.insidehighered.com

Salt, J., & Wood, P. (2014). Staffing UK university campuses overseas: Lessons from MNE practice. *Journal of Studies in International Education, 18*(1), 82–97.

Siltaoja, M., Juusola, K., & Kivijärvi, M. (2019). 'World-class' fantasies: A neocolonial analysis of international branch campuses. *Organization, 26*(1), 75–97. https://doi.org/10.1177/1350508418775836

Steers, R. M., Sanchez-Runde, C., & Nardon, L. (2012). Leadership in a global context: New directions in research and theory development. *Journal of World Business, 47*(4), 479–482.

Van Auken, S., Wells, L. G., & Borgia, D. (2009). A comparison of Western business instruction in China with US instruction: A case study of perceived program emphases and satisfaction levels. *Journal of Teaching in International Business, 20*(3), 208–229.aaa

Wang, R. (n.d.). Yinyang (yin-yang). *Internet encyclopedia of philosophy: A peer-reviewed academic resource.* https://www.iep.utm.edu/yinyang/#H5

8

INTERNATIONAL IMMERSIONS FOR GRADUATE STUDENTS OF GLOBAL LEADERSHIP

JENNIE L. WALKER AND YULIA TOLSTIKOV-MAST

The need to understand global contexts in Leadership Studies is driving more flexibility and creativity with international immersion curriculum. Traditional study-abroad programs or international internships require commitments of several months or more and have conventional structure. They are also mostly designed for undergraduate or full-time master's level students who can be abroad for extended periods of time. This is not possible for most working professional students especially in graduate or doctoral distance education programs.

The rise of flexible graduate degree programs has expanded opportunities for working professionals to pursue degrees concurrently with their careers. Those programs have students whose daily activities are connected to knowledge application and who require practice-driven education and experiences. This means that faculty must find creative solutions to effectively deliver global experiences to students with limited discretionary time. This chapter discusses globalization in the leadership curriculum, the need for shorter-term international immersions in graduate education, current approaches in the field, and challenges and potential solutions to improve the effectiveness of these experiences.

GLOBALIZATION AND LEADERSHIP CURRICULUM

The Council of Graduate Schools (2013) says that it is essential for graduate students to develop global perspectives and skills due to the globalization of research, development networks, and new technologies for communication and collaboration. International education is an effective way to build this perspective and skill-set. International education is defined as

> *Education that occurs outside the participant's home country. Besides study abroad, examples include such international experiences as work, volunteering, non-credit internships, and directed travel, as long as these programs are driven to a significant degree by learning goals. (Forum on Education Abroad, 2019)*

Study abroad has been found to impact students' self-confidence, sense of identity, and personal independence (Black & Duhon, 2006; Hadis, 2005). It also has profound influence on students' intercultural competence (Black & Duhon, 2006; Williams, 2005), communication skills (Drews & Meyer, 1996; Hadis, 2005), and even their career plans (Norris & Gillespie, 2009).

Research among employers confirms that international education is considered valuable for building sought after skills in the workplace. The QS Global Employer Survey Report (2016) found that more than 80 per cent of employers around the world said they actively sought graduates who had studied abroad. Multinational corporations continue to report a shortage of global leaders and poor global leadership development programs that force companies to roll back their global strategies (DDI, 2018). What is described as turmoil in the current global market conditions calls for adjustments in multinationals' strategies, structures, and approaches to local-global integrations (Fischer, 2019, March 28; Ghemawat, 2017, July/August). This underscores the need for global leaders across industries and nations who can lead those adjustments and creation of innovative global–local integration. To do this effectively, leaders will need globalized perspectives that are not isolated to their own worldviews.

Leadership, scholarship and education have been challenged around the world for their limitations in building globalized perspectives (Ashford & Sitkin, 2019; Chin et al., 2018; Riggio, 2019). Criticisms include weak interdisciplinary collaborations, narrow views of leadership as a position, systematic biases in leadership conceptualization, and prevailing male-centric and Western-centric bias (Hino, 2019; Kellerman, 2012; Nahavandi & Krishnan, 2018; Riggio, 2019). This imbalance skews leadership realities rather than represents a diverse and contextual picture of leadership. Rost and Barker (2000) argue that leadership education is currently inadequate, since it does not address the complex relationships among people created by globalization. Simultaneously, universities have been arguing that leadership education should better represent new leadership trends and challenges created by globalization (Herd et al., 2018; MacLeod & Farrell, 1994).

To resolve these concerns, universities must offer globalized curriculum and experiences that move beyond superficial discussion of international issues. Rusciano (2014) suggested considering "global perspective" in curriculum as "a lens through which we examine not only the traditional subject matter of our disciplines, but also the manner in which we approach those disciplines." This means creating deeper and more meaningful learning experiences that analyze plural epistemologies, linguistic nuances, and question generality of existing perspectives. Based on globalization demands, it becomes very important to make those experiences available to wider demographics and diverse learners.

NEED FOR SHORT-TERM STUDY-ABROAD PROGRAMS FOR GRADUATE STUDENTS

The Institute of International Education (IIE) recognizes the need for developing globalized perspectives through international education and is actively working with higher education institutions to double the number of US students who study abroad by 2020 (IIE, 2019). "The more we can expand access to study abroad for Americans, the better prepared they will be to strengthen their career trajectories and to participate in the global economy" (Institute of International Education, 2017). Since 2014, over 800 US and international colleges and universities, educational associations and organizations, and country partners have adopted this goal in partnership with IIE. They are called "Generation Study Abroad commitment partners" (GSA partners). Much of this effort is focused on undergraduate students, as graduate students comprise only 12 per cent of all study abroad participation (Institute of International Education, 2018).

Challenges and Benefits of Study Abroad
for Graduate Students

International education can be problematic for graduate students due to the complexity and weight of demands in their lives, including work, family, and rigorous studies. According to Canfield et al. (2009), many students found that studying abroad was not feasible due to time or funds and was especially difficult for those studying part-time or raising families. This situation creates a need for an alternative opportunity – shorter-term educational experiences, defined as a program lasting eight weeks or less (Institute of International Education, 2018). Short-term programs are typically offered over natural breaks in the academic calendar (summer, semester breaks, holiday breaks). It creates many benefits for students including cost-reduction, fewer scheduling limitations, less conflict with family and work obligations, and a more comfortable entrée into another cultural environment (Institute of International Education, 2018). These programs can also provide opportunities for students to specialize in a language or specific area.

Despite their short duration, research findings reveal several benefits for students including changes in beliefs, attitudes, values, and worldview (Kiely, 2005; McElhaney, 1998), increased self-confidence (Rhoads & Neururer, 1998), deepened empathy and care for others (King, 2004), and increased interest in international courses, travel and careers (Lewis & Niesenbaum, 2005). A few studies found no significant learning gains for students in shorter-term study abroad (Davies et al., 2015; Medina-Lopez Portillo, 2004). However, Jones et al. (2012) suggest that outcomes-based research may not fully illuminate the value of shorter-term immersion programs. Short-term experiences serve as "springboards" for learning and shifts in worldview (Jones et al., 2012), especially when program design is intentional and students are active participants in their experiences (Harris et al., 2018; Rowan-Kenyon & Niehaus, 2011).

Graduate Student Demographics and Interests
in Short-Term Study Abroad

Research found short-term study abroad programs have higher participation rates among all student populations, with 64 per cent of US students participating in 2016–2017 (Bandyopadhyay & Bandyopadhyay, 2015; Institute of International

Education, 2018). They are particularly appealing to graduate students, who are more likely to engage in limited- and short-term overseas experiences than the overall study abroad population (Institute of International Education, 2018; Sanger & Mason, 2019). Graduate students also participate in larger ratios, compared to the overall study abroad enrollment data. As many as 68 per cent of Master's students and 30 per cent of Doctoral students study abroad, even though 70 per cent of them were not required to do so in their degree programs (Sanger & Mason, 2019). This means that their interests drive participation, and understanding of this population and their interests becomes critical.

Graduate business students comprise the largest population (34 per cent) among graduate students who study abroad, followed by graduate students in the fields of health (16.5 per cent) and education (5 per cent) (Sanger & Mason, 2019). Their choice of study-abroad program tends to align with their degree interests.

> *Unlike their undergraduate counterparts who participate in organized group experiences that encompass a broad curriculum at any location around the world, graduate students participate in learning experiences that are more closely aligned with their academic and career pursuits. (Sanger & Mason, 2019, p. 22)*

Participation by type of a study program shows that it is largely driven by coursework (48 per cent) (Institute of International Education, 2018). Experiential activities account for the other half with research and field work leading (16 per cent), followed by travel seminar/study tour (13 per cent), work/co-op/internship (8 per cent), volunteering and service learning (5 per cent), and language study (2 per cent) (Institute of International Education, 2018). About half (51 per cent) of graduate students participate in experiences that are 2 weeks or less, a third (36 per cent) participate in experiences that are 2–8 weeks long, and only 13 per cent participate in study abroad programs that exceed 8 weeks (Sanger & Mason, 2019, p. 14).

From a diversity perspective, while participation in study abroad is mostly representative of the enrolled graduate student population in the United States (Sanger & Mason, 2019), overall enrollment in higher education suffers from a significant diversity problem. More than half of all students are White. Although some institutions are addressing barriers to study-abroad participation through scholarships, aid, targeted marketing, and special programs aimed at low-income and first-generation students of color, those efforts are limited (Engel, 2017).

Graduate degree programs have responded to the need for shorter-term international immersion experiences in the curriculum in a variety of ways, starting with the obvious reduction in time abroad. While shorter immersions can be stand-alone experiences, they are often integrated into a more comprehensive curriculum design, such as courses with build-in travel components, practicums, internships, conferences, service projects, labs, or consulting services. There is no existing research on short-term study abroad in graduate programs. Since this chapter focuses on leadership studies, a review of the field is conducted and presented below.

SURVEY OF THE FIELD: SHORT-TERM STUDY ABROAD IN GRADUATE LEADERSHIP EDUCATION

Since 1985, Open Doors has conducted research on U.S. students studying abroad for academic credit. It is conducted by IIE and is sponsored by the U.S. Department of State (Institute of International Education, 2019). While much is known about undergraduate study-abroad participants from this research, understanding graduate-student participation is a new phenomenon (Donnelly-Smith, 2009; Ferrari & Fine, 2016). In fact, IIE only recently launched the Graduate Learning Overseas (GLO) research project in 2018 to "identify the scale and scope of U.S. graduate students' educational activities overseas" (Sanger & Mason, 2019). The gap in understanding this population is largely due to institution-level reporting challenges. Data may not be collected or shared, due to the unique nature of many of the short-term programs that graduate students participate in. This effectively renders graduate students' activities overseas invisible in the national discourse on U.S. study abroad (Institute of International Education, June 2018).

Research Process and Sample

A search of the most recent Open Doors data on short-term graduate study abroad was performed for the top participating institutions. Two categories emerged, for Master's degree granting institutions and Doctoral degree granting institutions, and the lists differed. The total sample comprised

40 institutions. Next, since leadership studies were a specific area of interest, each institution's leadership studies graduate program was investigated through online publicly available information to determine available graduate degrees in leadership and available short-term study-abroad options for graduate students. Looking across the sample, leadership focused degrees were found in various colleges and departments including education, business, health, human services, and some specialized areas such as engineering and agriculture. Degree subject areas included strategic leadership, executive leadership, organizational leadership, educational leadership, sport and recreational leadership, non-profit leadership, and community leadership.

Types of Short-Term Study-Abroad Programs

When looking across the 40 top institutions for short-term study abroad at the graduate level, experiences take many forms based on their learning objectives. These include coursework, fieldwork, practicums, professional development, and scholarship. Since nearly half of all graduate student participation in short-term study abroad is through coursework, it is not surprising that this is the most prevalent option offered among institutions studied. The travel component is often only one-to-two weeks, and can take many forms, including cultural immersions, in-country project work, site and organization visits and networking. Faculty-led programs are considered to be optimal for learning in the context of coursework (Campbell, 2016; Mills et al., 2010; Slotkin et al., 2012). However, there are many vendors for short-term study abroad that partner with institutions to either fully lead these experiences or do so in conjunction with faculty. A more recent phenomenon is virtual study abroad in coursework, where faculty in different parts of the world arranges for virtual collaborations between their students, such as the X-Culture program (Taras, 2019).

Fieldwork, practicums, and professional development place students in positions to directly utilize or enhance their skills in a different cultural environment. Fieldwork is "practical work conducted by a researcher in the natural environment, rather than in a laboratory or office" (Fieldwork, 2019). Fieldwork takes disciplinary specific variations and is intended to enhance the skill sets and capabilities of students (e.g., health education, clean water projects, home construction, business development). Service learning also falls under the category of fieldwork, but places greater emphasis on the benefits to community partners as a result of the learning activities (National Youth Leadership Council, 2019). A practicum is defined as "a course involving activities emphasizing practical application" (Practicum, 2019). Practicums are different from fieldwork since they may not involve projects for other organizations or community groups. The focus is more directly on practicing skills to enhance specific capabilities (e.g., foreign-language practice).

Professional development includes workshops, internships and work abroad. While some skills practiced in practicum experiences fall under professional development, the structure for activities like internships and work abroad will likely be more rigorous with attention to performance standards and work deliverables. Scholarships in the context of short-term study abroad could include conducting international research or participating in an international conference. These activities may be spear-headed by faculty (e.g., joint research or presentation), or they may be independently pursued by students. These activities are particularly important to doctoral students engaged in international research.

A more recent phenomenon within coursework is virtual study abroad. This does not involve a physical travel component; it is facilitated through technology. Faculty members may collaborate with faculty in other parts of the world or with third-party vendors to coordinate and organize learning experiences among their students. Third-party vendors offer a variety of 'experiences' in other cultures that may include site tours, interactive lectures from experts in-country, or interactive meetings with local organizations to learn more about how they operate. Our research across vendors and institutions that offered these experiences showed that immersions tended to last a few days to one week with multiple sessions scheduled in 1- to 3-hour blocks of time with breaks in between.

Faculty member collaborations tend to focus more strongly on collaboration of students across cultures. This usually involves a group project, so that students can interact in meaningful ways to achieve a learning outcome. X-Culture is an example of this and was started in 2010 by Dr Vas Taras (X-Culture, 2021). In X-Culture, small teams of students across cultures work together to "solve" real-world business challenges provided to them by participating organizations. The projects run on a semester basis, and the student teams work on their project for two months.

Virtual immersions were already gaining traction prior to the start of the 2020 global pandemic; however, the pandemic forced many higher education institutions to more immediately reconsider their study abroad program format. For example, one of the authors was scheduled to lead a short-term immersion to Costa Rica in the fall of 2020. When it became clear that the pandemic would make travel impossible, she decided that instead of canceling she would use this as an opportunity to experiment with a virtual immersion format. She worked with a local university partner in Costa Rica, University for Peace, to co-design the immersion. The four-week design included two weeks of introductory coursework, immersion in week three, and a final project that culminated in presentations in week four. The immersion took place over three half-day blocks, scheduled into 90-minute sessions with breaks in between. During immersion, students engaged in interactive tours, presentations by local organizations, interviews with business and not-for-profit leaders, and daily debrief conversations. The online classroom and assignments leading up to the immersion supported their preparation for the immersion. The feedback was quite positive overall, with students sharing they learned more than they anticipated and would have liked more immersion sessions integrated into their classes over a full term. While this experience is anecdotal, it demonstrates the value in faculty experimenting with the virtual format, whether it is as a standalone experience or integrated into a class.

DESIGN AND PLANNING CONSIDERATIONS FOR SHORT-TERM STUDY ABROAD

In order to facilitate effective learning from short-term study abroad experiences, attention is needed to the design of course or experience objectives and intended learning outcomes. Researchers have found consistently that it is not necessarily the method or length of time an educational experience takes, but rather the quality and intentionality that matters when it comes to providing students with impactful learning environments (Stone & Petrick, 2013). In the analysis of many study-abroad offices across institutions, Anderson et al. (2006) found they have four primary objectives for students: academic or intellectual advances (e.g., problem solving, language skills, cultural knowledge), intercultural sensitivity (e.g., empathy, language, interest in the world), personal goals (e.g., self-awareness, flexibility, creativity), and professional benefits (e.g., networking, career development). All four objectives are equally significant, yet the emphasis of one over another varies greatly between students, programs and institutions (Cheng, 2013). At the graduate level, learning objectives should consider more advanced levels of knowledge, higher levels of abstract thought, both breadth and depth in a discipline, and emphasis on higher level taxonomies of learning (analysis, evaluation, creation) (Creighton University Graduate School, 2019). At the doctoral level, students may also be expected to demonstrate a professional level of scholarly ability.

Given the time compression in short-term study abroad programs, focused objectives are helpful to set realistic aims for the program and to maximize learning. Building intercultural competence is clearly an important objective for any cross-cultural experience in the context of higher education. However, exclusive focus on this aim may lead to a missed opportunity potentially significant for student learning. Short-term programs are unique in their focus on a particular area. Conversely, excessive attention on academics or travel itineraries could be at the expense of actual gains in cultural exposure (Ziamandanis, 2013). Thus, balance is important, and intended learning objectives need to be prioritized appropriately. Since students who complete short-term study abroad are more likely to complete a subsequent experience (Campbell, 2016; Dwyer, 2004; Gaia, 2015; Lewis & Niesenbaum, 2005; McKeown, 2009; McMurtrie, 2007; Sutton & Rubin, 2004), it may be possible to offer multiple opportunities that can scaffold learning further. This would reduce the pressure over program experiences and create more room for cultural exposure and faculty guided reflection discussions to link experiences to learning.

Dimensions that Influence Design and Experience: Structure and Process

Guzman (2018) cites two dimensions that influence international immersion design and, ultimately, experience: structure and process. Structural factors are those that either cannot be changed by the participant, or that influence the participant's immediate experience abroad (Barden & Cashwell, 2013). Guzman (2018) lists structural factors for students that impact their ability to achieve learning objectives in study abroad duration and location of the trip, language barriers, and cross-cultural interactions. Process factors influence how participants perceive their experiences abroad after their return (Barden & Cashwell, 2013). These factors include expectations of experiences, faculty support, and reflection on experiences.

Structural Factors

Duration and location of the trip. The length of short-term study abroad is often influenced by breaks in the academic calendar. Clarke et al. (2009) argue that study abroad programs need to be long enough for participants to process culture shock as well as to cope with the implications that come with it. However, very short programs can achieve objectives in building intercultural competence if the experience focuses on activities aimed at cultural awareness and intercultural competence growth (Krishnan et al., 2017).

Choosing the location of the program will influence potential learning objectives for the trip. Consolidated experiences may best focus on a specific aspect of the culture or a unique event or organization. When selecting the destination, prior research suggests that there are higher participation rates in locations that are considered vacation destinations (Goldoni, 2013) and in English speaking countries (Doyle et al., 2010). Top study abroad destinations specifically of interest to graduate students (based on their participation), include the UK, China, Italy, Spain, Germany, France, Mexico, India, Ireland, Australia, South Africa, Costa Rica, Japan, and Peru (Institute of International Education, 2018; Sanger & Mason, 2019). While many programs focus on major metropolitan areas, such as capitals or major economic centers, Guzman (2018) found that in shorter-term programs some participants found that smaller communities provided a more authentic immersive experience.

Language barriers. According to Dowell and Mirsky (2002), short-term study-abroad experiences can be more impactful than longer programs if they purposefully engage students with host families, cultural sites, or if students use the native language of the host country. These purposeful engagements place the student in rich interaction within the culture. They also promote greater self-development. Barden and Cashwell (2013) found in a review of the literature that participants who could overcome language barriers with locals in the host country found a deep sense of satisfaction, self-awareness, and self-efficacy which extended several months after returning home.

One of the challenges of short-term programs is the limitations of preparation in and practice of a foreign language. Language improvement is limited by program duration and the degree to which students interact with the language while in the culture (Dwyer, 2004; Gaia, 2015). While shorter-term programs may not cultivate full capability in communicating in another language, they do provide an avenue for introductory learning, practice or refinement.

Cross-cultural interactions. Literature proposes that the most effective study-abroad experiences are those that purposefully expose students to another culture in a variety of ways, encourage student reflection, and explore meaning-making processes (Ferrari & Fine, 2016). According to Goldoni (2013), impactful activities include pursuing hobbies and interests abroad, living with a host family, and practicing cross-cultural communication. When considering interaction opportunities between students and locals, it may be helpful to include both formal and informal interactions to provide students with some support and encourage them to actively interact with the local community on their own.

Formal interactions may include planned visits to universities or historical sites. If a program has participants who have never traveled abroad or may be fearful of traveling abroad, more structure in their itinerary is helpful to build in a sense of comfort (Guzman, 2018). Informal interactions are without structure and may involve daily living activities, such as shopping and using local transportation, or meeting individuals in restaurants through recreational activities. Studies show that students often wish they had more free time to interact with individuals in a more informal setting, particularly if their program included mostly formal interactions (Barden & Cashwell, 2013; Dekaney, 2008).

Process Factors

Expectations of experiences. As early as 1962, Battsek shared a concern that too many students focus on the "abroad" part rather than the "study" while they are away. This still remains a legitimate concern, especially among shorter-term programs that may not have many or any credit units associated with them. Cheng (2013) confirms Battsek's concern in research findings that show students perceived travel to be more important than academic objectives in a short-term study abroad. Over-traveling could actually present a barrier to intercultural competency development, said Ziamandanis (2013). If students do not have opportunities to become immersed in a culture, deal with issues on their own or push their personal boundaries, the aims of study abroad may not be achieved.

Expectations of the experience can be set through a comprehensive pre-departure education and discussion of realistic and relevant learning outcomes. Pre- and post-departure meetings are important even with short-term experiences. They may, in fact, be even more important for these students. Pre-departure meetings can include discussing logistics and expectations for the trip, learning about the host country's culture, social norms, politics, as well as giving the group a chance to interact before departing (Barden & Cashwell, 2013; Highum, 2014).

Faculty support. Faculty are at the heart of academics and academic institutions. One of the earliest known study abroad programs in the United States, The University of Delaware's Junior Year Abroad, began in 1923 at the suggestion of Professor Raymond W. Kirkbride (Morris, 2019). He was a veteran of World War I and believed that better understanding among nations would lead to greater peace in the world. In our days, faculty continue to play a significant role in encouraging – or not encouraging – students to participate in education abroad (Morris, 2019).

Faculty involvement in a study abroad program design has increased in recent years (McMurtrie, 2007; Slotkin et al., 2012). This involvement can help with aligning curriculum to courses offered at the home institution (Campbell, 2016) and support the creation of dynamic education abroad opportunities (Morris, 2019). To better support immersive experiences, faculty can actively share available opportunities, design courses or curricula that lend themselves to international immersions, and account for immersions within the overall design of course sequences or degree programs.

Faculty do need proper training and preparation to support students while abroad. Selection of a faculty member to lead a program may be based on a combination of their interest, subject matter expertise and knowledge of the culture. However, all those that lead students on these experiences should have prior experiences abroad themselves, continual training on interculturally competent practices with students, and lead students by example through open-mindedness (Barden & Cashwell, 2013; Barrett, 2018; Guzman, 2018). Faculty also need the confidence and skills to manage a group and facilitate learning in a less structured and sometimes unpredictable environments. While it may seem that stress associated with immersive experiences would largely come from culture shock, Barden and Cashwell (2013) found that most of participants' negative experiences abroad related to inter-group dynamics within the program. While faculty are at the forefront of managing group logistics and dynamics, it is ideal that they also have support at the home campus. "Institutional support can have a transformative effect on faculty and their ability to engage with education abroad" (Morris, 2019). For example, with proper training, many faculty members would benefit from leading study abroad programs as professional development opportunities.

Reflection on experiences. Post-experience debrief sessions are important to solidify learning.

> *When both graduate and undergraduate students are provided opportunities to engage, reflect, and immerse themselves into a new environment and experience material not only cognitively but also physically, the learning and educational impact is often profound. (Gilin & Young, 2009; Keeton & Tate, 1978; Sanders, 2013, as cited in Ferrari & Fine, 2016)*

In fact, it can be transformational. When students have "a constructive engagement with otherness" (Parks Daloz, 2000), it leads to challenging assumptions and boundary crossing. Students who critically reflected on their study abroad experiences built a foundation to become a more culturally competent practitioner in their field (Canfield et al., 2009).

Faculty are instrumental in the reflection process, as they provide structured experiences in which students can process their thoughts and feelings. Post-departure debrief sessions are useful to allow students the opportunity to reflect on their upcoming experiences and identify ways to apply their learning to their everyday life in the United States (Barden & Cashwell, 2013). The debrief session may include sharing expectations with others, presenting the results of a research paper or project related to the experience, and completing evaluations for continuous improvement of the program. Post-program time may also include becoming involved with organizations or activities with an international focus, service learning, international volunteerism or international research with a faculty member. Rowan-Kenyon and Niehaus (2011) found that the extent to which students learn from a short-term study abroad experience may depend more on what those students do after they have returned home than what they did while abroad.

CONCLUSION

Globalization has created a growing need for leaders who understand how to effectively work with diverse others while navigating the complexities of modern societies and organizations. Higher education is on the forefront to develop these global leaders for organizations across sectors and industries. In order to fulfill the need, graduate-level leadership education must foster global perspectives and experiences. Research shows that these are effectively built through well designed international immersions. For current graduate students, these experiences must be flexible and accessible for their many demands in life, making short-term study abroad an accessible and popular option

While diverse and creative designs for short-term study abroad in the academy today are popular, their effectiveness can be enhanced with greater attention to learning objectives. The ideal aim is not just a cross-cultural exposure or acquisition of new knowledge; it is transformational learning. Transformational learning in study abroad involves positive shifts in perspective and disposition. Short-term study abroad has the potential for transformational learning that can reach a wider population of professionals. Additionally, those programs should be well designed and facilitated.

Graduate schools and their broader institutions can help faculty facilitate transformational learning in short-term study abroad by providing training and support. They can also make concerted efforts to track institutional data regarding short-term study abroad activities and participation among graduate students to identify trends and opportunities for improvement. By communicating this data at the institutional level and beyond, academia and industry will have a better understanding of graduate-level study abroad in the United States.

REFERENCES

Academics: Graduate Students. (n.d.). Retrieved November 5, 2019, from https://www.du.edu/abroad/graduate-students.html

Anderson, P. H., Lawton, L., Rexeisen, R. J., & Hubbard, A. C. (2006). Short term study abroad and intercultural sensitivity: A pilot study. *International Journal of Intercultural Relations, 30*(4), 457–469.

Ashford, S. J., & Sitkin, S. B. (2019). From problems to progress: A dialogue on prevailing issues in leadership research. *The Leadership Quarterly, 30*(4), 454–460.

Baer, J., Bhandari, R., Andrejko, N., & Mason, L. (2018). *Open Doors 2018 report on international educational exchange.* Institute of International Education. https://www.iie.org/opendoors

Bandyopadhyay, S., & Bandyopadhyay, K. (2015). Factors influencing student participation in college study abroad programs. *Journal of International Education Research, 11*(2), 87–94.

Barden, S. M., & Cashwell, C. S. (2013). Critical factors in cultural immersion: A synthesis of relevant literature. *International Journal for the Advancement of Counseling, 35*(4), 286–297. https://doi.org/10.1007/s10447-013-9183-y

Battsek, M. (1962). A practical analysis of some aspects of study abroad. *The Journal of General Education, 13*(4), 225–242.

Black, H. T., & Duhon, D. L. (2006, January/February). Assessing the impact of business study abroad programs on cultural awareness and personal development. *Journal of Education for Business, 81*(3), 140–144. https://doi.org/10.3200/JOEB.81.3.140-144

Campbell, K. (2016). Short-term study abroad programmes: Objectives and accomplishments. *Journal of International Mobility, 1*(4), 189–204.

Canfield, B. S., Low, L., & Hovestadt, A. (2009). Cultural immersion as a learning method for expanding intercultural competencies. *Family Journal: Counseling and Therapy for Couples and Families, 17*(4), 318–322. https://doi.org/10.1177/1066480709347359

Cheng, A. Y. N. (2013). Perceived value and preferences of short-term study abroad programmes: A Hong Kong study. *Procedia – Social and Behavioral Sciences, 116*, 4277–4282.

Chin, J. L., Trimble, J. E., & Garcia, J. E. (2018). (Eds.). *Global and culturally diverse leaders and leadership: New dimensions and challenges for business, education and society.* Emerald Publishing.

Clarke, I., III, Flaherty, T. B., Wright, N. D., & McMillen, R. M. (2009). Student intercultural proficiency from study abroad programs. *Journal of Marketing Education, 31*(2), 173–181.

Council of Graduate Schools. (2013). *Graduate education for global career pathways.* Council of Graduate Schools. https://cgsnet.org/graduateeducation-global-career-pathways-1

Creighton University Graduate School. (2019). *Guidelines for Differentiation among Undergraduate, Graduate, and Professional Courses.* https://gradschool.creighton.edu/sites/gradschool.creighton.edu/files/Guidelines-for-Differentiation-UG-Grad-Courses.pdf

Davies, D. C., Lewis, A. A., Anderson, A. E., & Bernstein, E. R. (2015). The development of intercultural competency in school psychology graduate students. *School Psychology International, 36*(4), 375–392. https://doi.org/10.1177/0143034315592664

DDI. (2018). *Global Leadership Forecast 2018.* Retrieved November 5, 2019, from https://www.ddiworld.com/glf2018/digital-data

Dekaney, E. M. (2008). Students' pre-departure expectations and post-sojourn observations in a short-term international program abroad on the culture, music, and art of Brazil. *International Education, 37*(2), 17–29.

Donnelly-Smith, L. (2009). Global learning through short-term study abroad. *Peer Review, 11*(4), 12–15.

Dowell, M., & Mirsky, K. (2002). *Study abroad: How to get the most out of your experience* (1st ed.). Pearson.

Doyle, S., Gendall, P., Meyer, L. H., Hoek, J., Tait, C., McKenzie, L., & Loorparg, A. (2010). An investigation of factors associated with student participation in study abroad. *Journal of Studies in International Education, 14*(5), 471–490.

Drews, D. R., & Meyer, L. L. (1996). Effects of study abroad on conceptualizations of national groups. *College Student Journal, 30*(4), 452–462.

Dwyer, M. M. (2004). More is better: The impact of study abroad program duration. *Frontiers: The Interdisciplinary Journal of Study Abroad, 10,* 151–163.

Egron-Polak, E., & Marmolejo, F. (2017). Higher education internationalization: Adjusting to new landscapes. In H. de Wit, J. Gacel-Ávila, E. Jones, & N. Jooste (Eds.), *The Globalization of internationalization: Emerging voices and perspectives* (pp. 7–18). Routledge.

Engel, L. (2017). *Underrepresented Students in U.S. Study Abroad.* Institute of International Education. http://mobilitytoolkit.ie/wp-content/uploads/2017/12/Underrepresented-Students-and-Study-Abroad.pdf

Fast Facts: Distance Learning. (n.d.). *National Center for Educational Statistics.* Retrieved November 5, 2019, from https://nces.ed.gov/fastfacts/display.asp?id=80

Ferrari, C. M., & Fine, J. B. (2016). Developing global perspectives in short-term study abroad: High-impact learning through curriculum, co-curriculum and community. *Journal of Global Initiatives: Policy, Pedagogy, Perspective, 10*(1), 8. https://digitalcommons.kennesaw.edu/jgi/vol10/iss1/8

Fieldwork. (2019). In *Lexico.com.* Retrieved November 4, 2019, from https://www.lexico.com/en/definition/fieldwork

Fischer, K. (2019, March 28). How international education's golden age lost its sheen. *The Chronicle of Higher Education*. Retrieved November 5, 2019, from https://www.chronicle.com/interactives/2019-03-28-golden-age

Forum on Education Abroad. (2019). *Who We Are*. https://forumea.org/about-us/who-we-are/

Gaia, A. C. (2015). Short-term faculty-led study abroad programs enhance cultural exchange and self-awareness. *The International Education Journal: Comparative Perspectives*, *14*(1), 21–31.

Ghemawat, P. (2017, July/August). Globalization in the Age of Trump. *Harvard Business Review*. Retrieved November 5, 2019, from https://hbr.org/2017/07/globalization-in-the-age-of-trump

Gilin, B., & Young, T. (2009). Educational benefits of international experiential learning in an MSW program. *International Social Work*, *52*(1), 36–47.

Goldoni, F. (2013). Students' immersion experiences in study abroad. *Foreign Language Annals*, *46*(3), 359–376. https://doi.org/10.1111/flan.12047

Guzman, N. A. (2018). *Perceptions of short-term study abroad experiences on intercultural competence in school psychology graduate students*. ProQuest Dissertations & Theses Global.

Hadis, B. F. (2005). Gauging the impact of study abroad: How to overcome the limitations of a single-cell design. *Assessment & Evaluation in Higher Education*, *30*(1), 3–19.

Harris, V. W., Kumaran, M., Harris, H. J., Moen, D., & Visconti, B. (2018). Assessing multicultural competence (knowledge and awareness) in study abroad experiences. *Compare: A Journal of Comparative and International Education*, *1*(1), 1–23. https://doi.org/10.1080/03057925.2017.1421901

Herd, A., Cumberland, D., Lovely, W., & Bird, A. (2018). The use of assessment center methodology to develop students' global leadership competencies: A conceptual framework and applied example. In J. S. Osland, M. E. Mendenhall, & L. Ming (Eds.), *Advances in Global Leadership* (Vol. 11, pp. 175–196). Emerald Publishing Limited. https://doi.org/10.1108/S1535-120320180000011006

Highum, A. (2014). Predeparture services for students studying abroad. *New Directions for Student Services*, *146*, 51–57. https://doi.org/10.1002/ss.20090

Hino, K. (2019). Are leadership theories Western-centric? Transcending cognitive differences between the East and the West. In R. Riggio (Ed.), *What's wrong with leadership? Improving leadership, research, and practice* (pp. 138–149). Routledge.

Institute of International Education. (2017). *Study abroad matters: Linking higher education to the contemporary workplace through international experience*. https://www.iie.org/Research-and-Insights/Publications/Study-Abroad-Matters

Institute of International Education. (2018). *Leading institutions by duration of study abroad and institutional type, 2015/16-2016/17. Open Doors Report on International Educational Exchange.* http://www.iie.org/opendoors

Institute of International Education. (2019). *Programs.* https://www.iie.org/programs

Jones, S. R., Rowan-Kenyon, H. T., Ireland, S. M., Niehaus, E., & Skendall, K. C. (2012). The meaning students make as participants in short-term immersion programs. *Journal of College Student Development, 53*(2), 201–220. https://doi.org/10.1353/csd.2012.0026

Kellerman, B. (2012). *The end of leadership.* HarperCollins.

Keeton, M. T., & Tate, P. J. (1978). The boom in experiential learning. *Learning by Experience: What, Why, How, 1,* 1–8.

Kiely, R. (2005). A transformative learning model for service learning: A longitudinal case study. *Michigan Journal of Community Service Learning, 12,* 5–22.

King, J. T. (2004). Service learning as a site for critical pedagogy: A case of collaboration, caring, and defamiliarization across borders. *Journal of Experiential Education, 26*(3), 121–137.

Krishnan, L. A., Masters, C., Holgate, H., Wang, C., & Calahan, C. A. (2017). Structured study abroad enhances intercultural competence. *Teaching and Learning in Communication Sciences & Disorders, 1*(1), 1–26.

Lewis, T. L., & Niesenbaum, R. A. (2005). Extending the stay: Using community-based research and service learning to enhance short-term study abroad. *Journal of Studies in International Education, 9,* 251–264.

MacLeod, M. L. P., & Farrell, P. (1994). The need for a significant reform: A practice driven approach to curriculum. *Journal of Nursing Education, 33*(5), 208–214. https://doi.org/10.3928/0148-4834-19940501-05

McElhaney, K. A. (1998). Student outcomes of community service learning: A comparative analysis of curriculum-based and non-curriculum-based alternative spring break programs. Hathi Trust: Digital Library. https://catalog.hathitrust.org/Record/003987168/Cite

McKeown, J. S. (2009). *The first time effect: The impact of study abroad on college student intellectual development.* State University of New York Press.

McMurtrie, B. (2007). Study-abroad numbers continue to climb, trips are shorter, report says. *Chronicle of Higher Education, 54*(12), A36.

Medina-Lopez Portillo, A. (2004). Intercultural learning assessment: the link between program duration and the development of intercultural sensitivity. *Frontiers: Interdisciplinary Journal of Study Abroad, 10,* 179–200.

Mills, L., Deviney, D., & Ball, B. (2010). Short-term study abroad programs: A diversity of options. *The Journal of Human Resource and Adult Learning, 6*(2), 1–13.

Morris, C. (2019). *Faculty and education abroad: The role of faculty in promoting global learning on U.S. campuses*. Institute of International Education.

Nahavandi, A., & Krishnan, H. (2018). Indo-European leadership (IEL): A non-Western leadership perspective. In J. L. Chin, J. E. Trimble, & J. E. Garcia (Eds.), *Global and culturally diverse leaders and leadership: New dimensions, opportunities, and challenges for business, industry, education and society* (pp. 105–123). Emerald Publishing.

National Youth Leadership Council. (2019). *What is service learning?* https://www.nylc.org/page/WhatisService-Learning

Norris, E. M., & Gillespie, J. (2009). How study abroad shapes global careers: Evidence from the United States. *Journal of Studies in International Education*, 13(3), 382–397.

Parks Daloz, L. A. (2000). Transformative learning for the common good. In J. Mezirow & Associates (Eds.), *Learning as transformation* (pp. 103–123). Jossey-Bass.

Practicum. (2019). In *Collinsdictionary.com*. Retrieved November 4, 2019, from https://www.collinsdictionary.com/us/dictionary/english/practicum

QS Global Employer Survey Report. (2016). https://www.qs.com/qs-global-employer-survey-2016-reveals-desirable-graduates/

Rhoads, R. A., & Neururer, J. (1998). Alternative spring break: Learning through community service. *Journal of Student Affairs Research and Practice*, 35(2), 83–101.

Riggio, R. (Ed.). (2019). *What's wrong with leadership? Improving leadership, research, and practice*. Routledge.

Rost, J. C., & Barker, R. A. (2000). Leadership education in colleges: Toward a 21st century paradigm. *Journal of Leadership Studies*, 7(1), 3–12. https://doi.org/10.1177/107179190000700102

Rowan-Kenyon, H. T., & Niehaus, E. (2011). One year later: The influence of short-term study abroad experiences on students. *Journal of Student Affairs Research and Practice*, 48(2), 213–228. https://doi.org/10.2202/1949-6605.6213

Rusciano, F. L. (2014). Globalizing the curriculum: How to incorporate a global perspective into your courses. *Association of American Colleges & Universities*, 100(3). https://www.aacu.org/publications-research/periodicals/globalizing-curriculum

Sanders, M. (2013). The university as a setting for experiential learning: The potential for reciprocal benefits. In *Proceedings of the human factors and ergonomics society annual meeting* (pp. 1590–1594).

Sanger, J., & Mason, L. (2019). *Who's counting? Understanding the landscape of graduate learning overseas*. Institute of International Education.

Schwald, R. (2012). Toward a new practice of internationalization: A case study on a short-term study abroad program at European institutions of higher education. *Review of European Studies*, 4(2), 44.

Slotkin, M. H., Durie, C. J., & Eisenberg, J. R. (2012). The benefits of short term study abroad as blended learning experience. *Journal of International Education in Business*, 4(2), 163–173.

Stone, M., & Petrick, J. (2013). The educational benefits of travel experiences: A literature review. *Journal of Travel Research*, 731–744.

Sutton, R. C., & Rubin, D. L. (2004). The GLOSSARI project: Initial findings from a system-wide research initiative on study abroad learning outcomes. *Frontiers: The Interdisciplinary Journal of Study Abroad, 10*(1), 65–82.

Taras, V. (2019). X-Culture academy: Kids learning international business through experience. In *The Palgrave handbook of learning and teaching international business and management* (pp. 789–799). Palgrave Macmillan.

Williams, T. R. (2005). Exploring the impact of study abroad on students' intercultural communication skills: Adaptability and sensitivity. *Journal of Studies in International Education*, 9(4), 356–371. https://www.ie.org/Research-and-Insights/Graduate-Learning-Overseas

X-Culture. (2021). *For Instructors*. https://x-culture.org/for-instructors/

Ziamandanis, C. M. (2013). Qualitative and quantitative cultural gains from short-term study abroad. *Revista d'Innovacio Educativa, 10*, 138–143.

9

RECENT DEVELOPMENTS IN COLLEGE LEADERSHIP EDUCATION IN JAPAN

MIKINARI HIGANO

In recent years, college leadership education has experienced a boom in Japan. A decade ago, if you were to attend the annual global conferences of the International Leadership Association (ILA), you would observe that the vast majority of people in attendance were from North America. Some of those present were from Europe, primarily the UK, but attendees from Asia and Africa were difficult to locate. However, since 2014, the number of attendees from Japan has gradually increased, reflecting a significant growth of college leadership education in Japan. This chapter will sketch out those recent developments.

THE BEGINNING

Before 2006, some colleges in Japan included "leader" programs as part of their curricula. Some were designed exclusively for students with high Grade Point Averages (GPAs) worthy of honors status. Others were "study-abroad programs" for students with higher-than-average English skills. Common among them was the implicit idea that "leaders" are, and should be, selected from an elite membership.

Other leadership studies were found in "organizational behavior" courses, mainly in colleges of business. Such classes usually focused on leadership as a phenomenon that occurred under certain conditions, instead of merely targeting the development of leadership skills as part of a list of student competencies.

When Rikkyo University in Tokyo was planning a new student leadership development program for its College of Business (COB), I was hired by the dean to create it. For me, the greatest challenge was that the program was originally intended for elites only – yet at the same time, its three main consecutive courses were to be mandatory for all students in the department. I wondered if the program, as first conceived, was intended to reflect the US Military Academy at West Point, where a student, as part of an established hierarchy, might be promised certain special privileges, such as the bestowal of superior rank. However, in the end, our recruitment of students into the new COB was to be implemented on the basis of equality, as in other existing colleges.

I was given a year to complete and prepare the program before the actual leadership courses began. So during that time, I examined similar programs being taught in American colleges. In doing so, I discovered that elitist leadership education was becoming obsolete. Horizontal, shared leadership (without authority), was coming into its own as a more significant fit for the new digital age. So with the dean's permission, I drafted a plan that steered away from the traditional "elitist" (top-down) approach, gearing more toward one that emphasized shared-leadership education. By April 2006, everything was set. The entire first class of 380 freshmen students was admitted into the course (Rikkyo COB Business Leadership Program, BLP). It was the very first required educational leadership course ever in Japan.

THE STRUGGLE FOR LEGITIMACY: 2007–2009

Once the Rikkyo BLP (Business Leadership Program) began, it became extremely popular among students. BLP courses were all interactive and experienced-based. Significant time was spent on group discussion and mutual feedback, while other traditional courses used one-way lecture formats in large classrooms. Students seemed more attracted to the learning style than to the learning outcome (leadership), but their collective energy provided the driving strength and force of the program.

Many students brought their own ideas and proposals to improve BLP courses – so much so that some of those who offered us such assistance wound up later as candidates for Teaching Assistant (TA) positions. As a result of their daily interaction with professors, students felt a sense of belonging in the COB, having so many opportunities for self-disclosure and feedback. Thus, COB became an exceptional college in an urban commuting university of its size (20,000 undergraduates). The result was a unique kind of organizational development among its students.

Although the BLP was enthusiastically welcomed by students, the program continued to face various challenges. Besides the shortage of resources, as is usual with many new programs, a majority of faculty members remained skeptical about both the relevance of its learning outcome (leadership without authority) and its teaching method (peer learning). Some even regarded leadership education as a trivial, pointless academic exercise.

BLP was the only credit-bearing leadership development program for under-graduate students in Japan at the time. For the first 6–10 years, in fact, teaching and working there was like old-style para-trooping. You flew behind enemy lines toward unfamiliar terrain. Once you bailed out, you were often fired upon while floating to the ground. When you landed, you found yourself surrounded, outnumbered, and cut-off, alone. But as it turned out, BLP was not *totally* alone. Another institution, Shibaura Institute of Technology, launched a new leadership development program for graduate students just two years later. Until 2008, Rikkyo BLP and Shibaura Tech were unaware of each other's innovative work. Para-troopers were like that too – scattered and isolated, with limited communications.

THE ACTIVE-LEARNING MOVEMENT: 2010–PRESENT

Around 2010, a group of education scientists, including Shin-ichi Mizokami (2014) and Kayo Matsushita, became advocates of "active learning" in Japanese college education. At first, Rikkyo BLP faculty members were not aware of this movement, in spite of their having practiced active learning daily in the classroom. Eventually, its staff members were "re-discovered" through a nation-wide survey of active learning to determine best practices. For Rikkyo BLP, this led to commendation by the Ministry of Education (MEXT) and the Japan Society for Promotion of Science in 2012. The program also received the "Client of the Year: Academic Sector" award from the World Institute for Action Learning in 2014.

In the beginning, the term Active Learning referred only to a teaching method or a learning style – and not a learning outcome.[1] Still, active learning, in its preparation of students for future courses, became very important for its influence on leadership education in Japan. Previously, a majority of Japanese college students appeared comfortable with one-way lecture-style teaching, and they dared not think of raising their hands to ask questions, even when encouraged to. But once students went through leadership courses, they felt free to assert themselves and learn from their peers. In this sense, "active learning is based on new leadership by students" (Higano, 2017, p. 213); and so active learning is reinforced if it goes hand-in-hand with leadership education. This is exactly what happened in Rikkyo COB and some colleges and high schools later on.

BUSINESSES STARTED TO RECOGNIZE LEADERSHIP WITHOUT AUTHORITY: 2010–PRESENT

When Rikkyo BLP started in 2006, "leadership without authority" was taken for granted only in a limited number of companies, such as large consulting firms. In the 2010s, however, businesspeople became aware of the VUCA (Volatile, Uncertain, Complex and Ambiguous) – world, which influenced the idea of "leadership without authority" on the part of younger employees. This strategy has become accepted by more and more companies. Managers are encouraged to empower her or his people in order to motivate and engage them while adapting to outside environmental changes through new, innovative business processes. Striking examples of leadership-without-authority models can be found at Rikkyo and Waseda, where young employees of corporate sponsors often sit with students in leadership development classes and learn from each other, rather than acting as instructors.

Testimonials have demonstrated that those who took leadership education courses in Rikkyo COB appeared to be more valued by the private sector – more so than other Rikkyo alumni. This is probably because their leadership potential was highly appreciated in job interviews and internships.

THE DAWN OF COLLEGE LEADERSHIP EDUCATION: 2016

By the mid-2010s, COB Rikkyo had transformed itself into one of the best colleges of business in Japan. It rose from "competitive" to "extremely competitive" in terms of selectiveness of students (standard deviation rose by seven in 10 years: 2006–2015). Rikkyo BLP opened classrooms for outside visitors, a move that helped BLP to become more influential. By 2014, core instructors of BLP began a consulting service for outside faculty and staff at other colleges where new leadership education courses were being considered as part of the curricula. After eight years of witnessing the changes in their own students, BLP faculty members came to think it was better to extend leadership education *outside* of Rikkyo rather than containing it. To some extent, this was considered a way of making the country of Japan a better place.

As stated above, businesspeople began to welcome young people's leadership without authority. Thus, it was not surprising to see some colleges start their own leadership education programs during the last decade. Fifteen colleges in Japan launched credit-bearing leadership education programs in 2016 and 2019. (Fig. 9.1). They are all commuting colleges in urban areas. Five of them are women's colleges (in pink). And while some programs belong to the individual schools or departments, others are across the campus. Note that emergence of COVID-19 in 2020 did not check the rapid growth at all.

COVID-19 ENABLES THE INTRODUCTION OF A NEW LEARNING OPPORTUNITY

The first wave of the COVID-19 struck Japan in February 2020, two months before the new academic year started. Most colleges, including those shown in Figure 9.1 (from Rikkyo at the bottom of the graph to Kinjo Gakuin at the top) were forced to change most of their in-person courses to online formats for the Spring Semester and perhaps beyond. At the time, there were no ready-made online leadership education packages produced in Japanese. So, in order to keep classes interactive and experiential, synchronous online courses, using Zoom or WebEx, were an obvious choice. In fact, these were the only choices. Before long, instructors discovered that online leadership courses can be highly interactive and effective learning opportunities, especially when using such functions as breakout and chat. It was also found that a synchronous online class can act as a more comfortable, safer learning environment for "quiet" students (Cain, 2012) when compared to traditional in-person classes. In that sense, online synchronous leadership courses may not act as imperfect substitutes for in-person courses, but they do come with their own unique set of advantages. Such innovative formats have given leadership teachers some significant learning opportunities.

Fig. 9.1   New Credit-Bearing Leadership Education Programs (undergraduate)

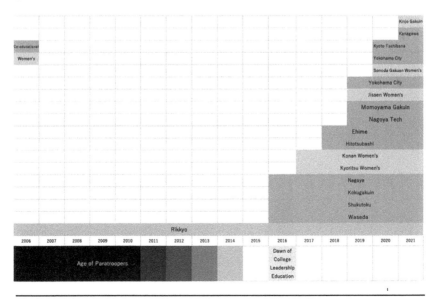

Table 9.1.   National Survey Questions and Answers.

Question	Y	N
1. Do you have leadership courses which set leadership skills as learning outcomes?	18	26
(Hereafter we ask only 18 colleges that answered "Yes" to Q1.)		
2. Is it credit-bearing?	16	2
3. What is the class size?	Max = 90	Min = 20
4. Do any of your leadership courses select students?	13	5
5. Is your leadership course restricted to particular grades of students? (i.e., freshmen only, sophomore only, etc.)	13	5
6. Are any of your leadership courses mandatory?	8	11
7. Are tenured faculty in charge of the leadership courses?	14	4
8. How much class time is used for lecturing?	max100%	min20%
9. Do you mainly teach leadership without authority (or shared leadership)?	15	3
10. Do you have staff to support the teacher and course?	Devoted = 3	Part time = 15
11. Do your students use mutual or 360 feedback to reflect on themselves in class?	14	4
12. Does your leadership program regularly collaborate with leadership programs in other colleges?	9	9
13. Do you employ a TA?	14	4
14. Do you always select TA's from students who took the same course in preceding semesters?	10	8
15. Do current and past TA's form a community?	6	12

NATIONAL SURVEY OF COLLEGE LEADERSHIP EDUCATION INSTITUTION: THE FIRST ROUND

As the number of leadership programs rapidly increase, it is becoming more and more difficult to accurately perceive the whole picture of college leadership education in Japan, what with the commonalities shared by each institute as well as how and where they differ. To fill that gap, we have implemented a national survey, based partially on recent studies by Guthrie et al. (2018, 2019), who conducted similar research using the data of 489 American colleges and universities to locate 1,526 leadership programs. In Japan, however, we have no such pre-existing data, so we had to begin our research from scratch. Moreover, our intention was not only to locate the programs, but also to explore the characteristics of each one. We were especially eager to know if these programs focused primarily on the development of "elite" students, or were they less exclusionary?

We benchmarked the 15 colleges mentioned earlier in this chapter and devised a questionnaire for all other colleges. Copies were sent to every department of all colleges (numbering in the thousands) in Japan. Below are the answers given by the preliminary survey group, consisting of 43 departments from 42 colleges with one master's degree program, plus the benchmarked 15 colleges. Even with this first survey group, we can see at a glance a lot of differences and varieties among the programs.

PRELIMINARY ANALYSIS

Most of the questions above need some clarifications.

1) Do you have leadership courses which set leadership skills as learning outcomes? (Yes = 18, No = 26)

   This is to locate leadership courses. Questions below are asked only of those 18 colleges that answered "Yes" to question #1.

2) Is it credit bearing? (Y = 16, N = 2)

   There are some interesting education programs that do not give students any credits, but here, "credit" means that the college officially recognizes the contents of the program to be academic and necessary to be taught.

3) What is the class size? (Maximum = 90, Minimum = 20)

   The larger the class, the more difficult for the class to be interactive.

4) Do any of your leadership courses select students? (Y = 13, N = 5)

   This is usually a demand-and-supply problem. Supply of leadership education service is usually limited, at least for a short period of time. If the demand from students goes above the supply, there will be selection. Exceptions occur with leadership courses taught in the traditional one-way lecture style. Another exception occurs within the context of the honors program.

5) Is your leadership course restricted to particular grades of students? (i.e., freshmen only, sophomore only, etc.) (Y = 13, N = 5)

6) Are any of your leadership courses mandatory? (Y = 8, N = 11)

   These two items often go yes in inside-department (or college) program. It would be relatively rare to for campus-wide program.

7) Are tenured faculty in charge of leadership courses? (Y = 14, N = 4)

   From students' point of view, it does not matter. But for faculty and staff, it is clearly important. And this is an especially important survival factor for a young program, which most leadership programs are.

8) How much class time is used for lecturing? (Maximum = 100%, Minimum = 20%)

   If it is 100%, it is not interactive by definition, and not peer learning either.

9) Do you mainly teach leadership without authority (or shared leadership)? (Y = 15, N = 3)

   As stated in a preceding section, businesspeople in Japan started to recognize the importance of leadership without authority. As a result, new leadership programs are preparing for the trend.

   Previously, there were only leadership programs where students with higher GPAs and/or fluency in English were recruited and given opportunities to develop leadership potential. Those programs do not teach leadership without authority because the selected students – the "elite" – are expected to have access to authority in the near future. These programs usually lacked any intentional or planned skill-enhancement elements because it was assumed a certain limited set of experience was sufficient for students who were true "elites." By contrast, today's new-school leadership education programs are based on the principles of Kolb's experiential learning and put much weight on reflection and feedback after the experience.

10) Do you have staff to support the teacher and course? (Devoted staff = 3, Part-time staff only = 15)

   Students may not notice, but devoted staff is highly valuable for instructors and eventually for students as well.

11) Do your students use mutual or 360 feedback to reflect on themselves in class? (Y = 14, N = 4)

If you use mutual or 360 feedback, you urge students to learn from peers.

12) Does your leadership program regularly collaborate with leadership programs in other colleges? (Y = 9, N = 9)

This often shows openness to learn from other colleges. If you think you know enough about leadership education, you do not spare time to collaborate with the outside.

13) Do you employ a TA? (Y = 14, N = 4)

14) Do you always select a TA from the students who had the same course in the preceding semesters? (Y = 10, N = 8)

15) Do current and past TA's form a community? (Y = 6, N = 12)

Some TAs (especially TAs for a large class) perform only clerical work such as taking attendance and setting up computers. The instructor does not expect a TA to fully understand the contents of the course. By contrast, if the instructor wants to stimulate peer learning, s/he would employ a TA who deeply understands the course contents. It is logical that a past TA should be a mentor for a new TA, or new and past TAs form a learning community, if motivated to do so.

Instead of judging or rating the performance of individual programs, the ultimate goal of this national survey is to provide a means of networking scattered leadership programs as a means of organizing a community so that separate institutions may learn from each other.

CONCLUSION

The first undergraduate academic leadership development course in Japan was initiated in 2006 with the Business Leadership Program (BLP) at Rikkyo University. This was followed by two major changes during the early 2010s: (1) Business people began to recognize the idea of leadership without authority and expect such leadership on the part of young employees; (2) The active-learning movement started independently of leadership education at first, but there was a growing realization that active learning is reinforced if it goes hand-in-hand with leadership education. Mainly due to these factors, the number of academic leadership development programs increased by 13 in 2019. This period might be labeled "The dawn of college leadership education in Japan" because even today, the number of such programs is still on the rise. In fact, several more programs are launched in 2020 and 2021. To ensure against such start-ups working in isolation from others, we have just begun a national survey of leadership education institutions in an effort to stimulate more collaboration among them. The events summarized here may indeed signal a dramatic boost in leadership education in Japan.

NOTE

1. As Mizokami (2017) wrote, "Active learning is an umbrella term. It has been considered impossible to find an agreed-upon definition for everyone. With that in mind, here is my definition: Active learning includes all kinds of learning beyond the mere one-way transmission of knowledge in lecture-style classes (passive learning). It requires engagement in activities (writing, discussion, and presentation) and externalizing cognitive processes in the activities."

REFERENCES

Cain, S. (2012). *Quiet: The Power of Introverts in a world that can't stop talking.* New York, NY: The Crown Publishing Group.

Guthrie, K. L., Batchelder, J. M., & Hu, P. (2019). *Examining degree types of academic leadership programs in the United States.* Leadership Learning Research Center, Florida State University.

Guthrie, K. L., Teig, T. S., & Hu, P. (2018). *Academic leadership programs in the United States.* Leadership Learning Research Center, Florida State University.

Higano, M. (2017). New leadership education and deep active learning. In K. Matsushita (Ed.), *Deep active learning: Toward greater depth in university education* (pp. 207–220). Springer.

Mizokami, S. (2014). *Active Learning to Kyoju Gakushu Paradigm no Tenkan.* Toshindo [in Japanese].

Mizokami, S. (2017). Deep Active Learning from the perspective of active learning theory. In K. Matsushita (Ed.), *Deep active learning: Toward greater depth in university education* (pp. 79–91). Gateway East, Singapore: Springer.

PART III

THE PRACTICE OF GLOBAL LEADERSHIP

10

LEADING CORPORATIONS IN THE US AND OTHER NATIONAL SETTINGS: WHAT WILL BE COMMON TO THEIR LEADERSHIP, AND WHAT WILL BE DIFFERENT?

MICHAEL USEEM

Leading a company should be guided by much the same set of principles, by one line of reasoning, whatever the country. The universals of the human condition are indeed universal, and making a product or marketing a service is arguably achieved by kindred tasks whether the firm is headquartered in China, India, or the United States. So too for setting strategy and communicating persuasively. Industries and languages can radically vary across national boundaries, but the foundational principles for leading enterprises both domestically and globally are less varied.

Much of our leadership canon is thus implicitly, and sometimes even overtly, universal in framing. Many business school instructors, including this author, do not qualify many of their prescriptions for executive behavior country-by-country. They implicitly affirm, for instance, that vision, strategy, and execution are required of company executives whatever the national setting. Similarly, management consultants who say that company culture has a larger impact than business strategy on workforce performance do not typically say that is the case in some countries but not in others (Collins, 2001; Goodwin, 2018; Ibarra, 2015; Isaacson, 2012).

Consistent with this, academic research has confirmed that many strands of business leadership are in fact geographically transcendent. Most business managers have been found, in one major study, for instance, to favor a set of qualities for their leaders regardless of country. In a cross-national study of 16,000 middle managers of more than 800 companies in 64 countries, from Albania to Zimbabwe, the investigators found that managers generally valued dynamism, decisiveness, and honesty, a capacity to motivate and negotiate, and a disciplined focus on performance, regardless of country. And the surveyed managers everywhere generally disfavored company executives – whatever the national setting – if they were autocratic, egocentric, or irritable. Taken together, we might term these a "global way" of company leadership (House et al., 2004).

Several explanations for the worldwide consistencies come to mind. If managers are solving the same kinds of problems but in different countries, they may be solving them in much the same manner because there are few effective alternatives. Also, when managers search for "best practices" they may be looking to companies in other countries for innovative management practices, just as the leaders of auto makers everywhere have long turned to Japan for ideas on how to run their own assembly plants. Finally, "isomorphic" behavior may also be bringing managers to copy one another across national boundaries for the risk reduction that can come with imitation of other proven performers, wherever they might be headquartered (DiMaggio & Powell, 1983; Kunreuther & Useem, 2018; Womack et al., 1990).

SOME LEADERSHIP PRINCIPLES ARE THE SAME

Whatever the explanation for the country commonalities, shared principles are indeed evident globally in many areas of leadership among senior managers and even governing directors. Drawing on my own direct work with company leaders in a range of countries and research across several national boundaries, I have, by way of illustration, identified 16 such capacities that are generally expected of company leaders everywhere. I have assembled them under the rubric of a prescriptive "leader's checklist" in Table 10.1 (Useem, 2021).

A similar effort to identify the capacities for leading effective teams yields a comparable framework for team oversight, also regardless of national setting, summarized in Table 10.2 (Edmondson, 2014; Haas & Mortensen, 2016; Hackman, 2002; Klein, 2004; McChrystal et al., 2015).

Table 10.1. The Leader's Checklist.

1. Articulate a vision	9. Embrace the front lines
2. Think and act strategically	10. Take charge and lead change
3. Identify personal implications	11. Manage relations and emotions
4. Convey your character	12. Strengthen leadership in oneself and others
5. Honor the room	13. Dampen over-optimism and pessimism
6. Communicate persuasively	14. Build a diverse top team
7. Decide decisively	15. Place common interest first
8. Motivate the ranks	16. Think like a CEO

Table 10.2. The Team Leader's Checklist.

1. Learning: Actively strengthen the team both cognitively and affectively.

2. Designed: Clear goals with well-designed tasks and assignments.

3. Esprit de Corps: Share experiences within the team.

4. Dynamic: Changing markets change the team's composition, culture, and architecture.

5. Diverse: Optimize team performance with diversity in background and experience.

6. Right Size: Not too large, not too small.

7. Engaged: Every team member actively involved.

8. Led: A team improves over individual performance and decision-making when the team is well formed and well led, especially under stress.

To briefly elaborate on this global framing, each of the capacities for individual leadership and team leadership in Tables 10.1 and 10.2 should also be seen as coming with a number of sub-capacities, and they are universal, as well. Consider by way of example the sub-capacities for the second element in Table 10.1, "think and act strategically." From observations and research, several investigators have set forward specific sub-feature prescriptions for the effective exercise of this leadership element anywhere, including scan widely, see sooner, separate signal from noise, identify weak signals, stand in customer shoes, build networks, and track markets (Day & Schoemaker, 2019; Krupp & Schoemaker, 2014).

Other observers have also elaborated on the "think and act strategically" principle in Table 10.1 by focusing on how managers can transform a strategic direction into an operational reality whatever the country. From watching company leaders in action and academic research on executive decisions, we have identified six prescriptive elements for "execution" regardless of nation (Singh & Useem, 2021):

1. Integrate Strategy and Leadership. Master the elements of strategy and leadership both separately and as an integrated whole.

2. Learn to Lead Strategically. Pursue directed learning, one-on-one coaching, and instructive experience to develop an integrated understanding of strategy and leadership.

3. Ensure Strategic Fit. Arrange a strong match between the strategic challenges of a managerial position and the individual with the leadership skills to fill it.

4. Convey Strategic Intent. Communicate strategic intent throughout the organization and empower others to implement the strategy.

5. Layer Leadership. Ensure that leaders at every level are capable of appreciating strategic intent and implementing it, and hold them responsible for its execution.

6. Decide Deliberatively. Focus on both short- and long-term objectives; press for disciplined analysis and avoid status-quo bias; and bring the future into the present.

We certainly appreciate that these leadership principles and sub-principles vary somewhat in their actual country-by-country incarnations. Consider principle 14 on the leader's checklist in Table 10.1, "build a diverse team." When applied to governance, for instance, a diverse board in Norway must include a balanced mix of both genders – by national policy. The country requires companies listed on its stock exchange to include women in at least 40 per cent of their board's seats, this at a time when large publicly-traded corporate boards on average in the United States included only 24 per cent women and Japan less than 7 per cent. But the team-leadership general principle still stands: Top teams – whether in the executive suite or the boardroom – should work to become more diverse if they are to be well led, even if they are not well along that path yet (Spencer Stuart, 2019).

SOME LEADERSHIP PRINCIPLES ARE ALSO DIFFERENT

American baseball legend Yogi Berra had a habit of offering up life's wisdom through memorable malapropisms. Among the better known: "You can observe a lot by just watching." Dale Berra, also a professional player, was asked if he was similar to his father, and he responded, the "similarities between me and my father are different." It was a Yogi-Berra-like way of reminding us that some similarities are similar while others are different. Much the same for leadership across national boundaries: for some capacities, the cross-national similarities are similar, our focus so far, but for others the similarities are different.

This was evident in the cross-national study referenced earlier of middle-manager leadership preferences across 64 countries. While individual capacities such as decisiveness and a focus on performance were universally admired, the value of other capacities differed significantly from nation to nation. Surveyed managers, for instance, stressed status differences, self-effacement, and empowerment in some countries – but the opposite in others (House et al., 2004).

We opted to focus further on this question of national differences by talking directly with executives and directors of large companies in China and India. In the case of China, we interviewed 72 executives and directors of large non-state-owned enterprises during the mid-2010s, and in the case of India, we interviewed 105 executives and directors among its largest corporations in 2007–2009. The better-known Chinese companies included Alibaba, Lenovo, and Vanke; the better-known Indian firms included Infosys, Reliance, and Tata (Cappelli et al., 2010; Useem et al., 2017).

We sought to identify distinctive leadership principles in China and India through the eyes of those who had been running the largest privately-owned firms in those countries, very informed participant observers. We appreciated that they may have brought blinders and biases to their reported perceptions, and we made every effort to take those limitations into account when extracting their guiding principles. In the background were several studies of American (and British) business leadership that I had earlier completed or was actively researching (Useem, 1984, 1993, 2021), and among the distinctive leadership principles we found in China were six, and in India, four (Cappelli et al., 2010; Useem et al., 2017).

Distinctive Leadership Principles Among Large Chinese Companies:

- A willingness to embrace uncertainty.

- An urgency to capitalize on business opportunities.

- Confidence and optimism, with a focus on action.

- Patient, persistent, and passionate about company purpose and mission.

- "Western system with oriental wisdom."

- Learning business leadership from experience with few historical models.

Distinctive Leadership Principles Among Large Indian Companies:

- Holistic engagement with employees. Indian business leaders see their firms as organic enterprises where sustaining employee morale and building company culture are critical obligations. People are viewed as assets to be developed, not costs to be reduced.

- Improvisation and adaptability. Improvisation is also at the heart of the India Way. In a complex, often volatile environment with few resources and much red tape, business leaders have learned to rely on their wits to circumvent recurrent and innumerable hurdles.

- Creative value propositions. Given the large and intensely competitive domestic market, Indian business leaders have of necessity learned to create value propositions that satisfy the needs of demanding consumers and do so with extreme efficiency.

- Broad mission and purpose. Indian business leaders place special emphasis on personal values, a vision of growth, and strategic thinking. They take pride in not only enterprise success but also family prosperity, regional advance, and national renaissance.

By way of one personal example, we draw upon our interview with the executive director of Tata Sons, which oversees Tata Group, India's largest company in market capitalization and revenue with investments in automobiles, communication, consulting, hotels, power, steel, and tea (with 300,000 employees at the time of the interview and revenue the equivalent of three percent of the country's GDP). From his own extensive experience with both Indian and Western business leaders, R. Gopalakrishnan reported that Indian executives rely far more upon their intuition than do their counterparts in the West. "Many foreigners come to India," he explained,

> *they talk to Indian managers, and they find them very articulate, very analytical, very smart, very intelligent; and then they can't for the life of them figure out why the Indian manager can't do something about [the plan] as prescribed by the analysis.*

Indian business leaders, he summed up, "think in English and act Indian" (Gopalakrishnan et al., 2010).

Another way to appreciate the national differences is to ask the executives and directors how they allocated their time among their major leadership tasks. From our interviews with the Chinese and Indian company leaders and a comparable survey in the United States, the top ranked priorities are displayed in Table 10.3. We see that setting strategy is the priority among the company executives in China and India, but regulatory affairs were more paramount for the American executives.

NATIONAL WAYS

The idea of distinctive national business leadership principles on top of a set of shared principles goes back more than a century. In *The Protestant Ethic and the Spirit of Capitalism*, German sociologist Max Weber argued that business managers in countries in Northern Europe and North America evolved a distinctive calling in which they demonstrated religious merit by founding a private enterprise, building the enterprise, and reinvesting in the enterprise – rather than consuming their newfound wealth. This ethos emerged as a distinctive leadership principle for those at the apex of enterprises in Northern Europe and North America (Weber, 1905).

Table 10.3.   Most Time-Consuming Areas for American, Chinese, and Indian Business Leaders.

Time Rank	American Companies	Chinese Companies	Indian Companies
1	Regulatory Issues	Setting strategy	Setting strategy
2	Reporting to the Board	Building top management teams	Regulatory Issues[a]
3	Shareholder relations	Nurture corporate culture	Reporting to the Board [a]
4	**Setting strategy**	Day-to-day management	Shareholder relations [a]
5	Media relations	Secure critical resources	Media relations
6	Day-to-day management	Customer relations	Day-to-day management

Source: Cappelli et al. (2010); Useem et al. (2017).

[a] Areas 2, 3, and 4 are tied.

Building on Weber's insights, Sociologist Reinhard Bendix more generally identified what he termed "ideologies of management," characteristic
national systems of thought that guide the actions of executives across a
range of companies and industries within a country. Drawing on the period
of industrialization in England, Germany, Russia, and the United States,
Bendix found that these country ideologies emerged as business founders
fought for acceptance by ruling aristocracies whose dominance predated the
rise of private enterprise. As one result, for instance, entrepreneurs came to
constitute a dominant and self-assured social class in the United States, but
remained subordinate to state authority in Russia and consequently were less
dominant and self-assured (Bendix, 1956).

Sociologist Mauro Guillen, further extended Weber's and Bendix's ideas
under the phrase "models of management," referencing the distinct national
mindsets he found among company managers in Germany, Great Britain,
Spain, and the United States. Guillen reported, for instance, that the pre-
cepts of Taylorism and scientific management experienced early adoption by
company leaders in Germany and the United States but far less so in Great
Britain and Spain (Guillen, 1994).

Subtler but still striking leadership differences emerged between the
United States and the United Kingdom, two countries otherwise much alike
in language and behavioral norms. Historian Martin J. Wiener, for example, documented that the supremacy of business became far more complete
in the United States than in the United Kingdom in the latter half of the
nineteenth century and the first half of the twentieth century. As a result,
high culture in England had not accorded business the respected status that
it had achieved in America. This "anti-industrial culture" was so strong in the
United Kingdom, Wiener reported, that manufacturers themselves "breathed
it in ever more deeply the higher they rose in social position," in sharp contrast to the high status accorded industrialists like Andrew Carnegie, Henry
Ford, and John D. Rockefeller in the United States (Wiener, 2004).

In keeping with these scholarly observations, our studies of Chinese and
Indian business leadership, noted earlier, found several distinctive commonalities in the models of management among their executives and directors that
differed from those prevalent in the West. Since the reforms of the 1990s in
both China and India opened up their economies, a group of entrepreneurs
created and operated their companies in each based on a set of practices that
differed substantially from what characterized the previous period, when state

constraints and a culture of hierarchy had stifled business innovation and flexibility. And though they shared underlying leadership principles with executives and directors in the West, they had also created distinctive bundles that have come to constitute what might be termed a "China Way" and an "India Way."

We believe that the Chinese and Indian business leaders acquired their characteristic hues because so many of them came of age at a time when private enterprise was barely tolerated or, for those a little younger, still viewed with suspicion. It would not have made their parents proud at the time to declare that their goal was to become a capitalist when they grew up, in sharp contrast to the ethos of the more-business friendly American way.

LEARNING TO LEAD GLOBALLY

One defining feature of the management mindsets among the executives and directors that we interviewed in China and India was a priority on experiential learning to lead. Much of what the executives knew about company leadership came, they explained, from their own trials and tribulations, though they were also eager to top off their learnings with the wisdom of others.

However, absorbing leadership practices from other sources was not just about their exposure to details about these practices. It began with company leaders first learning from their own experiences, something that was promoted through the widespread practice of self-reflection. Many studied their own experiences and then applied their emergent understandings to the often murky, complex problems involved in business management.

In some Chinese companies, this self-reflection also manifests itself through journal reading, self-conscious reports on personal learning, and even self-criticism. It is difficult to imagine a similar program of self-deprecation functioning in Western companies, in part because American executives are deeply concerned about impressions of their own competence – understandably so, given the tendency of company leaders to replace "weak" managers with more assured performers.

WHAT ABOUT SHAREHOLDER VALUE?

One of the most contrasting features of the Chinese and Indian business leaders with Western executives and directors was their relative lack of interest in creating shareholder value as a priority. What they did deem a priority is growth – even at the expense of earnings. Among both developing and developed economies, no country's business community is as fixed, by contrast, on maximizing shareholder value as that of the United States.

One reason the Chinese companies we studied have not been very concerned with maximizing shareholder value, at least in the short term, is that their founders, who are typically still the controlling shareholders, were still in charge. We sometimes hear in the United States that if business leaders acted more like major owners, they would push harder to maximize profits to shareholders. Yet many of the Chinese business leaders we studied were already large holders, billionaires many times over. It is not that they were unconcerned with being more successful but, rather, that their view of success is different from that of American executives and directors.

In our interviews with these Chinese executives, they reported no drumbeat from any quarter to optimize their short-term earnings for shareholders. Shareholder activism, a key driver of the market for corporate control in the West, has been rare in China and India so far. It thus came as no surprise that the executives and directors that we interviewed placed far less emphasis on investor relations and media savvy than is common among their American counterparts.

CHINESE AND INDIAN BUSINESS LEADERSHIP THAT WILL TRANSLATE

Some of the distinctive aspects of the Chinese and Indian business experience will not readily transfer to the West because they derive from country-specific contexts. But others are more likely to do so. One of the most important of these is the ability of the Chinese businesses we studied to operate with leaner control systems than do their Western counterparts, where "lean" means fewer managers and less supervision. The reason they can do so is, first, because of the belief that employees will not shirk or cheat, at least not as much as their equivalents in the West, in part because the primacy of individualism in China has not been as pronounced. As a result, the incentive to evade accountability or enrich oneself was not as great. Both the need for and cost of supervisors watching and managers monitoring had been sharply reduced.

Another factor allowing for less risk of malfeasance in China was the widespread sense of obligation to the company and especially its top person. In the West, we might refer to this as corporate "commitment" or "charismatic" authority. Dedicated employees were more willing to look after the interests of the company in China, and some of that willingness may have also stemmed from greater faith in the "big boss" and a belief that their leader was looking out for their welfare.

This sense of obligation was particularly strong in the upper ranks. Several executives told us that the commitment of a relatively small number of top executives to the values and norms of the company was a key to their company's leadership. Executives who consistently performed and repeatedly demonstrated their honesty and loyalty to the company were pulled by the CEO into the upper circle. And once in that circle, they became well protected. The chief executive forgave their mistakes, at least modest ones, and more generally cut them slack for under-performance; in return, the executives were more candid and faithful with their boss.

A lean operating system facilitated another leadership advantage in China, and that was the ability to change and adapt quickly. That agility, in turn, helped create an advantage for Chinese companies in detecting new opportunities and exploiting them quickly. This was unlike many Indian companies that focused on existing customers, Japanese companies that perfected established products, and new US companies that touted fresh products. The Chinese companies we observed grew via an aggressive business strategy that sought out new opportunities for existing products and then moved into those openings before others could react.

Indian enterprises leaders separately demonstrated the power of collective calling over private purpose, of transcendent value over shareholder return. Among the defining features of the India Way, as a result, was an emphasis on deeply held convictions. Companies built governing boards with directors who shared the enterprise's values and who could work with the executives in deciding how to grow or what to acquire for the long-term. They produced quality services and products with low prices, good not only for the business but also the country.

Historically, the creed of American business had pulled in much the opposite direction. Alexis de Tocqueville, the nineteenth century French chronicler of US ways, observed in *Democracy in America* that Americans "are fond of explaining almost all the actions of their lives by the principle of interest rightly understood," and America's culture of individual achievement has long placed a premium on being clear minded about the pursuit of one's private purpose. Unbridled capitalism, American style, observed hedge-fund manager and social critic George Soros, held "that the common good is best served by the uninhibited pursuit of self-interest" (de Tocqueville, 1835, p. 595; Soros, 1997).

Dissenting voices in the United States have long questioned the model of optimizing self-interest, holding that the role of executives and directors should be more about balancing the claims of competing stakeholders and less about optimizing private wealth. But America's penchant for self-interest "rightly understood" – what we often reference today as "enlightened" self-interest – is also being challenged.

In 2019, an association of some 200 large American company CEOs, the Business Roundtable, declared that corporations should move away from a singular focus on shareholder value and embrace a boarder commitment to customers, communities, employees, and suppliers as well. The chief executive of one its members, Progressive Insurance's Tricia Griffith, explained the rationale: "CEOs work to generate profits and return value to shareholders, but the best-run companies do more," she said. "In the end, it's the most promising way to build long-term value." Indian business leaders may provide a useful model for that multi-stakeholder pursuit of long-term value now being advocated for American business as well (in Useem, 2021).

CONCLUSION

After a century of corporate capitalism and multinational companies in the West that have dominated business ideas and management principles worldwide, the idea that we would find distinctive models in China and India for leading businesses represents a high hurdle. Whether Western companies can learn from their Chinese and Indian counterparts depends on whether Western leaders can recognize that the Western ways may not have all the answers – and then on whether they can identify their own blind spots that Chinese and Indian firms have already addressed.

We thus believe it is a fruitful time for Western business leaders to look hard at the leaders of Alibaba, Lenovo, and Vanke in China, and Infosys, Reliance, and Tata in India, and the hundreds of other large companies in those countries that are increasingly coming to define not only their own way of doing business but also better ways of leading business worldwide.

To be sure, Western companies possess many distinctive leadership advantages of their own. They are relatively quick to remove underperforming managers, part of the cold discipline of the market for corporate control, and they are now little diversified, a product of the unrelenting insistence by institutional owners that companies stick to the business they know best. Combining these and other affirmative features of the American way with the best of what the China and India ways have to offer could yield a powerful hybrid that would help American and other countries' business leaders learn to lead globally, drawing on not only the universal principles of leadership but also the best of what other national traditions have developed separately.

REFERENCES

Bendix, R. (2001). *Work and authority in industry: Managerial ideologies in the course of industrialization*. Transaction Publishers. (Originally published in 1956).

Cappelli, P., Singh, H., Singh, J., & Useem, M. (2010). *The India way: How India's top business leaders are revolutionizing management*. Harvard Business Press.

Charan, R., Carey, D., & Useem, M. (2014). *Boards that lead*. Harvard Business Review Press.

Collins, J. (2001). *Good to great: Why some companies make the leap and others don't*. Harper Business.

Day, G. S., & Schoemaker, P. J. H. (2019). *See sooner, act faster*. MIT Press.

de Tocqueville, A. (2000). *Democracy in America*. University of Chicago Press. (Originally published in 1835).

DiMaggio, P. J., & Powell, W. W. (1983). The iron cage revisited: Institutional isomorphism and collective rationality in organizational fields. *American Sociological Review, 48*, 147–160.

Edmondson, A. C. (2014). *Teaming: How organizations learn, innovate, and compete in the knowledge economy*. Jossey-Bass.

Goodwin, D. K. (2018). *Leadership in turbulent times*. Simon & Schuster.

Gopalakrishnan, R., in Cappelli, P., Singh, H., Singh, J., & Useem, M. (2010). *The India way: How India's top business leaders are revolutionizing management*. Harvard Business Press.

Guillen, M. F. (1994). *Models of management: Work, authority, and organization in a comparative perspective*. University of Chicago Press.

Haas, M., & Mortensen, M. (2016, June). *The secrets of great teamwork*. Harvard Business Review.

Hackman, J. R. (2002). *Leading teams: Setting the stage for great performances*. Harvard Business Review Press.

House, R. J., Hanges, P. J., Mansour, J., Dorfman, P. W., & Gupta, V. (Eds.). (2004). *Culture, leadership, and organizations: The globe study of 62 societies*. Sage Publications.

Ibarra, H. (2015). *Act like a leader, think like a leader*. Harvard Business Review Press.

Isaacson, W. (2012, April). *The real leadership lessons of Steve Jobs*. Harvard Business Review.

Klein, G. (2004). *The power of intuition: How to use your gut feelings to make better decisions at work*. Crown.

Krupp, S., & Schoemaker, P. J. H. (2014). *Winning the long game: How strategic leaders shape the future*. PublicAffairs Press.

Kunreuther, H., & Useem, M. (2018). *Mastering catastrophic risk: How companies are coping with disruption*. Oxford University Press.

McChrystal, S., with Collins, T., Silverman, D., & Fussell, C. (2015). *Team of teams: New rules of engagement for a complex world*. Portfolio.

Singh, H., & Useem, M. (2021). *The strategic leader's roadmap: Six steps for integrating leadership and strategy*. Wharton School Press.

Soros, G. (1997). The capitalist threat. *Atlantic*, February. https://www.theatlantic.com/ideastour/philanthropy/soros-full.html

Stuart, S. (2019). U.S. Board Index. https://www.spencerstuart.com/-/media/2019/ssbi-2019/us_board_index_2019.pdf

Useem, M. (1984). *The inner circle: Large corporations and the rise of business political activity in the U.S. and U.K.* Oxford University Press.

Useem, M. (1993). *Executive defense: Shareholder power and corporate reorganization*. Harvard University Press.

Useem, M. (2021). *The edge: How 10 CEOs learned to lead – and the lessons for us all*. PublicAffairs Books.

Useem, M. (2021). *The leader's checklist: 16 mission-critical principles*. HarperCollins/Basic Books.

Useem, M., Singh, H., Liang, N., & Cappelli, P. (2017). *Fortune makers: The leaders creating China's great global companies*. PublicAffairs Books.

Weber, M. (1958). *The protestant ethic and the spirit of capitalism*. (Talcott Parsons, trans). Scribner's. (Originally published in 1905).

Wiener, M. J. (2004). *English culture and the decline of the industrial spirit, 1850–1980*. Cambridge University Press.

Womack, J. P., Daniel, T., Jones, D. T., & Roos, D. (1990). *The machine that changed the world: The story of lean production*. Free Press.

11

THE PRACTICE AND IMPACT OF LEADERSHIP IN A SUB-SAHARAN CONTEXT

BRANDON W. KLIEWER, TRISHA GOTT, KAITLIN LONG AND MARY TOLAR[1]

INTRODUCTION

With a globally networked community of people practicing leadership, understanding how leadership manifests in practice, takes root in community, and moves beyond formal authority into networked relationships is critical. The goal of this chapter is to understand how significant learning moments from one Mandela Washington Fellowship Leadership in Civic Engagement Institute were enacted through the Fellows' network. In this chapter, authors account for the philosophical orientation and curricular framework used to inform the Leadership in Civic Engagement Institute for Mandela Washington Fellows. Findings included a discussion of how themes of significant learning emerged and how they intersect with the idea of a networked approach to leadership. Broader implications for this work are highlighted as they inform the study, practice, and development of global leadership learning and development.

CONTEXT

The Mandela Washington Fellowship is the flagship program of the Young African Leaders Initiative. Since 2014, the US Department of State has worked with IREX (International Research and Exchanges Board) and affiliated university partners to deliver six-week leadership institutes each summer. Institutes are organized along the themes of leadership in business and entrepreneurship, energy (inactive), public management, and civic engagement. This study is based on a leadership in civic engagement institute hosted at one school since 2016. Institutes are designed to advance priorities and public diplomacy objectives of the U.S. Department of State and IREX. Within the parameters set by the U.S. Department of State, there is still a large degree of autonomy for Institute partners to develop unique programmatic and curricular interventions.

The philosophical orientation and curricular framework outlined below informed the global leadership learning and development advanced within this Institute. These components provide insight as to how Fellows articulated significant learning from the experience. In the next section, we outline how efforts fit within the curricular and programmatic frames of relationship, dialogue, and applied practice.

PHILOSOPHICAL COMMITMENTS AND ORIENTATION

The philosophical basis of our leadership learning and development framework stems from a commitment to the democratic roots of leadership and practice theory. Practice theory relies upon how meaning-making and sense-making are created through the interactions of everyday life (Bourdieu, 1977; De Certeau, 1984). A focus on the ordinariness of everyday life points to tensions and opportunities to exercise leadership in ways that remake possibility imposed through systems and institutions. The philosophical commitments of Leadership-as-Practice (LaP) situate our overall understanding of leadership and what is required to support leadership learning and development through a collective and relational lens (Carroll, 2016; Raelin, 2016). With the philosophical project of co-development, scholars and practitioners work to recognize and represent a growing number of people, across social and personal identities, and alongside standards of equity, inclusion, and justice.

MID-LEVEL FRAMING OF LEADERSHIP LEARNING AND DEVELOPMENT

In moving from the philosophical basis of our program, the mid-level framework, aspects of leadership learning and development are organized into categories. Carroll (2015) organizes leadership learning and development by assigning meaning to leadership identity, mindset, and practice.

Each category of leadership learning and development draws upon specific theoretical perspectives and conceptual definitions. Leadership identity is understood as the social construction of meaning that is attached to what Foucault called "technologies of self" (Foucault, 1980). Leadership identity, as a series of technologies of self, includes ways individuals understand their leadership selves in relation to social identity, social location, community, practice, and larger systems (Gaventa, 2003). Leadership mindset is operationalized within our mid-level learning framework by drawing upon positive psychology (Dweck, 2008) and intentional critical reflexivity or "dialogue-with-self" (Cunliffe, 2009; Raelin, 2007). Leadership practice is positioned as an intentional sense and meaning-making approach to everyday experiences (Bourdieu, 1977; De Certeu, 2011; Raelin, 2016).

This mid-level framework becomes relevant as Fellows interrogate their understanding of self in relation to others and through a series of intercultural learning experiences to enhance intercultural intelligence and practice. Here, intercultural is defined through a set of competencies based on relationship, relational activity, perception, and self-management to work effectively interculturally (Moreley et al., 2010; Miska et al., 2013). Western conceptions of intercultural competence typically elevate empathy, perspective taking, and adaptability across cultural context (Deardorff et al., 2009).

The interactions between leadership identity, mindset, and practice create capacity and scaffold leadership learning and development. Next, we outline how these concepts and interactions manifest in daily work with curriculum and program-level interventions.

CURRICULUM AND PROGRAMMATIC LEVEL

Curricular and programmatic-level elements include dimensions of relationship, dialogue, and applied practice. Each dimension is described and illustrated with examples from the Institute. Shorthand monikers are shared as they have emerged from Fellows, staff, and faculty to describe when and how an experience should be understood within the context of a frame.

The element of relationship is operationalized in the programing as seeing systems in self, community, and society. StrengthsQuest, Myers-Briggs typology, the IREX Common Leadership Curriculum, and direct service experiences are components that underpin this dimension of learning. Fellows and staff might say, "leadership is a relationship" and "systems without intention tend toward atrophy" to signal understanding of this category. This shorthand became the call sign for the central idea of leadership as a relational activity. Noticing relational activity as an element of the experience highlighted liminal spaces of learning and development. The idea of liminality is that learning may emerge through formal experiences (the curricular interventions) and in liminal spaces where formal planning does not reach. Spaces such as shared living communities, transportation, over dining experiences, and other informal points of connection are the liminal spaces of in-between where much of the practice of relational activity emerges.

Next, leadership learning and development occurred through the element of dialogue. Much of the leadership learning and development at the curricular and programmatic level is connected to dialogue between Fellows, faculty, and staff. Components of this learning element include the Intercultural Development Inventory (IDI), personalized learning sessions associated with the IDI assessment, structured discussions of the concepts of Pan-Africanism, brainstorming intercultural collaboration within the Mandela Washington Fellow network, and culturally relevant "case-in-point" teaching. The moniker used to describe the practice of dialogue was highlighted during moments when the group engaged as "a community of communities."

Finally, a commitment to the applied practice of leadership learning and development was the third element of the programming. This category was realized through efforts to disrupt dominant ideological commitments to the "Tripod Ontology of Leadership" – Leader, Follower, Shared Purpose, and the "heroic" styles or actions of leadership (Drath et al., 2008). The commitment to applied practice reoriented Fellows, emphasizing co-development and shared responsibility to create direction, alignment, and commitment as an everyday practice (Drath et al., 2008). Conceptual models of leadership relying upon individual competition and command are pushed to the edges and held in tension with models that are connected to co-creation, cooperation, collective action, and shared responsibility. Fellows and program staff are reminded of this curricular and programmatic category with the shorthand moniker of "If you are not practicing what you are learning, you are learning something else" or sometimes, "If you are not modeling what you are teaching, you are teaching something else."

This framework at both the philosophical and curricular levels underpins how leadership identity, mindset, and practice are presented and developed throughout the Institute. In the next section, this framework becomes connected to the broader goals of the Fellowship program and the research.

BUILDING CAPACITY FOR GLOBAL LEADERSHIP, RATIONALE FOR THE STUDY

Curricular and programmatic frameworks ensure that this Institute meets the objectives outlined by IREX and advances the public diplomacy aims of the U.S. Department of State. Beyond those expectations however, a unique interest emerged in this effort. Centrally, leadership educators in this study asked how leadership interventions might support or interact with the following goals:

1. Deepen capacity to enact leadership across loosely affiliated networks that are held together by informal authority;

2. Encourage commitments to the co-development of shared purpose, common values, and a broad understanding of the "common good"; and

3. Be visually represented using methods of Social Network Analysis (Cross et al., 2002; Hoppe & Reinelt, 2010).

This led to the central question which emerged from the curricular framework and served as the guidepost for the study: How can we better understand how significant learning moments from one Mandela Washington Fellowship Leadership in Civic Engagement Institute were enacted? This question, along with a commitment to deepening understanding of how leadership development takes shape in a global and networked community, became the central thrusts of this qualitative study. Next, we discuss participants in the study along with the coding process that led to findings.

RESEARCH STUDY

Through a qualitative approach, researchers sought to deepen understanding of the language used to describe leadership learning and development. This effort was directed toward understanding significant learning moments from a group of participants in a global leadership intervention, and how those learning moments were enacted through formal and informal networks. The participant pool included Fellows from 2016, 2017, and 2018 cohorts. Participants were invited to complete a survey and to respond to open-ended questions about their leadership learning and practice. Open-ended responses were coded using a discourse analysis methodology to deepen understanding of how leadership was experienced and practiced beyond the Fellowship.

Discourses, the central data that informed this research, shed light onto how networks, systems, relationships, processes, and behaviors were built, changed, and removed through power. Discourses reveal understandings of concepts, ideas, and actions that shape our world and work (Gee, 2010). This similarly contributes to the understanding of how leadership occurs in the interactions and practices of everyday life. Researchers reviewed the discourse produced by participants in the study (Mandela Washington Fellows who participated in the Leadership in Civic Engagement Institute at Kansas State University in 2016, 2017, and 2018). The research team identified discursive themes in an emergent and iterative process.

Researchers then followed processes from the field of discourse analysis and sought to understand themes of power, practice, and leadership. In this context, discourse is what is being said, and the actions, context, framing, behaviors, practices, and circumstances that demonstrate a relationship between power and knowledge (Gee, 2014, pp. 24–26). Applied to analysis of the data, researchers used this orientation to code the text for emergent examples of behaviors or actions and to understand the discourse through the lenses of power, leadership identity, mindset, and practice.

Finally, researchers examined the themes that emerged from the data to understand how leadership as identity, mindset, and practice appeared (or not). This was distilled through the lens of curriculum and program language. With this process in mind, the question, *how was significant leadership learning described within the Fellow network?* became the overarching approach to analysis. Results from data analysis included three themes: (1) How ideas of inclusion activated different mindsets and practice; (2) How relational leadership and leadership as relationship emerged as distinct orientations; and (3) How cultural immersion and disruptive learning in program design created a context for significant learning experiences. The following section describes and provide examples of each theme.

INCLUSION UNDERSTOOD AND OPERATIONALIZED

Fellows across years and experiences identified that inclusion was a significant piece of their learning. Inclusion was defined and described by Fellows through language of leadership as a mindset and practice. Reflections of engaging others in their efforts were how inclusion was expressed as practice. Inclusion as an activity was expressed through intentional practice tied to formal processes. Examples of intentional engagement of others included inviting others to join a meeting, engaging others in decision processes, or identifying unusual voices and bringing them into leadership conversations. Examples included statements such as, "I am more eager to engage other voices," in reference to how to navigate workplace decisions and keep team members moving toward a collective effort. Another participant reflected, "I learned the importance of mapping key stakeholders and making plans to actively engage them." Here, the participant is making sense of how to organize a community in order to advance an issue. In this practice, inclusive behavior, specifically, an invitation to others was articulated as an effort to make progress on a leadership challenge.

In this finding, participants specifically pointed to inclusion as a tool or strategy to understand who and how to engage to make progress on leadership challenges. In the above examples, Fellows treated inclusion as a practice and process of leadership, rather than ideology.

Inclusion also appeared through discussions of empathy. Participants discussed leadership in relationship to others, understanding other perspectives, communities, societal issues, and other community approaches. This idea of inclusion was accompanied by sentiments about relationship, empathy, and seeking to understand others. In these instances, leadership was framed by participants as meaningful in ways it intersected with others. Participants discussed shifts in dispositions to leadership framed though an empathetic approach to others. "The approach(es) I am using are listening, empathy..." This participant reflected on empathy as used to reduce inequality and gender-based violence.

Another participant reflected on empathy to make decisions at work and advance practices of inclusion. In another example, a participant discussed empathy, harmony, and ethical fitness as ways to understand their role in building leadership relationships. Across findings, empathy was presented as a practice and a mindset to understand others, to build relationships, and to shift approaches to others in leadership practices. "I believe in nurturing teamwork through good and two-way communication. All my managerial practices are based on this spirit of teamwork, empathy and harmony." The presentation of empathy as a mindset is particularly interesting from a program and curriculum standpoint, as it was not a central thrust in the curriculum. Empathy represented a significant learning concept that endured as mindset and practice.

DISCOURSES OF LEADERSHIP AND RELATIONSHIP

A second finding was about the language of relationship as distinct from relational dimensions of leadership. Here, the way language was used to describe leadership learning and development represented different orientations to relational elements of leadership. The design of the curriculum and program includes a combination of leadership identity, leadership mindset, and leadership practice to catalyze significant learning and development. The language used to describe significant learning in the data tells a more nuanced story of the outcomes of that design. The data illustrate leadership learning being talked about both in ways that suggest direct connection to relationships, and a more diffused articulation of how leadership is understood and practiced as relational. Interpretation of this data highlights unanticipated ways in which significant global leadership learning is expressed.

Leadership Is Relationship

Mandela Washington Fellows that describe their significant leadership learning as being closely tied to relationship also emphasized a commitment to being empathetic and connecting to others along shared values. One Fellow talked about "Leadership is identifying and engaging unusual voices. It means empathy and exploring multiple interpretations. In my work, I subscribe [that] leadership is a relationship." Other Fellows emphasized the importance of creating space where others can participate in leadership activity: "Now I've become an active follower I encourage and empower people to lead our different initiatives." Running through this theme was a commitment to build leadership capacity through emotive relationships. This commitment is seen by this Fellow's comment: "I build my leadership role through building constructive leadership. I achieve this through empathy, harmony, and ethical fitness."

Also highlighted in this theme is a commitment to the importance of sustaining meaningful connection with others. This articulation came through clearly within the data; and this was unexpected. One way to make sense of this language is that the programmatic and curricular intervention within the leadership identity category created a strong orientation to leadership for this group. Words like empathy and harmony were used throughout the examples. This emerged as a leadership language that speaks to how Fellows understand their leadership identity or leadership selves. Statements of leadership learning that emphasized leadership as being about literal relationships and drew strongly upon values provided a distinct orientation from those who described significant leadership learning as having relational elements.

Leadership as Relational Practice

Distinct from seeing leadership as a relationship, significant learning emerged that described leadership as a relational activity. Leadership as a relational activity included descriptions of how leadership is operationalized in relation to others and was leveraged through practice. Fellows who expressed learning in line with this theme emphasized relational processes. One Fellow indicated,

> I see leadership as what we do outside our circle of jurisdictions and expectations. I see leadership as doing as opposed to being. So my current approach to leadership is how to engage others and the communication in doing or carrying out activities for community benefit, as opposed to selling this idea that to be a leader, you have to be this, that, etc... . I feel everyone is capable of leading.

Fellows talked about relational activities that are outside of their default orientation to leadership. In this Fellow's statement of learning, that is demonstrated:

*Leadership is identifying other voices and engaging the voices that
I don't normally involve. It also means observing and learning from
people who have walked the path or have core expertise in any
project or task.*

Fellows also talked about process orientations to highlight relational aspects
of leadership activity. For example, this Fellow indicated that "I learned the
importance of mapping out key stakeholders and making plans to actively
engage them." Across these narratives, leadership learning was understood
and described as relational.

SIGNIFICANT LEARNING, DISRUPTIVE MOMENTS, AND THE CYCLE OF CULTURE SHOCK

The third finding emerged from the moments of most significant learning
that participants reported on. A pattern emerged that reflected programmatic
and curriculum choices involving intercultural learning processes. Significant learning is often understood in intercultural experiences as a *crucible
moment* (Bennis & Thomas, 2002). The intersection of intercultural learning and practice might elevate significant moments of leadership learning
and development that are currently undertheorized in our framework. The
language of learning in these data describes the potential presence of a continuum, between learning that emphasizes elements of everyday experience
and the presence of "crucible moments."

In alignment with the cycle of culture shock, these data are evidence of
how the curriculum design and arc of the program connect to the developmental process that learners experience in an intercultural setting. Specifically, the discourse pointed to disruptive learning experiences as meaningful
for the participants. Disruptive learning, sometimes in intercultural circumstances, happens in liminal spaces that are not formally recognized with the
curriculum or classroom programming (Bass, 2012). Intercultural immersion
learning accounts for impacts of culture shock in this process. The *Cycle of
Culture Shock* includes an internalized perspective developed in response to
a new or different situation (Pedersen, 1994). This is accounted for in the
planning of the program and curriculum.

Participants reported significant learning related to events that happened
as they might be experiencing the adaptation stage of culture shock, in the

second three weeks of the program (Winkelman, 1994). Responses across the years expressed significant learning that took place through time at the Kansas Leadership Center (KLC). Participants named this event in their most significant learning and went on to name practices that emerged from this event including concepts and tools.

The KLC event occurs in alignment with when learners would be in the reemergence of their culture shock cycle toward reintegration (Winkelman, 1994). Other moments of significant learning were described as happening along the same timeline during which Fellows would be moving from the adaptation stage toward reintegration or return home.

To check these findings, the themes identified above, and the ideas shared below, were reviewed by program participants (Fellows) who provided reflections to the articulated learning. This was a practical member-check and provided a sense of how themes spoke to larger intercultural leadership learning and development efforts. Below you will find those responses.

Onyedika Ekwerike, 2017 Mandela Washington Fellow, stated the following about his Fellowship experience:

> It is impossible to lead change in isolation. To create change, leaders must consciously develop relationships with others who might share their values in order to inspire collective purpose. This was the central theme of my learning during the 2017 Mandela Washington Fellowship. Besides developing individual relationships, I also learned the value of building relationships across organizations. Some of the biggest challenges facing our world today cannot be solved by a single organization, it is therefore imperative that organizations collaborate if progress on tough challenges are to be made. Such collaborations are impossible without relationships.

Hiwot Getaneh, 2018 Mandela Washington Fellow, shared this about her fellowship:

> To be a good leader the first requirement is to acknowledge self as a leader and to be intentional in taking the role of a leader whether it involves a hierarchical position or not. Taking this role starts by building a relationship with our leader-self through self-assessment, identifying our values, strengths, drives and triggers. [It is] only when that exercise has been properly done and put in motion for

constant actualization that we can effectively put ourselves out there
and show up as a leader. It will enable us to see others, their values,
challenges and realities from an empathetic lens and enable us to
build sincere relationships that will enhance our capacity to influ-
ence others and reach a shared goal.

These reflections reify ideas about how significant learning has impacted
the orientations of leadership (self, others, and community or organization)
expressed by Ekwerike and Getaneh. Next, we will make sense of this study
and its implications for future work.

DISCUSSION AND CONCLUSION

Ultimately, this work, and these reflections reflect experiences at one specific Institute. These experiences can be understood through how leadership
educators move forward in programming for intercultural and globally networked audiences. Key findings of this work are summarized below.

1. If leadership programs seek to build networks from the standpoint
   of relational and collective leadership, then developing mindsets and
   practices of empathy and inclusion are worthy learning goals. Programs
   can make clear decisions about what is taught, and how teaching and
   learning takes place to develop inclusion as a practice and mindset in the
   curriculum, co-curriculum, and other liminal learning spaces.

2. A language of leadership learning that directs process as a relational
   practice and as a literal relationship were distinguishable themes. Fellows that spoke to leadership as a relational process relied on verbs
   such as "mapping," "engaging," and "doing." This discourse points to
   the significant learning as not only relational but requiring more complex expressions of associated activities. The Fellows that understood
   leadership as a literal relationship frequently used emotive language
   which highlights a commitment to empathy, harmony, and ethics. These
   two distinct themes highlight the complexities associated with how
   learning is understood in a global leadership development experience.

3. Global leadership learning and development closely parallels intercultural learning experiences. The ways Fellows gave language to

disruptive learning moments beyond the formal sessions highlight how the cycle of culture shock might provide pathways to understand global leadership learning and development contexts in new ways. The significance of learning that operates outside formal programming should not be discounted, rather it should be contextualized within the broader scope of the program and the culture shock cycle. This impacts how programs are designed and implemented, and how participants are prepared for their experiences and supported in making sense of their learning.

In addition to these findings, the study itself sheds light on how guideposts might be established so that leadership educators can design significant learning experiences for global learners. Specific recommendations include:

1. Curriculum planners focus on formal and informal spaces for learning. The co-curriculum or liminal learning environments are key to how learners, in this case, made sense of emergent leadership mindset, identity, and practice.

2. Leadership educators gain clarity on how practice and processes are established so that participants can define their orientations to leadership as a mindset and practice. Specific attention to the role of leadership in relationship and as relational activity can deepen understanding.

3. Program curriculum should align with broader developmental and learner readiness factors. In this case, the process of cultural immersion and in consideration of experiences of culture shock. Establishing a timeline for delivery, content, format, and process in light of this affects how curriculum is experienced, understood, and ultimately has impact.

Leadership education and development require elements of program evaluation to assess practices that demonstrate development. The assessment in this study illuminates impacts over time, place, and community. For this effort, leadership learning and development was mapped as a networked process rather than something linear. This network mapping provided an idea of the scope and scale that programs and participants have as they impact communities and in their own development. Leadership network mapping can be an especially powerful tool to visualize impact on community, policy, and collective efforts aimed toward social and systems change (Hoppe & Reinelt, 2010). In this study, an analysis of leadership networks was accompanied by an analysis of short narratives or discourses describing how a learning intervention has impacted behavior and progress post-Fellowship.

This study deepens our understanding of how specific approaches to leadership education and development, and orientations to leadership (as intercultural, as inclusive, as a practice, mindset, identity, and as relationship and relational) impact practices globally and inter-culturally. Generating more nuanced understanding of how leadership interventions serve to move individuals and communities forward, for progress, and for good is required if the field of leadership education and development desires to make progress for the global good. More must be asked, assessed, and learned about how significant learning about leadership globally takes place and how interventions stick beyond individual impact, but in service to collective and social good.

NOTE

1. The Mandela Washington Fellowship for Young African Leaders is made possible by the generous support of the American people through the U.S. Department of State and administered by IREX. This publication was produced independently by Brandon W. Kliewer, Trisha Gott, Kaitlin Long, and Mary Tolar and in no way represents official views of the U.S. Government, IREX, or any other official entity administering the Fellowship.

REFERENCES

Bass, R. (2012). Disrupting ourselves: The problem of learning in higher education. *EDUCAUSE Review, 47*(2), n2.

Bennis, W. G., & Thomas, R. J. (2002). Crucibles of leadership. *Harvard Business Review, 80*(9), 39–45.

Bourdieu, P. (1977). *Outline of a theory of practice.* Cambridge University Press.

Carroll, B. (2015). Leadership learning and development. In B. Carroll, J. Ford, & S. Taylor (Eds.), *Leadership: Contemporary critical perspectives.* SAGE.

Carroll, B. (2016). Leadership as identity: A practice-based exploration. In J. A. Raelin (Ed.), *Leadership-as-practice: Theory and application* (pp. 91–109). Routledge (pp. 89–109).

Carroll, B., Levy, L., & Richmond, D. (2008). Leadership as practice: Challenging the competency paradigm. *Leadership*, 4(4), 363–379.

Creveni, L., & Endrissat, N. (2016). Mapping the leadership-as-practice terrain: Comparative elements. In J. A. Raelin (Ed.), *Leadership-as-practice: Theory and application* (pp. 21–50). Routledge.

Cross, R., Borgatti, S. P., & Parker, A. (2002). Making invisible work visible: Using social network analysis to support strategic collaboration. *California Management Review*, 44(2), 25–46.

Cunliffe, A. L. (2009). The philosophical leader: On relationism, ethics, and reflectivity: A critical perspective to teaching leadership. *Management Learning*, 40(1), 1425–1449.

Day, D. V., Fleenor, J. W., Atwater, L. E., Sturm, R. E., & McKee, R. A. (2014). Advances in leader and leadership development: A review of 25 years of research and theory. *The Leadership Quarterly*, 25(1), 63–82.

De Certeau, M. (2011). *The practice of everyday life*. University of California Press.

Deardorff. (2009). Synthesizing Conceptualizations of Intercultural Competence. In Deardorff (Ed.), *The SAGE handbook of intercultural competence* (pp. 264–271). SAGE.

Deardorff. (2011). Assessing intercultural competence. *New Directions for Institutional Research*, (149), 65–79. https://doi.org/10.1002/ir.381

Drath, W. H., McCauley, C. D., Palus, C. J., Van Velsor, E., O'Conner, B. P. M. G., & McGuire, J. B. (2008). Direction, alignment, commitment: Toward a more integrative ontology of leadership, *The Leadership Quarterly*, (19), 635–653.

Dweck, C. (2015). Carol Dweck revisits the growth mindset. *Education Week*, 35(5), 20–24.

Dweck, C. S. (2008). *Mindset: The new psychology of success*. Random House Digital, Inc.

Edwards, G., Elliott, C., Iszatt-White, M., & Schedlitzki, D. (2013). Critical and alternative approaches to leadership learning and development. *Management Learning*, 44(1), 3–10.

Foucault, M. (1980). *Power/knowledge: Selected interviews and other writings by Michel Foucault, 1972–1977 (Ed.) Gordon*. Pantheon.

Ganz, M. (2011). Public narrative, collective action, and power. In *Accountability through public opinion: From inertia to public action* (pp. 273–289). The World Bank.

Gaventa, J. (2003). *Power after Lukes: An overview of theories of power since Lukes and their application to development*. Participation Group, Institute of Development.

Gee, J. P. (2010). *How to do discourse analysis: A toolkit*. Routledge.

Gee, J. P. (2014). *An introduction to discourse analysis: Tools and practice.* Routledge.

Gergen, K. J., & Hersted, L. (2016). Developing leadership as dialogic practice. In J. A. Raelin (Ed.), *Leadership-as-practice: Theory and application* (pp. 178–198). Routledge.

Hoppe, B., & Reinelt, C. (2010). Social network analysis and the evaluation of leadership networks. *The Leadership Quarterly, 21*(4), 600–619.

Jenkins, D. M. (2012). Exploring signature pedagogies in undergraduate leadership education. *Journal of Leadership Education, 11*(1), 1–27.

Komives, S. R., Lucas, N., & McMahon, T. R. (2009). *Exploring leadership: For college students who want to make a difference.* John Wiley & Sons.

Mandela Washington Fellowship | Bureau of Educational and Cultural Affairs. (n.d.). Retrieved April 14, 2019, from https://eca.state.gov/mandela-washington-fellowship

Miska, C., Stahl, G. K., & Mendenhall, M. E. (2013). Intercultural competencies as antecedents of responsible global leadership. *European Journal of International Management, 7*(5), 550–569.

Morley, M. J., Cerdin, J. L., Bird, A., Mendenhall, M., Stevens, M. J., & Oddou, G. (2010). Defining the content domain of intercultural competence for global leaders. *Journal of Managerial Psychology,* 810–828.

Pedersen, P. (1994). *The five stages of culture shock: Critical incidents around the world: Critical incidents around the world.* ABC-CLIO.

Pye, A. (2005). Leadership and organizing: Sensemaking in action. *Leadership, 1*(1), 31–49.

Raelin, J. A. (2007). Toward an epistemology of practice. *Academy of Management Learning and Education, 6*(4), 495–519.

Raelin, J. A. (2016). Introduction to Leadership-as-practice: Theory and Application. In J. A. Raelin (Ed.), *Leadership-as-practice: Theory and application* (pp. 1–19). Routledge.

Selingo, J. (2018, September). 2028: The Decade Ahead for Higher Education. In Proceedings of the 2018 ACM on SIGUCCS Annual Conference (pp. 1-1). In *International World Wide Web Conferences Steering Committee.*

Winkelman, M. (1994). Cultural shock and adaptation. *Journal of Counseling & Development, 73*(2), 121–126.

Woods, P. A. (2016). Democratic roots: Feeding the multiple dimensions of leadership-as-practice. In J. A. Raelin (Ed.), *Leadership-as-practice: Theory and application* (pp. 70–89). Routledge.

12

THE IMPACT OF GLOBALIZATION AND THE COVID-19 PANDEMIC ON LEADERSHIP IN INTERNATIONAL DEVELOPMENT: THE NEED FOR ADAPTIVE TRANSFORMATIONAL SYSTEM LEADERSHIP AND EXPANDED CONSCIOUSNESS

RANDAL JOY THOMPSON

The end of the Cold War and concomitant globalization radically transformed the priorities of international development and international aid, and placed new demands on leaders in this realm (Asefa, 2010; D'Alessandro & Leautier, 2016; Verson, 2017). Globalization brought new challenges of integration into global markets of previously isolated countries, expanded trade, unleashed mass migration, climate change, pandemics, more localized conflicts and demands for citizen influence on political processes, increased inequality and extreme poverty, among others. The COVID-19 pandemic exacerbated these challenges in addition to threatening a global economic collapse and causing millions of people to be unemployed and to sink into extreme poverty. The pandemic revealed that fundamental socio-economic systems are in collapse. Greatly increased interconnections and interactions between global leaders and states are required to address these multi-faceted challenges. Leaders in international development and international aid have had to broaden their horizons and embrace new perspectives and approaches in order to effectively deal with these new, complex realities.

This chapter situates leaders of international development in their new globalized reality and proposes an adaptive transformational system leadership approach to transform socio-economic political systems in developing countries. The chapter also argues that certain cognitive abilities, self-identity, and values characteristic of a level of consciousness typically associated with at least postmodernity but more appropriately with post-postmodernity are required to effectively practice adaptive transformational system leadership. Focusing on the still dominant project form of aid, the chapter argues that leaders must embrace an ethical expansive and complex systems mindset, co-create change with followers who are co-leaders, and help build adaptive systems that can respond to the volatility, uncertainty complexity, and ambiguity of the globalized pandemic-ridden world. For the purposes of this chapter, leaders in international development are considered as change makers

> *dedicated to transforming complex systems and their components in developing countries (and by implication in the global world) such that all individuals in the world can live in equitable societies, free from want, able to achieve their aspirations, and in harmony with the environment. (Thompson, 2018, p. 3)*

Such leaders are also global leaders in the sense that they influence others to adopt a shared vision through structures and methods that facilitate positive change while fostering individual and collective growth in a context characterized by significant levels of complexity, flow and presence (Mendenhall et al., 2012, p. 500). They influence "the thinking attitudes and behaviors of a global community to work together synergistically toward a common vision and common goals" (Osland, 2014, p. xiii), which in international development revolve around improving human welfare sustainably. The leaders referred to primarily in this chapter are those individuals who work with aid-receiving countries to assist them implement their development plans. These leaders generally work for international organizations such as the United Nations, World Bank or regional development bank, or bilateral or private donor organization. As will be argued, these leaders co-lead with leaders in developing countries as well as other involved in specific aid packages.

CHALLENGES IN INTERNATIONAL DEVELOPMENT

Confusion regarding how to divide the world into friends and enemies according to Communist blocs after the fall of the Soviet Union in 1991 caused the US military to coin the term VUCA for volatile, uncertain, complex, and ambiguous to describe the emerging world order (Lawrence, 2013). Subsequent efforts to characterize friends and enemies according to religion or terrorism did not fill the void even after the 9/11 attack on the United States or the US invasions of Iraq and Afghanistan. The pluralistic, complex world, with new emerging powers of countries such as Brazil, Russia, India, China, and South Africa, could no longer be placed in a dualistic construct (D'Alessandro & Leautier, 2016).

At the same time, new challenges emerged in international development from: the need for previously autonomous markets to integrate into the global one; more expansive global trade; efforts of peoples to rise up against repressive dictatorships and regimes; massive migrations caused by violence or lack of economic opportunity; the HIV/AIDS pandemic and Ebola epidemic; increased cross-border crime including drugs, weapons, and trafficking of persons and body parts; climate change; increased extreme poverty and inequality; and persistent financial insecurity, among others (Asefa, 2010).

Leaders of developing countries and of the so-called transitional countries of the former Soviet bloc were confronted with the need to solve these challenges and often the challenge to rebuild their countries after economic collapse or uprisings and violence. The world of international aid needed to shift its priorities in order to assist these countries. Integration of former Soviet bloc countries by aid agencies involved mass privatization of state-owned enterprises and inculcation of neo-liberal capitalism, which has been the model of development since the 1980s. A push for democratic systems of governance also became a major objective of aid agencies, especially of the United States. Reducing mass migrations through prevention strategies also moved front and center for aid agencies in many parts of the world, in addition to dealing with pandemics and humanitarian crises. Poverty reduction and sustainability became the centerpiece of aid in 2015 with the establishment of the United Nations Sustainability Development Goals (SDGs) for 2015 or 2030, also called "Agenda 2030," although not all aid agencies systematically work toward these (United Nations Development Programme, 2015).

Sustainable development, according to economist Jeffrey Sachs (2015), attempts

> to make sense of the interactions of three complex systems: the world economy, the global society, and the earth's physical environment...Normatively, [it] recommends a set of goals to which the

world should aspire...calls for a world in which economic progress is widespread; extreme poverty is eliminated; social trust is encouraged through policies that strengthen the community; the environment is protected from human-induced degradation. (p. 3)

Good governance and the provision of social services, infrastructure, promotion of science and technology, and regulations to protect the environment are also required (Sachs, 2015).

The SDGs include ending poverty and hunger; promoting good health and wellbeing, quality education, gender equality; providing clean water and sanitation, affordable and clean energy, decent work and economic growth; building industry, innovation and infrastructure; reducing inequality; creating sustainable cities and communities, responsible consumption and production, climate action; revitalizing life below water and on land; working toward peace, justice, and strong institutions, and working in partnerships to achieve these goals (United Nations Development Programme, 2015). Globalization demands that these goals be achieved through close connections between countries and not in countries in isolation.

The COVID-19 pandemic had made the SDGs focus on poverty alleviation even more urgent as the IMF estimated that the resultant economic downturn will thrust approximately 49 million people into extreme poverty, with over 50% of these in Africa. War torn countries such as Yemen and Syria will fare worse since their populations are at risk of famine (Reliefweb, 2020). Half of the world's 3.3 billion workforce are at risk of losing their jobs and livelihoods while the world's health status has plummeted and will continue to plummet as food systems have been seriously disrupted (Chriscaden, 2020). The need for countries to work together rather than to vie for power to solve these intractable problems has never been more urgent.

The achievement of the SDGs occurs within a highly dynamic environment whose disruptive changes leaders must take into consideration. D'Alessandro and Leautier (2016) offered a framework for tracking these changes. They identified four spheres of change:

people (preferences for location, consumption, production, and reproduction); resources (land, food, water, and natural resources); economies (finance, trade, production, sourcing, and markets); and technology (agriculture, communication, knowledge sharing, manufacturing, and transport). (n.p.)

Polity is also an important sphere of change to consider, especially as peoples around the world are fighting for more influence on the governance of their countries.

Fig. 12.1.   Spheres of Change.

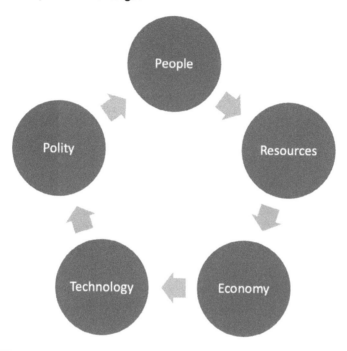

The same authors identified six drivers of change including logistics, increased mobility and connectivity, ownership and financing arrangements, interconnectedness and interaction between knowledge and culture, evolution of key risks affecting decision-making around the world, and growing demand for ethical and accountable leadership (D'Alessandro & Leautier, 2016, n.p.). Risks include the increasing instability of the financial system, natural disasters, pandemics, climate change, unrest and discontent, and unsuspected aggressions by so-called enemies. A seventh driver is also important, namely, the global ambitions of nation states and their leaders. For example, China's plan to dominate world trade and to become the new global power (Vernon, 2017) is a major driver of change in the world. Their plan has been greatly expedited by the COVID-19 pandemic and they have moved to take increasing control while the rest of the world floundered

(Campbell & Doshi, 2020). Finally, the eighth driver of change includes technological advances. Leaders must especially take into consideration the impact on the globalized world and developing countries of the Fourth Industrial Age and the eventual take-over by robotics.

Fig. 12.2. Drivers of Change.

D'Alessandro and Leautier (2016) also added the locus of change to the framework within which leaders in international development and foreign aid work. These include "social space (individuals, communities, nations, regions, global society); ecological space (local, global); and economic space (household, city, country, regional bloc, global)" (n.p.). Political space also needs to be highlighted as a locus of change, especially given the drive to democratize many developing countries of the world. Leaders in international development and aid need to be aware of the spheres and drivers of change and how they are impacting the locus within which they are working and how the change they are introducing impacts other loci of change, as well as change spheres and drivers.

Fig. 12.3. Loci of spaces where leaders work.

TRANSFORMATIVE CHANGE OF INTERNATIONAL DEVELOPMENT AND AID

Along with their counterparts in developing countries, leaders of international development introduce change at many different governmental levels and in a number of different ways, including the policy level of developing country governments; in social and industrial systems; in developing country organizations; in communities; and within individuals. Through their organizations, such leaders deliver aid via cash transfers to developing country governments with conditionalities, in the form of loans, grants, cooperative agreements, programs, and projects. Projects remain the most common form of promoting development. They are temporary, time-bound, resource bound systems with specific objectives which provide funding, training, and technical assistance to change complex systems in developing countries (Thompson, 2016). Projects introduce change via projects in many development sectors including economic, political, industrial, agricultural, infrastructure, education, health, civil society, energy, technology, disaster relief and humanitarian assistance, among others.

The change leaders introduce is transformative and is directed at highly complex socio-economic-political systems. This change represents an adaptive challenge (Heifetz et al., 2009; Uhl-Bien et al., 2007) to recipient country systems. Such a challenge requires "new learning, innovation, and new patterns of behavior…exploration, new discoveries, and adjustment" (Uhl-Bien et al., 2007, p. 300). Adaptive challenges in organizations are distinguished from technical challenges that can be addressed by authoritative expertise. Adaptive challenges can only be addressed through "changes in people's priorities, beliefs, habits, and priorities," and, these change by mobilizing discovery, "shedding certain entrenched ways, tolerating losses, and generating the new capacity to thrive anew" (Heifetz et al., 2009, p. 20). Further, adaptive challenges include changes at increasingly higher level systems that conscribe relationship between so-called developing and developed countries and within countries between the political and monied elites and the rest of the population. Such challenges require leaders with courage who are willing to confront the powers-that-be.

Both country and aid organization leaders need to be ready to inspire stakeholders to such an extent that they are able to endure the emotional turmoil that such change creates (Linsky, 2011). These leaders are challenged not only to ensure that stakeholders achieve a particular goal but that adaptive processes are functioning in the transformed system so that the system can survive and adapt to the forces in a globalized VUCA world (Heifetz et al., 2009; Senge et al., 2015). System change requires that a critical mass of interrelationships support the change and that stakeholders comprising these relationships are committed to implementing it (Stone & Barlow, 2015). As noted above, adaptive change in one system and sphere will no doubt impact changes in other systems and spheres and leaders need to be aware of and ready to respond to the ramifications of indirect changes and unintended impacts.

ADAPTIVE TRANSFORMATIONAL SYSTEM LEADERSHIP

Given the challenges of a globalized VUCA world suffering a global pandemic and the challenges faced by leaders in international development and aid, a leadership style that draws on adaptive, transformative, system approaches can facilitate more sustainable change owned and embraced by developing country stakeholders. Such a leadership approach is a variation of complexity leadership theory which "focuses on identifying and exploring the strategies and behaviors that foster organizational and subunit creativity, learning, and adaptability" (Uhl-Bien et al., 2007, p. 299).

Adaptive leadership is defined as "the practice of mobilizing people to tackle tough challenges and thrive" (Heifetz et al., 2009, p. 14). It involves "improvisational expertise, a kind of process expertise that knows prudently how to experiment with never-been-tried-before relationships, means of communication, and solutions" (Heifetz et al., 2009, p. 2). Adaptive leadership is also "a generative dynamic that underlies emergent change activities" (Uhl-Bien et al., 2007, p. 299). Stakeholders in the change process are empowered by transformational leadership to define and own the change and to align it to their values (Burns, 2004). The practice of system leadership expands the defining context of the change process to a broad systemic level where stakeholders can discern the influences initiating the change and resisting the change and in so doing reconcile their differences by taking a broader view (Senge et al., 2015). Thereby, stakeholders can encourage initiating influences and address resisting influences. This leadership also builds a shared understanding among stakeholders and catalyzes a shift to co-creation of the change trajectory so that the change emerges as appropriate and is owned and sustained.

When combined into one leadership approach, adaptive transformational system leaders are able, through collective leadership, to unleash the adaptive abilities of the system targeted for change. By leading collectively, the aid agency, projects, and aid-receiving country organizations emerge as a system and share in visioning, planning, decision-making and executing change (Senge et al., 2015; Thompson, 2016). At the same time, these leaders inspire, motivate, and empower individuals to embrace the change that the individuals perceive as enhancing their lives. Hence, actions of collective leaders facilitate and respond to leadership as a system property (Senge et al., 2015). As Uhl-Bien et al. (2007) asserted,

> a complex interplay from which a collective impetus for action and change emerges when heterogeneous agents interact in networks in ways that produce new patterns of behavior or new modes of operating. (p. 299)

Adaptive leadership takes place at many levels. This leadership manifests in the interactions between people; the spaces between people and their actions; relationships that allow for learning, expression of new ideas and dissent; feedback, reflection, and interaction with new technology and new processes; and clashes among ideas (Heifetz et al., 2009; Hogan, 2008; Obolensky, 2010; Torres & Reeves, 2011; Uhl-Bien et al., 2007). Adaptive leaders are collective leaders who tap into the collective intelligence of the stakeholders. They help the stakeholders "generate new norms that enable the organization to meet the ongoing stream of adaptive challenges posed by a world ever ready to offer new realities, opportunities, and pressures" (Heifetz et al., 2009, p. 17).

As a consequence, adaptive leadership requires that the leaders let go of the notion that a pre-set technical fix for the organization is the correct approach and instead help all stakeholders become collective leaders. Leaders in international development, in particular, have traditionally viewed themselves as outside experts who are responsible for introducing new technical approaches to people with little knowledge or skills. Hence they may view these people as passive recipients incapable of leading. By recognizing that change is far more complex than technical fixes, leaders recognize that they do not have all the answers and that they need the collective wisdom that collaboration provides. Collective leaders seek creative solutions by dialoging, challenging the norm, and making transparent the emotions that inevitably accompany giving up the familiar (Thompson, 2017). Transformational leaders motivate and inspire stakeholders to embrace change and empower them to make the change their own (Burns, 2004; Northouse, 2010). As Burns (2004) pointed out, transformational leaders encourage "a sense of collective identity and collective efficacy, which in turn brings stronger feelings of self-worth and self-efficacy... By pursuing transformational change, people can transform themselves" (pp. 25–26). The creation of this collective identity is aligned with the capacity of system leadership to foster a shared understanding and collective *we*.

The unity and collective identity emphasized through transformational leadership is critical for the success of the joint effort required to implement international development projects. Transformational leadership appeals to higher social values and mores and motivates stakeholders to see the project as a vehicle through which to operationalize these values and mores (Burns, 2004). Participants move beyond a consideration of their individual gain to a commitment to the whole, collective endeavor. Such a perspective elevates the undertaking to a higher level and provides stakeholders with the possibility of accomplishing something positive for society and even the world that they would not normally have the possibility to do (Burns, 2004). Transformational leadership, associated with "inspiration...empowerment, articulating a vision, promoting group goals, providing intellectual stimulation... and organizational citizenship behavior," enhances stakeholders' sense of achievement (Jha, 2014, p. 22).

Like adaptive and transformational leadership, system leadership fosters collective leadership (Fillingham & Weir, 2014; Senge et al., 2015). System leadership makes invisible forces visible (Senge et al., 2015). This leadership style also legitimates the need for transparency and communication. The importance of culture is highlighted when practicing system leadership. Cultural values of the aid-receiving country are honored and their potential impact on how the change process is led is taken into serious consideration (Osland, 2013). Indigenous leadership styles are learned by expatriate experts (Osland et al., 2014) and aid-receiving country stakeholders also come to understand the leadership styles of expatriates.

Through system leadership, stakeholders create a shared understanding of leadership and decide on the most appropriate and potentially successful leadership approach for the transformational change. Stakeholders must become leaders in order to embrace the transformation and co-create and own it (Thompson, 2016). In so doing, leaders develop cognitive and emotional connections. They must work together to hone the transformation such that it effectively adapts to the aid-receiving country context and so that it inspires stakeholders in the target systems to adopt and even thrive on the change. System leaders need to first see the larger system within which the change effort is embedded (Senge et al., 2015). Seeing the larger system includes making transparent the donor system, project implementing system, and recipient country system or systems, and facilitates the agreement to find a common ground in cases where these systems have contrasting goals and constituencies. Finally, system leaders build community and networks that support transformative change (Senge et al., 2015).

System leadership involves deeply examining one's own assumptions and worldview, trying to see the world as others see it, and "appreciating how our mental models may limit us" (Senge et al., 2015, para. 11). Collective leaders in international development projects ideally form a bond such that they can engage in shared reflection and thereby "appreciate emotionally as well as cognitively each other's reality" (Senge et al., 2015, para. 11). Collective knowledge and wisdom emerge from these relationships and provide a view of the whole system reality not available to any individual beforehand. Such knowledge and wisdom come forth over time "through a ripening process that gradually brings about new ways of thinking, acting, and being" (Senge et al., 2015, para. 38).

As collective knowledge and wisdom develop, a "we" identity will form between leaders from the donor, project implementation, and aid-receiving country organizations based on intense self-examination, combined with true appreciation of the others' perspectives. These leaders in the project implementation process are then able to co-create the system transformation. There is a shift from the negative problem-focused approach to a more positive orientation. The positive orientation is driven by visioning and sorting through the cultural aspects of their past that they want to hold on to (Heifetz, 2011). The shift

> *involves not just building inspiring visions but facing difficult truths about the present reality and learning how to use the tension between vision and reality to inspire truly new approaches. (Senge et al., 2015, para. 12)*

The shift also recognizes the fact that "problems out there" are also "problems in here" (Senge et al., 2015, para. 16). Leaders find that problems exist in our assumptions about the world and our worldviews regarding which paradigms are "the correct ones." They also discover that there are problems in their cultural beliefs and values that influence how they expect themselves and others to behave. This recognition leads leaders to let go of these biases, open themselves to the worldviews and cultural beliefs and values of the other leaders, and together to find a common worldview based on a higher vision for the world that transcends differences and seeks the wellbeing of all.

Adaptive transformational system leadership ignites a highly participatory and synergistic adaptive change process that balances the power differential between aid agencies and developing countries, while showing them that such power equilibrium leads to better results. System leadership expands the change effort to a higher-level system view; promotes collective leadership; and builds resonance and mutual understanding among stakeholders (Senge et al., 2015). Such a leadership practice will lead to mutual agreement and more harmonious planning between the aid agency, the project, and the host country and allow for co-creation of the change process to occur. The practice of adaptive transformational system leadership will result in international development projects that make sense in their context and to which the recipient organization will be committed to sustain (Thompson, 2017).

Fig. 12.4. Synergies between leaders.

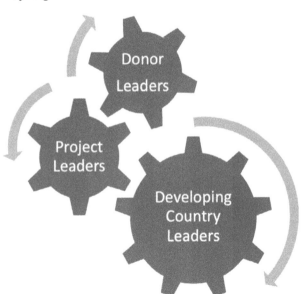

CONSCIOUSNESS AND LEADERSHIP

To process the complexity of globalization and lead complex adaptive and sustainable change and to adopt adaptive transformational system leadership successfully, an effective leader requires particular cognitive abilities (what one is aware of), a unique self-identity (what one identifies with), and certain values (what one considers most important) (Brown, 2006). Cognition, self-identity, and values are constructs often associated with consciousness, which is typically defined as the notion of value-laden awareness (Brown, 2006).

Leaders need to be able to cognitively "see" in systems terms instead of in narrow linear terms and need to be able to track changes in systems catalyzed by their projects and also be aware of external changes that may influence the outcome of their projects. They also need to be able to share and possibly impart systems cognition to their teams and counterparts in the developing country. Leaders need to have values of relationships, consensus, dialogue, and collaboration and need to recognize that their teams' perspectives are critical for effective decision-making and that leadership is not an individual process but rather a group process. That is, they need the belief that community, not individualism, is fundamental. As individuals, they need to allow multiple perspectives that represent different views of reality and understand diversity and multiculturalism and respect different cultural values. They also need to see the creative potential in people and in systems and be able to envision new possibilities for an egalitarian world. One's identity needs to have begun to separate from one's preconceived notions and conditional beliefs and one is ready and willing to listen and begin to reconstruct who one is and what one believes based on broader values. The attachment to place should have begun to loosen so that one can more naturally relate across cultures and also have the confidence to challenge cultural beliefs and practices that do not promote life and wellbeing.

According to developmental psychologists, consciousness evolves over time as a result of the demands of the contemporary age (Kegan, 1994) and as a result of one's openness to the transformational potential of one's learnings, experiences, and relationships, and as the result of "brutal awakenings" caused by crises in one's life (Kegan, 1994). Developmentalists argue that the cognition, self-identity, and values components of consciousness develop through recognizable stages, each stage revealing a different understanding of self and one's values and a "markedly different understanding of the world" (Brown, 2006).

Generally, the values component of consciousness is viewed as expanding over time from an egocentric perspective through a more ethnocentric, worldcentric, and ultimately cosmocentric orientation, encompassing, accepting, and eventually transcending diversity of cultures and values and perceiving more in terms of relationships and interconnections between peoples and places (Brown, 2006; Wilber, 2007). The cognitive component evolves into increasing "mental complexity" (Kegan, 1994) and more complex meaning making and ability to perceive the world in terms of systems and then in terms of paradigms and eventually cross-paradigms. Self-identity moves from what may be characterized and paraphrased as

> *I am my memberships to I am my competencies (rationality capabilities, responsibilities), to I am my inclusiveness (identified with the world/world centered, culture, ecosystems) to I am my multi-perspectival multiple points of view (vision logic). (Wilber, 2007)*

One's sense of self ultimately becomes co-extensive with everyone and everything (Wilber, 2007).

Given the complexity of the globalized world exacerbated by the global pandemic and the challenges facing the world as encompassed in the SDGs, leaders in international development and aid needs to be at least at the level of consciousness associated with postmodernity, as described below, to be effective. However, the demands of globalization are such that movement to the level of consciousness characteristic of the next era of post-postmodernity would better facilitate leaders' abilities to handle the demands and complexity of the world.

Fig. 12.5. Necessity to see whole systems and inter-relationships.

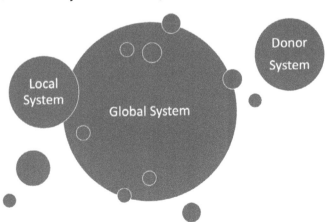

Postmodern Consciousness

The "worldcentric" stage of consciousness, considered to be the consciousness of postmodernity is fostered by values of community harmony and equality (Brown, 2006). Reacting to the rigid rationality of modernity, an individual at this stage of consciousness is sensitive to others and the environment and values reconciliation, consensus, dialogue, relationships, diversity and multiculturalism, and contributing to the earth's resources and opportunities equally among all (Brown, 2006).

The self-identity of those at this postmodern stage is such that individuals, with an individualistic sense of self, view themselves in interaction with systems and hence have an increased "understanding of complexity, systemic connections, and unintended effect of actions" (Brown, 2006, n.p.) due to interacting systems. They have a perspectival view of reality, meaning that they recognize that reality is not a fixed absolute but is created by how different people perceive it and make meaning out of it. They consequently question their own assumptions and identities and those of others and speaks of interpretations rather than truth (Brown, 2006). An individual at this stage transcends strict categories and adapts rules when needed or invents new ones and discusses issues and airs differences. Graves and Beck argued that at this level, individuals seek inner peace and explore the caring dimensions of community and have an egalitarian and humanistic code (Beck et al., 2018).

Cognitively, individuals at the postmodern stage of consciousness possess what Kegan (1994) called the "self-authoring mind." Individuals with this cognitive ability think in terms of systems, "have the capacity to take responsibility for and ownership of their internal authority" (Kegan & others, 2001, p. 5), and establish their own sets of values and ideologies (Kegan, 1994). Relationships become a part of one's world rather than the reason for one's existence. Support at this stage is evident in acknowledgment of the individual's independence and self-regulation.

Post-Postmodern Consciousness

The initial stage of the "cosmocentric" stage of consciousness may be considered the post-postmodern or transmodern era. At this stage of consciousness, an individual recognizes "the magnificence of existence" (Brown, 2006) and is committed to live responsibly in a condition of always "becoming." An individual at this stage integrates differences "into interdependent, natural flows...complementing egalitarianism with natural degrees of ranking and excellence" (Brown, 2006), recognizing overlapping dynamic systems and natural hierarchies in any context.

The self-identity of an individual at this stage of consciousness

> comprehends multiple interconnected systems of relationship and processes and is able to deal with conflicting needs and duties in constantly shifting contexts ... and recognizes complexity and inter-relationships ... and paradox and contradictions in system and self. (Brown, 2006, n.p.)

An individual at this level "leads in reframing, reinterpreting situations so that decisions support overall principle, strategy, integrity, and foresight" (Brown, 2006, n.p.). Graves and Beck called this stage "second-tier being" (Beck et al., 2018). An individual at this stage understands "that chaos and change are natural and integrating the kaleidoscope of natural hierarchies, systems and forms into interdependent, natural flows is a must" (Beck et al., 2018, p. 26).

Kegan (1994) argued that this stage of cognitive consciousness is comprised of an interdependent mind, a "self-transforming mind," which transcends its own beliefs and positions and can maneuver change and uncertainty because individuals at this stage have a higher-level view of the global order and are intent of working toward an integrated world characterized by justice and equality (Kegan & Lahey, 2009).

Intentionality, Connection, Global Identity, and Expanding Consciousness

As stated before, Kegan (1994) argued that the modern age places demands on consciousness to expand, and globalization may well be pressuring certain leaders to move to the higher level of consciousness. Beck contended that as life conditions change, complex adaptive intelligences arise in certain leaders and that these two forces interact and "push each other and evolution forward" (Beck et al., 2018, p. 27).

Such movement also depends upon the intentionality and values of leaders and upon their openness to change. Intentionality is a critical component of self-identity and is an important driver of expanding one's consciousness. Intentionality derives largely from one's values and motivations. Leaders in international development and aid need to carefully reflect on why they are working in this sector and how they intend to approach leading. Fundamental to leading is the intent to connect with stakeholders. Developing close working relationships are the critical first step before anything else can be accomplished in international development and also serve as a critical first step in forming a global identity and expanded consciousness (Thompson & Storberg-Walker, 2018).

Curran's (2018) "global resonance" provides a model of how leaders can connect with stakeholders in order to overcome alterity, to create a "we" relationship, and to create a way to "be" a global leader. This is the essential step to beginning the process of developing a global identity, in which, as Curran (2019) pointed out,

> the process of belonging expands on vertical, geographically-dependent rootedness to include horizontal rootedness. In other words, belonging extends unrestrained across geographic locale and affiliations based on many more elements than shared traditional identity markers. (2019, n.p.)

Furthermore, practices such as the "presencing" of Scharmer's Theory U, and its opening of oneself to active listening and more intuitively experiencing the world and the future possibilities (Scharmer & Kaufer, 2013) help one confront one's "blind spots" and accept a changed awareness. Kegan and Lahey (2009) called for confronting and surpassing one's immunity to change as a necessary step to achieving more complex mental models and even allowing others to confront one about those traits and behaviors which prevent productive community-building. Leaders in international development and aid should stop and reflect upon their values, their intentionality, and conduct a brutal self-reflection to determine whether they are committed to the values required to lead in a globalized world and decide whether they are committed to opening themselves up to a process of expanding their consciousness.

CONCLUSION

This chapter has argued that leaders in international development and aid need to adopt complexity leadership as practiced in adaptive transformational system leadership in order to effectively cope with the globalized VUCA world , especially post-pandemic, and that leaders require a consciousness at least at the level associated with postmodernity but ideally at the level associated with post-postmodernity in order to effectively lead adaptive change in complex socio-economic political systems in developing countries.

Leaders can expand their consciousness by confronting themselves and their beliefs and opening themselves up to new possibilities. In international development and aid, leaders should begin by reflecting upon their true motives for being involved in this profession and determine whether in fact they have a sincere intent to connect with their followers and stakeholders and to form a "we" identity to co-create transformative change. Further, leaders need the courage to confront and help transform whole-systems that maintain the inequalities between so-called developed and developing countries, even when this means confronting intrenched powers.

More research needs to be undertaken regarding to what extent leaders in international development and aid have a sufficiently expanded consciousness to apply adaptive transformational system leadership and whether practicing this leadership leads to more positive and sustainable system changes. Research can also be usefully conducted to explore in more detail how leaders in this profession can expand their consciousness. Research that explores the extent to which "a national identity" may challenge the development of a transmodern perspective can also contribute significantly to the global leadership literature.

REFERENCES

Asefa, S. (Ed.). (2010). *Globalisation and international development: Critical issues of the 21ˢᵗ century*. W.E. Upjohn Institute for Employment Research.

Beck, D. E., Larsen, T. H., Solonin, S., Viljoen, D. B. L, & Johns, T. Q. (2018). *Spiral dynamics in action: Humanity's master code*. Wiley.

Brown, B. C. (2006). An overview of developmental stages of consciousness. Integral Institute. https://integralwithoutborders.net/sites/default/files/resources/Overview%20 of%20Developmental%20Levels.pdf

Burns, J. J. (2004). *Transforming leadership: A new pursuit of happiness*. Grove.

Campbell, K. M., & Doshi, R. (2020). The coronavirus could shape global order: China is maneuvering for global leadership as the United State falters. *Foreign Affairs*. November–December. https://www.foreignaffairs.com/articles/china/2020-03-18/coronavirus-could-reshape-global-order

Chriscaden, K. (2020). Impact of COVID-19 on people's livelihoods, their health and our food systems. World Health Organization, October 13. https://www.who.int/news/item/13-10-2020-impact-of-covid-19-on-people%27s-livelihoods-their-health-and-our-food-systems

Curran, K. (2018). Global resonance for global leadership. In R. Thompson & J. Storberg-Walker (Eds.), *Leadership in international development: Navigating the intersections of gender, culture, context, and sustainability* (Chapter 18). Emerald Publishers.

Curran, K. (2019). Global identity tensions for global leaders. In J. Osland, S. Reiche, B. Szudiarek, & M. Mendenhall (Eds.), *Advances in global leadership* (Vol. 12). Emerald Publishers.

D'Alessandro, C., & Leautier, F. (2016). *Cities and spaces of leadership: A geographic perspective*. Palgrave MacMillan.

Fillingham, D., & Weir, B. (2014). *System leadership: Lessons and learning from Aqua's integrated care discovery communities*. The King's Fund.

Heifetz, R., Grashow, A., & Linsky, M. (2009). *The practice of adaptive leadership: Tools and tactics for changing your organization and the world*. Harvard Business Review Press.

Hogan, T. J. (2008, Spring). The adaptive leadership maturity model. *Organization Development Journal, 26*(1), 55–61.

Jha, S. (2014). Transformational leadership and psychological empowerment: Determinants of organizational citizenship behavior. *South Asian Journal of Global Business Research, 3*(1), 18–35.

Kegan, R. (1994). *In over our heads: The mental demands of modern life*. Harvard University Press.

Kegan, R., & Lahey, L. (2009). *Immunity to change: How to overcome it and unlock the potential in yourself and your organization*. Harvard Business Publications.

Lawrence, K. (2013). Developing leaders in a VUCA environment. UNC Kenan-Flagler Business School. http://execdev.kenan-flagler.unc.edu/hubfs/White%20Papers/unc_white_paper_Developing%20leaders%20in%20a%20VUCA%20environment.pdf

Léautier, F. (2014). *Leadership in a globalized world*. Palgrave Macmillan UK. Kindle Edition.

Linsky, M. (2011, April 13). Adaptive leadership, leading change. [video file]. https://www.youtube.com/watch?v=af-cSvnEExM

Mendenhall, M. E., Reiche, B. S., Bird, A., & Osland, J. S. (2012). Defining the 'global' in global leadership. *Journal of World Business, 47*, 493–503.

Obolensky, N. (2010). *Complex adaptive leadership: Embracing paradox and uncertainty*. Routledge.

Osland, J. S. (2013). Leading global change. In M. E. Mendenhall, J. S. Osland, A. L. Bird, G. R. Oddou, M. L. Maznevski, M. J. Stevens, & G. K. Stahl (Eds.), *Global leadership: Research, practice, and development* (2nd ed., pp. 183–214). Routledge.

Osland, J. S. (2014). Preface. In J. S. Osland, M. Li, & Y. Wang (Eds.), *Advances in global leadership* (Vol. 8, pp. 1–18). Emerald Group Publishing, Ltd.

Osland, J. S., Li, M., & Yang, Y. (2014). Introduction: The state of global leadership research. In J. S. Osland, M. Li, & Y. Wang (Eds.), *Advances in global leadership* (Vol. 8, pp. 1–18). Emerald Group Publishing, Ltd.

Reliefweb. (2020). COVID-19 and the need for global leadership: Fighting for a common cause, June 1. https://reliefweb.int/report/world/covid-19-and-need-global-leadership-fighting-common-cause

Rhinesmith, S. H. (1993). *A manager's guide to globalization: Six keys to success in a changing world*. American Society for Training & Development.

Scharmer, O., & Kaufer, K. (2013). *Leading from the emerging future: From egosystem to eco-system economics*. Barrett-Koehler Publishers.

Senge, P., Hamilton, H., & Kania, J. (2015, Winter). The dawn of system leadership. *Stanford Social Innovation Review*, 17. http://www.ssireview.org/articles/entry/the_dawn_of_system_leadership

Stone, M., & Barlow, Z. (2015). *Seven lessons for leaders in systems change*. Center for Ecoliteracy.

Thompson, R. (2016). Theorizing women's ways of knowing and leading for international development projects: The adaptive transformational system leadership model. In J. Storberg-Walker & P. Haber-Curran (Eds.), *Theorizing women & leadership: New insights & contributions from multiple perspectives*. Information Age Publishing.

Thompson, R., & Storberg-Walker, J. (2018). *Leadership in international development: Navigating the intersections of gender, culture, context, and sustainability*. Emerald Publishers.

Torres, R., & Reeves, M. (2011, July). Adaptive leadership: How many of these practices do you employ? *Leadership Excellence*, *28*(7), 8.

Uhl-Bien, M., Marion, R., & McKelvey, B. (2007). Complexity leadership theory: Shifting leadership from the industrial age to the knowledge era. *The Leadership Quarterly*, *18*(4), 298–318.

United Nations Development Programme. (2015). UN Sustainable Development Goals. https://www.undp.org/content/undp/en/home/sustainable-development-goals.html

Vernon, P. (2017). Characteristics of the new foreign aid architecture and the way forward. *IPE and development's blog*. https://ipeanddevelopment.wordpress.com/2017/12/23/characteristics-of-the-new-foreign-aid-architecture-and-ways-forward/

Wilber, K. (2007). *The integral vision*. Shambala Publications, Inc.

13

IMMIGRATION AS A LEADERSHIP CRUCIBLE AMONG GLOBAL LEADERS

MARCO APONTE-MORENO

INTRODUCTION

Globalization can be defined as the growing interdependence of the world's economies, cultures and populations. This phenomenon, which resulted from the increasing trade of goods, flows of capital, and movement of people across borders, started in the fifteenth century with the Spanish and Portuguese expansion into the Americas (Wesseling, 2009). In recent decades, particularly with the rise of emerging markets and the development of the internet, globalization has taken center stage.

In an increasingly globalized world, leading at a transnational level has surged as a distinctive form of leadership. The term "global leader" has emerged in leadership studies to refer to those leaders who operate beyond domestic organizations and political contexts. They lead in a global environment and deal with followers and other constituents from multiple cultural backgrounds. Unlike international leaders, who represent national interests at a global level, global leaders represent transnational interests (Perruci, 2018).

The literature on global leadership mainly focuses on four streams: comparisons between two or more cultures, intercultural communication studies, research on managing people in a global context, and the study of expatriation. These streams provide insights about traits, abilities and roles related to leading globally (Bird & Mendenhall, 2016).

However, there is another stream that is receiving increasing attention: the impact of globalization on the leader–follower relationship. In this context, scholars have paid particular attention to the way global environments affect individual cultures in general and leadership in particular (Perruci, 2018).

One of the most tangible effects of globalization is immigration, often referred to as the human face of globalization. Roughly one third of the world migrants travel from developed countries to other developed countries, one third from developing countries to developed countries, and one third from developing countries to other developing countries (Keeley, 2009). In the United States, where most of the global leadership literature is generated, immigrants are frequently cited as fundamental elements of the American story. People often take pride in their immigrant pasts and in the traditions of enterprise, struggle and courage that immigrants have brought to the country (Schuck, 2011).

However, immigrant leaders are rarely, if ever, mentioned in the leadership literature. This despite the fact that nearly half of US Fortune 500 companies were founded by immigrants or their children (Hathaway, 2017). Instead, leadership scholars have focused their attention on global leaders, but have overlooked those global leaders who are or have been immigrants. An online search on Google Scholar confirms this tendency. At the time of writing this chapter, a search for "global leader" resulted in 42,400 entries, compared to only 250 when searching for "immigrant leader." Although expatriates, who have been widely studied, could technically be considered immigrants, the focus of the studies has been on adaptation techniques, culture shock, and other elements related to their expatriation experience, which is assumed to be temporary (Adler, 2008).

The purpose of this chapter is to explore the immigration experience of global leaders as a life event that shapes their leadership style. It is based on a qualitative study aimed at determining the extent to which global leaders consider immigration a life event that shapes their leadership styles, and at exploring the ways in which their leadership styles are shaped by their immigration experiences. The study is grounded on the analysis of a corpus consisting of current press articles and interviews of 20 prominent global leaders who immigrated to the United States. It also draws from eight face-to-face semi-structured interviews conducted among immigrant leaders in the United States.

LEADERSHIP CRUCIBLES

The model of "leadership crucibles" was proposed in 2002 by Warren Bennis and Robert Thomas in their book *Geeks and Geezers*. According to the authors, leadership crucibles are transformative life events that change a person's sense of identity and therefore his or her leadership style. They coined the term "crucibles" after the vessels used by alchemists in the Middle Ages when trying to turn metals into gold (Bennis & Thomas, 2002).

Crucibles can be life-threatening, like for example overcoming cancer or surviving a car accident. But they can also be more common life events such as being influenced by a teacher or having climbed a tall mountain. In all cases, what matters is that these life events generate a narrative of transformation in leaders, who talk about how they overcame challenges or seize opportunities as a result of the crucibles (Bennis & Thomas, 2002).

Other authors have also looked at life experiences and their influence on leadership. Shamir et al. (2005) argue that a leader's life story has a strong impact on how influential the leader is. Followers' perceptions and beliefs about the leader mediate his or her influence, and these perceptions and beliefs are often based on the stories that the leader tells about his or her life. Similarly, Avolio and Luthans (2006) argue that experiences and events in life play a significant role in leadership styles, especially in the ability to lead authentically. They link this role to the leader's self-awareness, that is to say, the leader's capacity to reflect on her life and learn from her experiences.

Although in their study Bennis and Thomas interviewed 43 leaders in the United States, a country with a strong immigration tradition, the immigration experience as a leadership crucible was not mentioned by their respondents. This is likely due to the fact that for the most part their leaders were American citizens born in the United States. This chapter hopes to fill this gap by analyzing cases of global leaders who immigrated to the United States.

IMMIGRATION AS A LEADERSHIP CRUCIBLE

At first glance, immigrating to another country seems like a clear leadership crucible. It involves a transformative life event likely to change the person's sense of identity, and therefore his or her leadership style. However, since the definition of leadership crucible also involves the creation of a narrative of transformation in the leader (as a result of the transformative life event), then it is essential to analyze what the person says about his or her immigration experience before it can be classified as a leadership crucible.

Considering the stigma associated with being an immigrant in today's world, the question is whether or not the leader chooses to adopt a narrative of transformation in relation to his or her immigration experience. If the immigration experience does not generate this narrative in the leader, then it is not a leadership crucible. But if the leader speaks about how he or she was able to overcome obstacles and take advantage of opportunities because of the immigration experience, then it is a crucible.

When people immigrate, they leave behind their homes, friends and families to start over in a foreign country. Although some immigrants have an easier immigration experience than others, researchers have documented that immigrants, in general, tend to experience traumatic events including depression, great loss and grief:

> *Some immigrants may experience a profound or incapacitating sense of loss, disassociation, flashbacks or nightmares about separation from the homeland or family of origin that may be consistent with the symptoms of Post-Traumatic Stress Disorder (PTSD). (Beckerman & Corbett, 2008, p. 1)*

There are many ways in which people immigrate to a new country. In the case of the United States, for example, the most fortunate immigrants arrive with visas, typically as family members of American citizens, international students, entrepreneurs, or even winners of the diversity lottery. Some go back home when their visas expire; but many are able to obtain permanent residency and stay in the United States legally (Mark, 2018).

Less fortunate immigrants, on the other hand, arrive as undocumented migrants, as refugees, or as visa holders who overstay their temporary visas. These disadvantaged immigrants tend to have experienced traumatic events including physical or sexual assault, human trafficking, detention and deportation, transactional sex, or exposure to political violence (Fortuna et al., 2008).

A case in point is the one of migrant children separated from their parents by American authorities at the US–Mexico border. Medical experts have expressed serious concerns about this practice and warned that those children were likely to experience permanent psychological harm. Although this controversial practice has ended, experts cautioned that the alternative (detaining children with their parents) is also likely to involve serious risks to the children's mental health (Ducharme, 2018).

In sum, based on the leadership theories discussed in the previous section (Avolio & Luthans, 2006; Bennis & Thomas, 2002; Shamir et al., 2005), and considering that immigration is a life event that changes the person's life, it can be argued that the immigration experience has the potential to be a leadership crucible. After all, it is a life event that shapes leadership styles in unique ways, which reflect the circumstances that immigrants have gone through as a result of their immigrant condition.

IMMIGRANT GLOBAL LEADERS: A QUALITATIVE STUDY

In order to understand the extent to which immigrant global leaders consider their immigration experience a life event that shapes their leadership styles, a qualitative study was conducted based on the analysis of current articles and interviews of 20 prominent global leaders who are also immigrants in the United States. All of them lead in global environments and interact with followers and other constituents from multiple cultural backgrounds. Thus, they can all be considered global leaders.

The sample was randomly selected by students as part of an assignment in an undergraduate leadership class at a liberal arts college in Northern California. The students conducted Google searches to identify the immigrant leaders that they wanted to research. The two criteria in the selection process of the leaders were as follows: that the leader had immigrated to the United States, and that the leader was a global leader. A typical search usually included the full name of the leader together with the word(s) "immigration" or "immigrant."

The searches conducted by the students resulted in a sample of twenty immigrant leaders from sixteen different countries. Most of them were CEOs working in various industries including tech, publishing, and finance among others. Only 20% of the sample consisted of women leaders. Although the number is rather low, it is significantly higher than the percentage of women CEOs in Fortune 500 companies in the United States, which in 2018 was approximately 6% (Percentage of Fortune 500 CEOs who are women, 2018). Table 13.1 lists the names of the leaders in the sample, their current jobs, and their countries of origin.

Table 13.1. Twenty Prominent Global Immigrant Leaders in the Large
Sample.

Leader	Origin	Position	Immigration Crucible
Albright, Madeleine	Czech Republic	Former Secretary of State and Chair of ASG	Yes
Brin, Sergey	Russia	Co-founder of Google	No
Gheorghe, Christian	Romania	Founder and CEO of Tide-mark	Yes
Huang, Jen-Hsum	Taiwan	Founder and CEO of Nvidia	No
Huffington, Arianna	Greece	Founder of Huffington Post and CEO of Thrive Global	Yes
Jaber, Phil	Palestine	Founder of Philz Coffee	Yes
Kandil, Ammar	Egypt	Co-founder of Yes Theory	No
Koun, Jan	Ukraine	Co-founder and former CEO of WhatsApp	No
Laplanche, Renaud	France	Founder and CEO of Lending Club	Yes
Levchin, Max	Ukraine	CEO of Affirm; Founder of PayPal	Yes
Ly, Andrew	Vietnam	Founder and CEO of Sugar Bowl Bakery	Yes
Mirza, Claudia	Colombia	Co-founder and former CEO of Akorbi	Yes
Musk, Elon	South Africa	Co-founder of TESLA and CEO of SpaceX	No
Nadella, Satya	India	CEO of Microsoft	Yes
Nooyi, Indra	India	Former CEO of Pepsico	Yes
Pichai, Sundar	India	CEO of Google	Yes
Santos, Victor	Brazil	Founder and CEO of Airfox	Yes
Schwarzenegger, Arnold	Austria	Former Governor of California	Yes
Tran, David	Vietnam	Founder of Huy Fong Foods	No
Ulukaya, Hamdi	Turkey	Founder and CEO of Chobani	Yes

When examining the way in which leadership styles are shaped by the immigration experience, we analyzed face-to-face interviews with eight immigrant leaders who live and work in Northern California. These interviews were borrowed from the Global and Diverse Leadership Project, a research initiative aimed at expanding our understanding of leadership in diverse and global contexts. The project, which is currently in progress, gathers a group of researchers from around the world who work in different disciplines. Prior to her passing in 2020, it was led by Professor Jean Lau Chin from Adelphi University and includes the author of this chapter as one of the contributing scholars (International Leadership Network, 2019).

It is important to note that the eight immigrant leaders are also considered global leaders because their jobs require them to interact with diverse constituents from other countries. All eight have a university education. Six of them are male and two are female. This gender disparity is mainly due to the fact that most of the respondents were enrolled in an executive MBA program. These programs generally consist of only one third of female students (Kowarski, 2017).

Five of the immigrant leaders interviewed were from India, one was from Iran, one was from Mexico, and one was from the Philippines. All of them were in their thirties or forties except for one who was in his twenties. Two of them worked in higher education, two in the health industry, one in a pharmaceutical company, one in a non-profit organization, and two in general business. Table 13.2 summarizes the main characteristics of the immigrant leaders in the sample.

Table 13.2. General Characteristics of Immigrant Leaders in the Small Sample.

Country	Gender	Age	Sector	Position
India	Male	40s	Business	Senior
India	Female	30s	Non-profit	Senior
India	Male	40s	Business	Senior
India	Male	20s	Higher ed.	Junior
Iran	Male	40s	Higher ed.	Senior
Mexico	Male	30s	Health	Senior
Philippines	Male	30s	Health	Senior
India	Female	40s	Pharma.	Senior

IMMIGRATION AS A LEADERSHIP CRUCIBLE FOR GLOBAL LEADERS

The analysis of press interviews and articles related to our sample of 20 prominent global leaders shows that most of them consider immigration a defining leadership crucible. Specifically, two thirds of leaders in the sample (or 14 of them) not only consider immigration an important life event, but also speak about its transformational quality.

All of them speak about how their lives improved when they immigrated to the United States. Many talk about how they were able to overcome difficulties, achieve personal and professional goals, and provide a better future for their families. Their narratives unmistakably show that immigration is for them a leadership crucible.

It is important to note that although our data indicate that one third of the sample (six of them) do not consider immigration a leadership crucible, it is possible that they do, but that the information is either unavailable or difficult to find online. Table 13.1 includes a column that specifies whether or not we found evidence of considering immigration a leadership crucible for each of the twenty leaders in our sample.

The following excerpt which was taken from an article about Andrew Ly, the founder and CEO of Sugar Bowl Bakery, is a good example of how immigration is conceptualized in the narratives of those leaders in our sample who consider immigration a leadership crucible:

> When I came here, I didn't speak the language or have any money. I am proud that I've taken my family where they hesitated to go years ago. Whenever I mentor young people, I tell them, never give up. Work hard, have a good heart, and be disciplined. Those are the ingredients to success. (Eng, 2015, p. 1)

A closer analysis of the narratives by global immigrant leaders who think of immigration as a leadership crucible (a transformational life event) reveals three types of narratives: Those who focus on adversities and difficult circumstances, those who emphasize the outcome of the transformation (the new and better life in the United States), and those who focus on the United States as the agent responsible for the transformation.

Leaders who focus on adversities and difficult circumstances talk about either the challenging conditions left behind, or the difficulties encountered when they first arrived in the United States. Andrew Ly's excerpt above is a good example of this type. Another example can be found in a quote from Christian Gheorghe, the Romanian-born limo driver turned founder and CEO of Tidemark:

> *In retrospect, not knowing English when I first arrived at the modern version of Ellis Island–a brightly lit immigration room at JFK airport–was a blessing in disguise. Freedom, the first word I ever learned by listening to Pink Floyd records in communist Romania before escaping to America, was one of the few English words I did know and muttered to the immigration officer when he asked me, "Why are you here?" (Nasri, 2013, p. 1)*

In regard to the narratives in the sample that emphasize the outcome of the transformation, all of them conceptualize immigration as a positive experience. They often mention that life in the United States is better than in the old country, and talk about the opportunities found in America. Arianna Huffington, the Greek immigrant who founded the Huffington Post, provides a good example of this in one of the narratives analyzed in this study:

> *When I was growing up in Athens, my mother would tell me, "Failure isn't the opposite of success; it's a stepping stone to success," and when I came to America, I was given many opportunities to fail my way to eventual success. But my story is just one of millions. And it falls to all of us – especially those of us who have come here and started businesses – to do whatever we can to make sure the same opportunities we've enjoyed are there for the immigrants of today and tomorrow. (Nasri, 2013, p. 1)*

In the cases in which the United States is presented as the agent responsible for the transformation, the country is given human characteristics and is often presented as a saviour. One quote by Sergey Brin, co-founder of Google, illustrates this very well:

> *This country was brave and welcoming and I wouldn't be where I am today or have any kind of the life that I have today if this was not a brave country that really stood out and spoke for liberty. (Samuelson, 2017, p. 1)*

It is interesting to note that Brin's excerpt was part of a speech given as a reaction to President Donald Trump's refugee ban in 2017. In fact, most of the articles and interviews analyzed in the study were written in the context of President Trump's anti-immigrant rhetoric and policies. This was particularly true for leaders in the tech industry, which relies heavily on immigrant labor (Rodriguez, 2017). The following quote from Satya Nadella, CEO of Microsoft, illustrates well this point. It was taken from a public letter that he wrote in response to President Trump's policy of separating undocumented children from their parents at the US Southern border in 2018:

> *Like many of you, I am appalled at the abhorrent policy of separating immigrant children from their families at the southern border of the U.S. As both a parent and an immigrant, this issue touches me personally. (Nadella, 2018, p. 1)*

In sum, the analysis of press interviews and articles related to our sample of 20 prominent global leaders indicates that most of them consider immigration a defining leadership crucible that transforms their lives. While some narratives emphasize adversities and difficult circumstances, others focus on the outcome of the transformation (the new and better life in the United States). There are also narratives in which the United States is conceptualized as the agent responsible for the transformation.

INFLUENCE OF THE IMMIGRATION CRUCIBLE ON THE LEADERSHIP STYLES OF GLOBAL LEADERS

Although the analysis of the interviews of the 20 prominent global leaders provided solid evidence that immigration is considered a leadership crucible for them, it did not provide any insights on the possible ways in which their leadership styles could have been shaped as a result of the immigration crucible. The only two exceptions in the sample were Hamdi Ulukaya, founder and CEO of Chobani Yogurt; and Claudia Mirza, the Colombian entrepreneur who co-founded Akorbi. In both cases, they spoke about wanting to help others who might find themselves in similar situations to theirs.

In the case of Ulukaya, because of his experience as a refugee, he is now committed to employing as many refugees and immigrants as possible. His current workforce consists of approximately 30% of refugees and other immigrants. Once a refugee himself, Ulukaya often speaks about the responsibility he feels to help others in similar situations (Alesci, 2018).

In the case of Mirza, the Colombian entrepreneur, she clearly expressed that she does not want others to have to live what she went through when she immigrated:

> I want to be sure people don't have to immigrate. No one should be deprived of the right of being in the place they were born [...] Immigrating is one of the worst things that can happen to a human being, I'm telling you. If it is a choice, that's fine. But no one should have to leave their country due to poverty and violence. (DeBaise, 2019, p. 1)

In order to shed light on possible ways in which the immigration crucible could impact the leadership styles of global leaders, this chapter draws on eight face-to-face interviews with immigrant leaders who live and work in Northern California. All of these leaders are also global leaders given that in their leadership roles they interact with a diverse group of people from many parts of the world.

It is important to note that although this is not a big sample, it sheds light on possible ways in which the immigration crucible could impact leadership styles. This is because all leaders in the sample expressed (during the interviews) that they view their immigration experience as a defining event in their lives. Thus, by looking at their leadership styles, we hope to obtain some insights on how the immigration crucible has shaped the way they lead.

The analysis reveals three key leadership characteristics that all immigrant leaders in our sample identified as very important for leadership: humility, benevolence and egalitarianism. The three characteristics were identified from a list given to the sample. They were asked what each of the terms meant to them with regard to leadership. Humility was described to respondents as "being humble;" benevolence as "showing kindness, empathy, and concern for the welfare of others;" and egalitarianism as "being egalitarian with members of the organization."

Table 13.3 summarizes their responses for each of the eleven categories included in the question. A "Yes" means that that the category was considered important by the respondent, a "No" means that it was not considered important, and a "D" means that the respondent thought that it depended on the situation (sometimes it could be important and some other times it

Table 13.3. Importance of Selected Categories in Leadership (Per Respondent in the Small Sample).

	India	India	India	India	India	Iran	Mexico	Philippines
Humility	Yes	Yes	Yes	Yes	Yes	Yes	Yes	Yes
Assertiveness	D	Yes	Yes	D	No	Yes	Yes	D
Directness	Yes	No	No	Yes	D	D	D	No
Social status	No	No		No			No	No
Competitiveness	No	Yes	No	Yes	D	D	No	Yes
Interpersonal favors	No	No	Yes	No	No	Yes	No	No
Not losing face	Yes	No		Yes	Yes	No	Yes	D
Benevolence	Yes	Yes	Yes	Yes	Yes	Yes	Yes	Yes
Egalitarianism	Yes	Yes	Yes	Yes	Yes	Yes	Yes	Yes
Members first	Yes	No		No	Yes	Yes	D	D
Individual needs	No	No		D	No	No	D	D

could be unimportant). A blank means that the interviewer omitted a specific category, thus the respondent did not have an opportunity to answer it. This happened because of the semi-structured nature of the interviews.

Humility

Being humble is the opposite of being pretentious. It is about being unassuming and modest. Humble people keep their achievements in perspective. They know their limitations as individuals and as human beings. They are oriented toward others and value the well-being of other people. In this respect, humility is a good trait to have in leadership given the strong focus on followers (Austin, 2012).

It can be argued that humility is a characteristic likely to be valued and adopted by immigrants precisely because of their need to adapt to a new country. In the new society they are generally perceived as different by the majority. They often have limited financial means and reduced networks of friends and family. They have to deal with delicate bureaucratic procedures to remain in their host countries. They have to cope with a mix of emotions related to being away from loved ones. For these reasons, they learn to be risk-takers and doers, but they also learn to be humble so that they can be accepted in the new society.

Benevolence

Studies have found that humility is a strong and consistent predictor of benevolence. Humble people tend to be more generous toward others (Exline & Hill, 2012). Then it is not surprising that both humility and benevolence are considered very important by all immigrant leaders in our sample. In this respect, one of our respondents stated:

> So humility, being humble, is important because you've come to a position of leadership in an organization by working hard, right? But there were people around you who supported you and made you who you are. So you should never forget that. It's important. I think it also goes back to the idea of being compassionate. I've seen these two characteristics go hand in hand.

All immigrant leaders in the sample also mentioned the importance of empathy, which is an essential component of benevolence. Empathy can be defined as the ability to understand another person's feelings (the cognitive element) and to re-experience them oneself (the affective element). While sympathy involves the capacity to understand and support the feelings of another person, empathy entails the ability to experience those feelings (Salovey et al., 2004). It is about being able to put oneself in someone else's place and experience what the other person is feeling. In this respect one respondent said:

> It's really important to be able to put yourself in your team members' shoes and to see from their perspective, even if you are sort of higher in terms of your role in the organization. You might be senior, you have to relate to those who are reporting to you and understand their perspective.

Egalitarianism

In addition to showing the respondent's affinity to empathy, the comment above also suggests an awareness of equality. In fact, egalitarianism, which can be defined as the belief that all people are equal, have equal rights, and deserve equal opportunities ("Egalitarianism," 2018), was mentioned by all respondents in the sample during their interviews. As one respondent said:

Everyone is equal. When you start to think everyone is equal, you will learn about lots of different opportunities. You will learn lots of different skills. All that's going to help you do better.

It is not surprising that immigrant leaders tend to value egalitarianism. As late comers to a society, they are likely to understand and appreciate the importance of equal rights and equal opportunities.

Also, since many of them come to the United States fleeing political and economic inequality in their home countries, finding an equal society in the United States is part of their expectations. After all, egalitarianism is an ideal that is very present in the nation-building discourse of the United States. In a way, it is part of the American dream. This ideal is clearly stated in the Declaration of Independence, which is a keystone of American culture:

We hold these Truths to be self-evident, that all Men are created equal, that they are endowed by their Creator with certain unalienable Rights, that among these are Life, Liberty, and the Pursuit of Happiness. (US Declaration of Independence)

CONCLUSION AND LIMITATIONS

This chapter explored the immigration experience of global leaders as a life event that shapes their leadership styles. The examination of a corpus consisting of press articles and interviews of 20 prominent global leaders who immigrated to the United States indicated that global immigrant leaders do consider immigration to be a leadership crucible. Their narratives can be classified into three categories: those focusing on adversities and difficult circumstances, those emphasizing the outcome of the transformation (their new and better life in the United States), and those representing the United States as the agent responsible for the transformation.

In addition, the chapter drew from eight face-to-face semi-structured interviews conducted among immigrant leaders in the United States to shed light on ways in which the immigration crucible could affect the leadership styles of global immigrant leaders. The analysis suggested that there are three key leadership characteristics that global immigrant leaders consider important for leadership, precisely because of their immigrant condition: humility, benevolence, and egalitarianism.

Although the size of the samples used in this study is small, the chapter provides a solid foundation for understanding both immigration as a leadership crucible, and the leadership styles of global immigrant leaders. For future studies, a larger and more diverse sample, both in terms of nationalities and industries, is likely to produce more meaningful results. It is the author's hope that this chapter will inspire researchers to continue the study of global immigrant leaders in the United States and beyond.

REFERENCES

Adler, N. (2008). *International dimensions of organizational behavior*. South-Western Cengage Learning.

Alesci, C. (2018, October 1). US yogurt billionaire's solution to immigration: "Humanity first." *CNN.com*. https://www.cnn.com/2018/09/30/politics/chobani-ceo-immigration-solution/index.html

Austin, M. (2012, June 27). Humility. *Psychology Today*. https://www.psychologytoday.com/us/blog/ethics-everyone/201206/humility

Avolio, B. J., & Luthans, F. (2006). *The high impact leader: Moments matter in accelerating authentic leadership development*. McGraw-Hill.

Beckerman, N. L., & Corbett, L. (2008, Summer). Immigration and families: Treating acculturative stress from a systemic framework. *Family Therapy*. http://findarticles.com/p/articles/mi_6897/is_2_35/ai_n30931668/

Bennis, W. G., & Thomas, R. J. (2002). *Geeks and geezers: How era, values an defining moments shape leaders*. Harvard Business School Press.

Bird, A., & Mendenhall, M. (2016). From cross-cultural management to global leadership: Evolution and adaptation. *Journal of Global Business*, *51*(1), 115–126.

DeBaise, C. (2019, May 14). A successful entrepreneur shares what it's really like to be an immigrant. *The Story Exchange*. https://thestoryexchange.org/successful-entrepreneur-shares-immigrant/

Ducharme, J. (2018, June 21). Separating kids from their parents can cause psychological harm. But experts say detaining them together isn't much better. *Time.com*. http://time.com/5317762/psychological-effects-detaining-immigrant-families/

Egalitarianism. (2018). In Oxford Dictionaries. https://en.oxforddictionaries.com/definition/egalitarianism

Eng, D. (2015, May 24). How a family of refugees turned a bakery into a dessert powerhouse. *Fortune*. https://fortune.com/2015/05/24/andrew-ly-sugar-bowl-bakery/

Exline, J., & Hill, P. (2012, May). Humility: A consistent and robust predictor of generosity. *The Journal of Positive Psychology*, 208–218.

Fortuna, L., Porche, M., & Alegria, M. (2008). Political violence, psychosocial trauma, and the context of mental health services use among immigration Latinos in the United States. *Ethnicity & Health, 13*, 435–463.

International Leadership Network. (2019). Global and Diverse Leadership Project. *Research Gate*. https://www.researchgate.net/project/International-Leadership-Network-Global-and-Diverse-Leadership

Keeley, B. (2009). *International migration: The human face of globalization*. OECD Insights, OECD Publishing. https://doi.org/10.1787/9789264055780-en

Kowarski, I. (2017, March 14). U.S. News Data: A portrait of a typical MBA student. *US News*. https://www.usnews.com/education/best-graduate-schools/top-business-schools/articles/2017-03-14/us-news-data-a-portrait-of-the-typical-mba-student

Mark, M. (2018, May 3). Jeff Sessions said immigrants should 'wait their turn' to come to the US – Here's how complicated that process can be. *Business Insider*. https://www.businessinsider.com/how-to-green-card-visa-legal-immigration-us-news-trump-2017-4

Nadella, S. (2018, June 19). My views on U.S. immigration policy. *Linkedin.com*. https://www.linkedin.com/pulse/my-views-us-immigration-policy-satya-nadella/

Nasri, G. (2013, August 14). The shocking stats about who's really starting companies in America. https://www.fastcompany.com/3015616/the-shocking-stats-about-whos-really-starting-companies-in-america

Percentage of Fortune 500 CEOs who are women. (2018). Pew Research Center, Washington, D.C. https://www.pewsocialtrends.org/fact-sheet/the-data-on-women-leaders/

Perruci, G. (2018). *Global leadership: A transnational perspective*. Routledge.

Rodriguez, S. (2017, January 29). Why tech companies need immigrants to function. *Inc.com*. https://www.inc.com/salvador-rodriguez/why-tech-needs-immigrants.html

Salovey, P., Mayer, J., & Caruso, D. (2004). Emotional intelligence: Theory, findings, and implications. *Psychological Inquiry, 15*(3), 197–215.

Samuelson, K. (2017, January 31). Google's co-founder criticizes president Trump's refugee ban in passionate speech. *Fortune*. https://fortune.com/2017/01/31/sergey-brin-donald-trump/

Schuck, P. (2011). 11. Immigrants' incorporation in the United States after 9/11: Two steps forward, one step back. In J. Hochschild & J. Mollenkopf (Eds.). *Bringing outsiders in: Transatlantic perspectives on immigrant political incorporation*. (pp. 158–175). Cornell University Press. https://doi.org/10.7591/9780801461972-012

Shamir, B., Dayan-Horesh, H., & Adler, D. (2005). Leading by biography: Towards a life-story approach to the study of leadership. *Leadership, 1*, 13–29.

U.S. Declaration of Independence. (1776). http://www.ushistory.org/declaration/document/

Wesseling, H. (2009). Globalization: A historical perspective. *European Review, 17*(3–4), 455–462.

14

FROM A SEA OF GREY TO A SKY OF BLUE: GLOBAL WOMEN LEADERS PROVIDING RAYS OF HOPE

LORRAINE STEFANI

INTRODUCTION

This chapter offers a case study exploring the connection between global leadership and context as exemplified by four women leaders who have come to prominence for championing agendas that prioritize the wellbeing of citizens, an economy of inclusion rather than exclusion, and an ethos of social justice. Their impact is significant; they are shifting the narrative of global leadership. In the case study, each of these women is viewed through a wide-angle lens focused on twenty-first century global challenges and their respective responses. A fine-focus on their leadership emphasizes the appropriateness of the metaphor of rays of hope amidst the sea of grey that is the current landscape of global leadership during a time of great division, turmoil, unpredictability, and instability.

BACKGROUND

Global leadership is in a parlous state. The continuing rise of the strongman leader (Rachman, 2018) in so many countries from the United States to Russia, Eastern European countries such as Hungary and Poland, Southern European countries including Italy and also in Britain, is creating severe disruption to our implicitly understood concept of democracy (Conradi, 2018). A perfect storm of circumstances seems set to lead to a global catastrophe of immeasurable proportions. All nations are, and will be, challenged by climate change and global warming. The evidence of climate change in action is irrefutable.

The dark underbelly of globalization so lauded and applauded for wealth creation by politicians and businesses, has contributed to unsustainable gaps between rich and poor in many countries. Advances in technology are stripping out low-skill jobs. Across much of the Western world, there is a noticeable rise in xenophobic authoritarianism and a loss of tolerance of social, intellectual and political diversity (Golec de Zavala et al., 2017). Far-right activists are on the rise everywhere, and they are being emboldened and radicalized by mainstream politicians and a disturbingly large section of the mainstream media in their targeting of minorities and migrants (Sabbagh, 2019).

What the strongmen hero leaders putting power and influence into re-arranging the current world order have in common is an approach to leadership that is lacking in compassion and concern for the whole of the populations they lead. They tend to favor authoritarianism and undermining the traditional power structures. They use their self-inflated powers to push through repressive legislation that has disproportionately negative effects on the poorest and most vulnerable citizens. They display an apparent relish for dividing their citizenship into "us" and "other," a right-wing nationalist fervour and a propensity for making the rich richer on the backs of the poor (Rachman, 2018).

The policies in many countries across Europe and in the United States primarily associated with globalization and profit making have resulted in a shift from financial deficits to social deficits, with a concomitant threat to our understood social fabric (Elliott, 2016). These global, political leaders have forgotten, or perhaps deliberately chosen to ignore the idea that essential ingredients of leader(ship) are a commitment to serve and service, to unite rather than divide, to positive role modeling and setting an example to followers, showing courage, compassion and humanity in the face of great turbulence (e.g., Avolio & Gardner, 2005).

The Brexit chaos in Britain and the Trump administration in the United States are prominent spectacles that the world can watch to see global leaders prepared to put political, social, and economic stability at risk for individual power and political gain by any means. We must ask these questions: Is this the best we can expect from global leaders in the twenty-first century? Does what we see and hear daily through multiple communication channels inspire confidence that current global leaders can take us to a new, sustainable political order? Can they heal the wounds of division they have so successfully inflicted on societies? Can they commit to understanding that all of their citizens, not just their followers, are their primary stakeholders?

FROM A SEA OF GREY TO A SKY OF BLUE

Leadership in times of strife requires great courage and vision. Colorful rays of hope can be seen by focusing a leadership lens on outstanding leaders challenging the status quo, being seen and heard above the noise and the power-clamor of the current sea of grey strongmen. The four women leaders chosen for this case study: Greta Thunberg, Alexandria Ocasio-Cortez, Jacinda Ardern, and Nicola Sturgeon, are bringing the herstory into history through their visible, tangible twenty-first-century approaches to leading and leadership. Conceptualizing leadership as the interplay between the leaders, the social environment, the context, the purpose (of the leadership moment), and the followers, each one of these global women leaders is in the bright glow of the spotlight over significant leaderful moments (Stefani, 2017). Global women leaders are role modeling new, twenty-first-century narratives with social justice for all citizens at the heart of these new approaches to the practice of leadership – practices that bring to light the values and characteristics of progressive leaders. This chapter interrogates the leadership of four prominent women and asks if we can capture and articulate their new narratives and approaches for the global good.

GLOBAL CHALLENGES AND GLOBAL LEADERSHIP

The Climate in Crisis

One of the greatest challenges facing the world is that of climate change and our collective failure in climate change adaptation (UNFCC, 2018). There is unequivocal evidence that the climate is changing dramatically, and the world is heating up at a significant rate. The reality of climate change is not new but has largely been ignored or denied. Today we are seeing the effects of our collective inaction, climate change in action. The changes are manifesting in abnormally high temperatures in many continents; there are record-breaking wildfires across the globe particularly in drought-stricken areas, with the east coast of Australia experiencing catastrophic bush fires in 2019; the ice caps in the Arctic are melting at an unprecedented rate. Many places across the world are in drought, in others such as the Pacific Islands, sea levels are rising to a dangerous level for coastal communities. There is an increase in extreme weather events including more flooding and superstorms. Other severe consequences of our inaction include the extinction of species, which we know to be happening and which in turn will destabilize ecosystems, the networks that support all of life. The consequences for people's lives are dramatic (Attenborough, 2019; WWF, 2019).

Our responsibility for the planet is a social justice issue. Due to the impacts of climate change, there will be huge areas currently supporting life that will become uninhabitable. This in turn will mean population displacement and mass migration of climate refugees. Conflict is almost an inevitability (UNFCC, 2019). Poor people will suffer most and yet they are the least responsible for the massive rises in CO_2 levels caused by our exploitation and use of fossil fuels, coal, gas and electricity and the apparently unstoppable levels of deforestation, in essence removing the lungs of the world (Hagen, 2018).

Greta Thunberg – Skolstrejk for Climate

While the world was asleep through the crisis of climate change, it took the actions of just one young schoolgirl to waken us up to the extent of this crisis. Greta Thunberg is a climate change warrior, a figurehead for a vast and growing movement. She is also a young woman who challenges existing notions of leader and leadership. She is autistic with a diagnosis of Asperger Syndrome (now called Level 1 Autism Spectrum Disorder), which is often characterized by differences in social interaction, communication and behaviors, along with struggles coping with an overload of sensory stimulation.

Like 80% of autistic people at some point in their lives (National Autistic Society, 2018), Thunberg has suffered with mental health issues. Obsessive-compulsive disorder (OCD), selective mutism and bouts of anxiety and depression have caused her to miss long periods of school and rapidly lose up to 10 kilos (22 pounds) in weight in only two months' time. She attributes her despair to the lack of attention the existential threat of climate change receives from politicians and the media (Bourke, 2019). Instead of allowing herself to be paralyzed by her fears, she turned these fears into a motivating force for change.

At the time of writing, Thunberg is aged 16, open, articulate, and highly self-aware. At the age of 15, she skipped school, sat down outside the Swedish parliament with a hand painted cardboard banner with the words *skolstrejk for climate* (school strike for climate), and to her own amazement, her action sparked off the global school climate strike movement, *Fridays for Future* (Gould, 2019). From a lone child protester, both passionate and terrified about the lack of action by politicians on climate change and global warming, Greta Thunberg is now a household name, having inspired "strike" action by schoolchildren in more than 70 countries over responsibility for the planet. Once her lone campaign started to attract media attention, it sparked the consciousness particularly, though not exclusively, of young people across the world. Twice in 2019, over a million students in 112 countries around the world joined her call in striking and protesting (Gould, 2019).

Thunberg is now widely recognized across the world, as a model of determination, inspiration, and positive action. She has responded to invitations to address the most powerful and wealthy global citizens, including the British Parliament and the World Economic Forum in Davos (Khan, 2019). She does not hold back in her condemnation of adult, corporate, and governmental pusillanimity, self-interest, and greed. She is unrelenting in her emphasis on their inaction on climate change. What is more uncomfortable when we are destroying the planet to have someone who is still a child telling us in the British and European Parliaments that we require "permanent and unprecedented changes because our house is falling apart"? (Linden, 2019). The emergence of Thunberg as a global leader highlights the temporal inequity of climate change, a burden shrugged off by the old on to the young. "[Our] future was sold," she explained in a speech to the British Parliament, "so that a small number of people could make unimaginable amounts of money" (Thunberg, 2019).

Collectively, through our own actions, the politicians and leaders we elect, the power of multi-national companies to lobby against action on climate change, the get-rich-quick mentality of the shareholders in the fossil-fuel industry leaves the next generation and those that follow with a devastating legacy. Thunberg has received numerous prestigious prizes and awards for her activism including a nomination for the Nobel Peace Prize. She featured on the cover of *Time* magazine in May 2019 and was selected by the same magazine as the "Person of the Year;" she made a carbon-neutral journey across the Atlantic to the United States to join the UN Climate Action Summit hosted in New York in September and traveled carbon free to the relocated Summit hosted by Madrid in December 2019. Some media have described her impact on the world stage as the "Greta Thunberg effect." The impact of the movement inspired by Thunberg is so significant that it is now perceived by the CEO of OPEC (Organization of the Petroleum Exporting Countries), as "the greatest threat" to the fossil-fuel industry (Snaith, 2019).

The leadership characteristics shown by Greta Thunberg include being a role model for her generation. She did not set out to be a role model, rather the courage she displayed in challenging the status quo regarding climate change inspired and empowered global youth to demand action from their politicians and leaders. She is not only a role model for climate action warriors; she has also shown the world that difference is a strength, not a weakness. She is articulate about her diagnosis of Asperger's and states that for her it means that she sees the world differently. She sees the world in black and white and action on climate change is a black and white issue – "either we take meaningful, sustained action now or we don't," in which case we are responsible for the cataclysmic consequences.

Through her words, her passion, her authenticity and her courage, she enabled her generation to take up the baton for action on climate change. A criticism leveled at Thunberg is that she has no vision for the future if carbon emissions are reduced to the necessary levels to mitigate global warming. Her response to this is what might be called cathedral thinking – "we must lay the foundations even though we may not know exactly how to build the ceiling" (Thunberg, 2019) and clearly, her generation and others think likewise.

AOC and the New Green Deal

Along with Greta Thunberg, Alexandria Ocasio-Cortez is one of the world's most powerful voices on climate change. She is clear that addressing the challenge is a social justice issue. Ocasio-Cortez, generally addressed as AOC, has been making waves since 2018 when she was voted in as the Democratic

Representative for New York's congressional district over a long-standing, well-funded incumbent (Wallace-Wells, 2019). At 29 years of age Ocasio-Cortez, the daughter of working-class parents from Puerto Rico and born in the Bronx, is the youngest woman ever to serve in the US Congress. She is one of a number of progressive women politicians elected in 2018 to US Congress. She defines herself as a democratic socialist and frequently comes up against significant challenge from Democrats as well as Republicans for her vision and her core belief in a socially just society and redistribution of wealth. Whether we look to the left or the right in US politics, it is still a sea of grey. Ocasio-Cortez is pushing for meaningful change that empowers everyone and creates a better future for her generation and the generations coming up after her. It is an uphill struggle to shift the current punitive agenda across the United States – but AOC is a strong woman giving hope to, and being nurtured and supported by, her growing millions of followers.

Up until she was elected to Congress, she was earning the minimum wage in a cheap restaurant supporting the family finances. She talks of her time in this work as a galvanizing political experience seeing and hearing the raw reality of the rising inequities in American society (Morris, 2019).

Alexandria Ocasio-Cortez is as impassioned by climate change as Thunberg, understanding climate change as a real, systemic and urgent global problem. She is the main author of the Green New Deal, a Resolution put before the US Congress that seeks to redefine what the climate movement is in the scope of environmental justice, social justice, and economic justice. What is proposed is a stimulus package that aims to address climate change and economic inequality. One of its demands is a transition to 100% renewable energy (Holden, 2018). It is no surprise that the Green New Deal resolution was defeated given that President Donald Trump was himself a climate-change denier as were many in his Republican-led administration, not to mention the key stakeholders in the fossil-fuel industry and members of her own party (Rubin, 2019). Through her astute use of social media, however, AOC amplifies her stance to many millions of followers and ensures the critical issue of climate change does not drown in the sea of grey that surrounds her.

Alexandria Ocasio-Cortez is of the new generation of progressive leaders pushing an alternative leadership narrative with social justice at its core. She gives hope to a sense of a generational rise, a desire to empower rather than punish, to be inclusive, and to push for action rather than rhetoric. As Charlotte Alter who interviewed AOC for *Time* magazine says of her, "no lawmaker in recent memory has translated so few votes into so much political and social capital so quickly" (Alter, 2019). In the same interview, AOC says

> *we can't compromise on transitioning to 100% renewable energy,*
> *on saving our planet, on saving our kids. We have to do these things.*
> *If we want to do them in different ways, that is fine. But we can't*
> *not do them.*

This is not so different from Thunberg saying that action on climate change is "very much a black and white issue, either we take action, or we don't."

Despite the age difference between Alexandria Ocasio-Cortez and Greta Thunberg, there are similarities between them especially when we take a closer look through a leadership fine-focus. Both women show courage in the face of great challenge; they are authentic in their beliefs; they have taken action despite the inevitable opposition; they have inspired a vision that they disseminate in highly effective ways; they epitomize inclusion, and they are role models for challenging the status quo. Given their youth, they have the time and the growing strength in numbers of their followers to navigate the sea of grey they are challenging.

Defying White Power Ideology

White national terrorist attacks are on the rise across the globe. There is plenty of evidence of this. A shocking white supremacist terrorist killing spree in Norway in 2011 killing 77 people (Beaumont, 2011) and the massacre of nine African Americans at a Charleston Methodist Episcopal church in 2015 (Zapatosky, 2017). The attack on a synagogue in Pittsburgh in 2018 (Robertson et al., 2018) and mass shootings in El Paso, Texas, and Dayton, Ohio, in August 2019 (Levin et al., 2019) killing 30 people in one day. These and many other attacks too numerous to detail provide clear evidence that the threat of white supremacist domestic terrorism is on the increase (Bergengruen & Hennigan, 2019). While white nationalist terror attacks are local, the ideology is global. The narrative of the far-right is one of white supremacy, authoritarianism, nativism and a hatred of immigrants, (Beckett & Wilson, 2019).

Since 9/11, the focus of Western national-security agencies has been on Islamic terrorism. Numerous attacks in countries including Britain, France,

Germany and Belgium were perpetrated by lone terrorists radicalized by Jihadi propaganda (Giglio, 2019). This in turn has led to increased Islamophobia due to the megaphone invective against Muslims everywhere (Nelson, 2019), while a blind eye is turned to white nationalist terrorism. Every attack by a white nationalist supremacist, particularly within the United States and Britain, is seriously miscalculated and reported as the actions of "the lone gunman with mental health problems" (Burke, 2019; Metzl & Macleish, 2015).

Jacinda Ardern – Words of Unity from a Global Leader

Jacinda Ardern, Prime Minister of New Zealand, was one of the first global leaders to call out white nationalist terrorism for what it is. New Zealand, a small country with a population of approximately 5 million, located in the southwestern Pacific Ocean suffered an unspeakable domestic terrorist attack on March 15, 2019. An Australian white nationalist supremacist fatally shot 51 Muslims during Friday Prayer in two different mosques in the city of Christchurch. Not only did the terrorist carry out the massacre, he live-streamed the first attack at Al Noor Mosque on Facebook Live for the world to watch, and posted online a 74-page manifesto citing admiration for other supremacists who have gone before him in carrying out unimaginable atrocities in the furtherance of white nationalism (Lawrence & Bennett, 2019).

How does a country respond to such an atrocity? New Zealanders followed their leader, Jacinda Ardern, whose words, actions and humanity marked her out as an outstanding global leader. Ardern rushed to be with the Muslim community, to be present with them after what she termed New Zealand's darkest day. She called out the atrocity for what it is: an act of white nationalist terrorism – something other global leaders show a strong reluctance to acknowledge in the aftermath of such heinous attacks in their own countries. She refused to speak the name of the terrorist. She wore a headscarf to show solidarity with Muslim women whose shattered community was deliberately targeted. Ardern's response resonated loudly not only across New Zealand but globally.

The image of Ardern wearing a headscarf and sharing in the grief of the Muslim community swept around the world. She promised to tighten gun laws in New Zealand and did so (Lyons, 2019). She promised to challenge the power of the tech companies such as Facebook and the responsibilities that come with such power, and is doing so (Willshire, 2019). Most significantly, she showed compassion and humanity. She emphasized inclusivity, solidarity and empathy when she told the Muslim Community in Christchurch *"I am here today to bring with me the grief of all New Zealand. I am here to stand alongside you...."* (Manhire, 2019) and the people of New Zealand did likewise and examined their own collective racist conscience. After all, as Gamal Fouda, the Imam of the Al Noor mosque stated in a speech, "these murders did not come overnight. Rather they were the result of anti-Muslim rhetoric from mainstream political leaders, the media and commentators" (Manhire, 2019).

Ardern became the leader of the then opposition NZ Labour Party in 2017 only weeks before the New Zealand general election. While no stranger to a life in politics having been an active social democrat and progressive thinker for over a decade (Manhire, 2019), Ardern became the youngest woman to lead a government at the age of 37. She became the Labour leader after the incumbent resigned from the position after a historically low poll result for the party. She became the world's second elected head of government to give birth while in office when her daughter was born on June 21, 2018. Her image as a global feminist icon was hugely uplifting for women everywhere; in New Zealand "Jacindamania" (Shuttleworth, 2017) sparked off, such is her appeal as a leader.

Ardern's political goals are informed and framed by her ethos of social justice. Her response to the Christchurch atrocity was authentic and empathetic; she did not have time to ponder it. She spoke from the heart and in accordance with her own personal values and moral compass in a moment of such tragedy. Irrespective of domestic politics, New Zealand has gained the admiration of the world. Ardern's leadership narrative of social justice, inclusion, courage, empathy, her vision for her country and all of its citizens, her authenticity, her insightfulness as a leader have gained her global respect. As with Thunberg and AOC, she gives cause for the world to take note of this new and powerful leadership narrative. There is a vast unbridgeable gulf between Ardern bringing her country together, united in grief, determined to do better, and the bellicose warmongering political rhetoric generally espoused by the strongmen leaders around the world.

Global Leadership and Shifting Geopolitics

Global leadership is in a parlous state and the current geopolitical landscape of chaos impacts on individual nations and states. In Britain, the Brexit referendum has ruptured an already fractious "unity" between the four countries that comprise the United Kingdom. Scotland voted overwhelmingly to remain within the European Union. The majority of Scottish people are angered by the ruling Conservative and Union party dragging Scotland out of Europe in a manner that almost all analysts, many members of parliament (MPs) and economic experts have warned will have disastrous consequences for the whole of Britain (Menon, 2019). Many people see Scotland and the Scottish people as a beacon of hope and are vocal in their view that Brexit is a very English crisis fought over bitterly by the two major British political parties, Labour and the Conservative and Unionist Party. Such is the geopolitical crisis caused by Brexit that the United Kingdom may well break up.

Nicola Sturgeon – Leading Through a Momentous Challenge

The Scottish National Party currently leads in Scottish politics and its leader Nicola Sturgeon, seeing the profoundly negative impact of Brexit in her country and on the Scottish people, will lead Scotland into a second referendum on independence. Not only a brave and bold move but also a clear indication that Scotland's First Minister and her party are putting the people before politics.

Sturgeon entered politics at the same age Greta Thunberg is today. Her "inspiration" for becoming politically active was Margaret Thatcher and the policies of her Tory government. Sturgeon believed it was not right that a party it had not elected should govern Scotland (Sim, 2017). In 1986, she joined the Scottish National Party and has worked tirelessly toward the goal of independence for Scotland ever since. At the time of this writing, she is First Minister of Scotland and the first woman leader of the Scottish National Party. She is also a role model for other global women leaders. Her commitment to an agenda for social justice is at the forefront of her political career.

Examples of Sturgeon's ethos of social justice in action include her government's significant efforts in mitigating the worst effects of the Westminster Tories' austerity measures (Paterson, 2019). Her stance on climate change is clear, supporting the *Fridays for Future* school children's global warming strikes, and declaring a "climate emergency" in her speech at the SNP conference in 2019 (Baynes, 2019) having been inspired by meeting climate campaigners. She is articulate and emphatic about Scotland's need for immigrants, stating that reducing Scotland's immigrant numbers will have devastating consequences for its economy (Gourtsoyan Nis, 2018).

Since becoming First Minister of Scotland, Sturgeon receives a rock-star type of welcome from her supporters wherever she appears (Mac Cormaic, 2019). Her leadership today has never been so critical to her country's future. Sturgeon and the Scottish National Party are pro-Europe and anti-Brexit. In an Independence for Scotland referendum in 2014, the electorate voted 46% for independence and 54% against (BBC Scotland News, 2014). However, the independence referendum took place before the Brexit referendum in 2016. The 2014 Independence Referendum in Scotland was originally billed as a "once in a generation opportunity" with a caveat however, relating to substantially changed political circumstances. Britain leaving the European Union despite Scotland or Northern Ireland voting to remain in the EU, creates this significant change and poses a real threat to the concept of a united Britain. Given the catastrophic impact Brexit is already having on Scotland's economy with worse to come, a growing resentment in Scotland at having toxic policies imposed by a Westminster government Scotland did not vote for, and the increasingly obvious cultural differences between Scotland and England, Sturgeon's job is to secure and win independence for Scotland.

Throughout the Brexit fiasco, leadership has been in short supply from Britain's main partisan political parties. Across much of the country outside of London, people have looked to Scotland and in particular to Sturgeon's leadership. She is respectful, measured and honest in her communications. She is authentic and passionate. She believes in uniting rather than dividing people with different views. Her social justice ethos, inclusivity and compassion necessitate a high level of courage in the face of a divided nation and country.

On the one hand, she and her party are dealing with an ever-changing landscape regarding Brexit and a British government determined to allow no dissent from their increasingly toxic policies and authoritarian regime. On the other hand, she is holding together supporters and followers who are divided in their desire for an independence referendum immediately versus those who would be circumspect about the right moment to hold that referendum. In addition, the British Prime Minister, Boris Johnston, is refusing the Scottish National Party permission to hold another independence referendum (Hughes & Dickie, 2020) but the political fight will continue. Meanwhile there is a very deliberate act of mischief taking place across the increasingly right-wing press. SNP stands for the Scottish *National* Party but increasingly politicians and the compliant media insist on calling it the Scottish *Nationalist* Party. A subtle but profound means of undermining the social justice values of the SNP.

The stakes are very high for Sturgeon, the challenge immense, but more and more people in Scotland are seeing independence as a better way forward than forever being beholden to a Westminster government that appears to care little for any nation but England. It takes courage, resilience and outstanding leadership to effect such a profound change in your nation, the intention of which is to create a better society. A society characterized by inclusion, dignity, renewal of the conditions that enable social mobility, respect for all constituents, and most of all a leadership and governance that is designed to work for all of the population, not only the natural followers of Nicola Sturgeon, the Scottish National Party or the Independence agenda.

RAYS OF HOPE IN RE-IMAGINING GLOBAL LEADERSHIP

Each of the four women leaders observed is facing major twenty-first century global challenges that impact locally and nationally as well as internationally. In the face of toxic strongmen leaders, their bellicose rhetoric and repressive policies it can be difficult to imagine a different approach to leadership, one that recognizes that actions and words have consequences. Irrespective of the immediate challenge or crisis, each of these women has role modeled new twenty-first century narratives of progressive global leadership. Each of them has shown great courage in challenging the status quo in the face of strong resistance from toxic leaders and their followers. Their desire to inspire and empower communities and societies through an emphasis on social justice and inclusion resonates well with a younger generation of voters.

Key characteristics of the new leadership narrative offered by these progressive women leaders include:

- Authenticity – communicating powerful messages with conviction, following their moral compass

- An ability to challenge the increasingly toxic status quo

- Courage in offering an inspiring vision with social justice at its core

- Honesty, respect and integrity – refusing to bow to the insidious rhetoric of people with different views

- Commitment to service – service to the entire constituency, not only followers

- A focus on unity rather than division

- A narrative of empowerment for all members of society

- Inclusion – understanding difference as a strength, not a weakness.

This narrative, which is in its infancy, but which is growing stronger and resonating with a younger generation of voters, offers a blueprint for a different future from that promulgated by our strongmen leaders. It will take great courage for new progressive leaders to follow their moral compass, their "True North" (George & Sims, 2007), and it is incumbent on everyone involved in leadership research, development, education, and practice to give more fulsome support to new leaders genuinely committed to making the planet a better, safer place for all.

REFERENCES

Alter, C. (2019). 'Change Is Closer Than We Think.' Inside Alexandria Ocasio-Cortez's Unlikely Rise. *Time Magazine*. Retrieved June 6, 2019, from https://time.com/longform/alexandria-ocasio-cortez-profile/

Attenborough, D. (2019). Climate change – The Facts BBC One TV. Retrieved August 25, 2019, from https://www.bbc.co.uk/programmes/p076w7g5

Avolio, B. J., & Gardner, W. L. (2005). Authentic leadership development: Getting to the root of positive forms of leadership. *Leadership Quarterly*, 16, 315–338.

Baynes, C. (2019). *The Independent* Scotland declares 'climate emergency' following school strikes. Retrieved September 12, 2019 from https://www.independent.co.uk/environment/climate-change-scotland-emergency-global-warming-nicola-sturgeon-snp-conference-a8891071.html

BBC Scotland News. (2014). Scottish referendum: Scotland votes 'No' to independence. Retrieved September 12, 2019, from https://www.bbc.co.uk/news/uk-scotland-29270441

Beaumont, P. (2011). Norway attacks: At least 92 killed in Oslo and Utøya island. *The Guardian*. Retrieved August 3, 2019, https://www.theguardian.com/world/2011/jul/23/norway-attacks

Beckett, L., & Wilson, J. (2019). 'White power ideology': Why El Paso is part of a growing global threat. *The Guardian*. Retrieved September 4 2019, from https://www.theguardian.com/us-news/2019/aug/04/el-paso-shooting-white-nationalist-supremacy-violence-christchurch

Bergengruen, V., & Hennigan, W. J. (2019). 'We Are Being Eaten From Within.' Why America Is Losing the Battle Against White Nationalist Terrorism. *Time Magazine*. Retrieved August 10, 2019, from https://time.com/5647304/white-nationalist-terrorism-united-states/

Bourke, I. (2019). Greta Thunberg: the teenage climate warrior leading a new global movement. *New Statesman*. Retrieved September 4, 2019, from https://www.newstatesman.com/2019/02/greta-thunberg-teenage-climate-warrior-leading-new-global-movement

Conradi, P. (2018). How serious a threat to global stability are populist leaders like Putin, Trump and Brazil's Jair Bolsonaro? *The Times*. Retrieved April 16, 2019, from https://www.thetimes.co.uk/article/how-serious-a-threat-to-global-stability-are-populist-leaders-like-putin-trump-and-brazils-jair-bolsonaro-xws8r595l/

Elliott, L. (2016). Brexit is a rejection of globalisation. *The Guardian*. Retrieved August 24, 2018 from, https://www.theguardian.com/business/2016/jun/26/brexit-is-the-rejection-of-globalisation/

George, B., & Sims, P. (2007). *True North: Discover your authentic leadership*. JosseyBass.

Giglio, M. (2019). The fight against white nationalism is different. *The Atlantic*. Retrieved September 4, 2019, from https://www.theatlantic.com/politics/archive/2019/08/the-difficulties-of-fighting-white-nationalism/595609/

Golec de Zavala, A., Guerra, R., & Simão, C. (2017). The relationship between the Brexit Vote and individual predictors of prejudice: Collective Narcissism, right wing authoritarianism, social dominance orientation. *Frontiers of Psychology*, (8), 2023–2032.

Gould, L. (2019). How Greta Thunberg's climate strikes became a global movement in a year. *Reuters*. Retrieved September 4, 2019, from https://www.reuters.com/article/us-global-climate-thunberg/how-greta-thunbergs-climate-strikes-became-a-global-movement-in-a-year-idUSKCN1VA001

Gourtsoyan Nis, P. (2018). Nicola Sturgeon says new immigration policy is an 'act of vandalism'. *The Scotsman*. Retrieved September 12, 2019, from https://www.scotsman.com/news/politics/nicola-sturgeon-says-new-immigration-policy-is-an-act-of-vandalism-1-4846342

Hagen, R. (2018). Deforestation suffocates the lungs of the world. *American Security Project*. Retrieved September 3, 2019, from https://www.americansecurityproject.org/deforestation-suffocates-the-lungs-of-the-planet/

Heyman, T. (2019). Teen activist Greta Thunberg makes waves in UK visit. *The National News*. Retrieved September 16, 2021, from https://www.thenationalnews.com/world/europe/teen-activist-greta-thunberg-makes-waves-in-uk-visit-1.852817

Holden, E. (2018). What is the Green New Deal and is it technically possible? *The Guardian*. Retrieved September 16, 2021, from https://www.theguardian.com/environment/2018/dec/29/green-new-deal-plans-proposal-ocasio-cortez-sunrise-movement

Hughes, L., & Dickie, M. (2020). Boris Johnston rejects SNP call for independence referendum *Financial Times get*. Retrieved January 20, 2020, from https://www.ft.com/topics/people/Boris_Johnson

Khan, S. (2019). Davos 2019: Teenage activist tells global elite they are to blame for climate change. *The Independent*. https://www.independent.co.uk/news/world/europe/davos-teenager-speech-climate-change-global-elite-greta-thunberg-swedish-a8747086.html

Knight, S. (2019). The Uncanny Power of Greta Thunberg's Climate-Change Rhetoric. *The New Yorker*. Retrieved September 16, 2021, from https://www.newyorker.com/news/daily-comment/the-uncanny-power-of-greta-thunbergs-climate-change-rhetoric

Lawrence, M., & Bennett, L. (2019). New Zealand's darkest day: 'Our hearts are heavy but our spirit is strong'. *New Zealand Herald*. Retrieved March 20, 2019, from https://www.nzherald.co.nz/nz/news/article.cfm?c_id=1&objectid=12214271

Levin, S., Laughland, O., & Walters, J. (2019). Thirty dead in 13 hours: US reckons with back-to-back mass shootings. *The Guardian*. Retrieved September 9, 2019, from https://www.theguardian.com/world/2019/aug/04/mass-shootings-el-paso-texas-dayton-ohio

Linden, I. (2019). We had all better hope that Great Thunberg's impact is permanent. *The Article*. Retrieved January 14, 2020, from https://www.thearticle.com/we-had-all-better-hope-that-greta-thunbergs-impact-is-permanent

Lyons, K. (2019). Jacinda Ardern bans all military-style semi-automatic guns and assault rifles – As it happened. *The Guardian*. Retrieved September 12, 2019, from https://www.theguardian.com/world/live/2019/mar/21/new-zealand-shooting-jacinda-ardern-to-make-policy-announcement-live-updates

Mac Cormaic, R. (2019). Sturgeon visit offers glimpse into Brexit diplomacy game. *The Irish Times*. Retrieved September 12, 2019, from https://www.irishtimes.com/news/world/europe/sturgeon-visit-offers-glimpse-into-brexit-diplomacy-game-1.2891054

Manhire, T. (2019). Jacinda Ardern: 'Very little of what I have done has been deliberate. It's intuitive'. *The Guardian*. Retrieved September 12, 2019, from https://www.theguardian.com/world/2019/apr/06/jacinda-ardern-intuitive-courage-new-zealand

Menon, A. (2019). Don't buy the bluff. Here's the truth about no-deal Brexit. *The UK in a Changing Europe*. Retrieved September 12, 2019, from https://ukandeu. ac.uk/dont-buy-the-bluff-heres-the-truth-about-no-deal-brexit/

Metzl, J. M., & Macleish, K. T. (2015). Mental illness, mass shootings and the politics of American Firearms. *American Journal of Public Health, 105*(2), 240–249. Retrieved September 16, 2021, from https://www.ncbi.nlm.nih.gov/pmc/ articlesPMC4318286

Morris, A. (2019). Alexandria Ocasio-Cortez wants the country to think big. *Rolling Stone*. Retrieved April 14, 2019, from https://www.rollingstone.com/politics/ politics-features/alexandria-ocasio-cortez-congress-interview-797214/

National Autistic Society. (2018). What is Autism? Retrieved September 4, 2019, from https://www.autism.org.uk

Nelson, F. (2019). Banning Islamophobia would suppress debate – Just ask a liberal Muslim. *The Telegraph*. Retrieved June 10, 2019, from https://www.telegraph.co.uk/ politics/2019/05/16/banning-islamophobia-would-suppress-debate-just-ask-liberal/

Paterson, K. (2019). *The National* Scotland can do no more to mitigate Tory austerity, UN report says. Retrieved September 12, 2019, from https://www. thenational.scot/news/17657096.scotland-can-do-no-more-to-mitigate-tory-austerity-un-report-says/

Rachman, G. (2018). *Asia's Rise and America's Decline from Obama to Trump and Beyond*. Other Press.

Robertson, C., Mele, C., & Tavernise, S. (2018). 11 Killed in Synagogue Massacre; Suspect Charged With 29 Counts. *The New York Times*. Retrieved September 9, 2019, from https://www.nytimes.com/2018/10/27/us/active-shooter-pittsburgh-synagogue-shooting.html

Rubin, J. (2019). Republican climate-change deniers should study the E.U. elections. *Washington Post*. Retrieved August 3, 2019, from https://www.washingtonpost.com/ opinions/2019/05/28/republican-climate-change-deniers-should-study-eu-elections/

Sabbagh, D. (2019). Owen Jones: Attackers targeted me for my politics. *The Guardian*. Retrieved August 28, 2019, from https://www.theguardian.com/uk-news/2019/ aug/18/owen-jones-attackers-targeted-me-for-my-politics

Shuttleworth, K. (2017). Jacindamania: Rocketing rise of New Zealand Labour's fresh political hope. Retrieved September 12, 2019, from https://www.theguardian. com/world/2017/sep/02/jacindamania-rocketing-rise-of-new-zealand-labours-fresh-political-hope

Sim, P. (2017). Who is Nicola Sturgeon? A profile of the SNP leader. *BBC Scotland News*. Retrieved September 12, 2019, from https://www.bbc.co.uk/news/ uk-scotland-25333635

Snaith, E. (2019). Greta Thunberg thanks Opec chief for complaining about 'threat' of climate activists. *Independent*. Retrieved September 4, 2019, from https://www. independent.co.uk/environment/greta-thunberg-opec-climate-change-campaigners-oil-sector-mohammed-barkindo-a8990011.html

Stefani, L. (2015). Inclusive, authentic, values-based or opportunistic – What counts as leadership Today? A case study of Angela, Donald, Francis and Helen. In A. Boitano, R. Lagomarsino Dutra, & H. E. Schockman (Eds.), *Breaking the zero sum game: Transforming societies through inclusive leadership* (pp. 438–459). International Leadership Association Building Bridges Series. Emerald Publishing Ltd, UK.

The Economist Group. (2019). Far-right and very wrong: Why white nationalist terrorism is a global threat. *The Economist*. Retrieved September 4, 2019, from https://www.economist.com/international/2019/03/21/why-white-nationalist-terrorism-is-a-global-threat

Thunberg, G. (2019). 'Our house is on fire': Greta Thunberg, 16, urges leaders to act on climate. *The Guardian*. Retrieved August 30, 2019, from https://www.theguardian.com/environment/2019/jan/25/our-house-is-on-fire-greta-thunberg16-urges-leaders-to-act-on-climate

UNFCC. (2018). United Nations Framework Convention on Climate Change. Retrieved August 5, 2018, from https://unfccc.int/sites/default/files/resource/UN-Climate-Change-Annual-Report-2018.pdf

Wallace-Wells, B. (2019). Alexandria Ocasio-Cortez and the Legacy of the Bernie Sanders Movement. *The New Yorker*. Retrieved September 4, 2019, from https://www.newyorker.com/news/news-desk/alexandria-ocasio-cortez-and-the-legacy-of-the-bernie-sanders-movement

Watts, J. (2019). Greta Thunberg, schoolgirl climate change warrior: 'Some people can let things go. I can't'. *The Guardian*. Retrieved September 16, 2021, from https://www.theguardian.com/world/2019/mar/11/greta-thunberg-schoolgirl-climate-change-warrior-some-people-can-let-things-go-i-cant

Willshire, K. (2019). Leaders and tech firms pledge to tackle extremist violence online. *The Guardian*. Retrieved September 12, 2019, from https://www.theguardian.com/world/live/2019/mar/21/new-zealand-shooting-jacinda-ardern-to-make-policy-announcement-live-updates

WWF. (2019). World Wildlife Fund – Impacts of Climate Change. Retrieved September 3, 2019, from https://www.wwf.org.au/what-we-do/climate/impacts-of-global-warming

Zapatosky, M. (2017). Charleston Church Shooter: 'I would like to make it crystal clear, I do not regret what I did'. *The Washington Post*. Retrieved September 4, 2019, https://www.washingtonpost.com/world/national-security/charleston-church-shooter-i-would-like-to-make-it-crystal-clear-i-do-not-regret-what-i-did/2017/01/04/05b0061e-d1da-11e6-a783-cd3fa950f2fd_story.html

15

LEADERSHIP CHALLENGES FROM THE EDGE OF EXPERIENCE IN THE GLOBAL CRISIS CONTEXT

MICHAEL COX AND JAMES WARN

Diverse global crisis contexts create emergent disruptions and changes that challenge leadership in novel and unexpected ways. The pressures and forces unleased by the interconnectivity and ambiguity of these crises can overwhelm traditional institutional problem-solving and set in chain further crisis events that can result in fragmentation across societies. The emergent problems associated with crises can challenge the capacity of leadership to leverage the required surge capacity across state, institutional and organizational boundaries. In crisis contexts, leadership operates at the edge of known experience where problems are novel, intricate, and interconnected.

Leadership at the edge of experience is about responding to these emergent contexts by working with coalitions to adapt and pursue viable action that achieves a coherent response. The failure of traditional approaches in making sense of complex inter-connected problems can be found in the *say-do* gap (i.e., the discrepancy between words, or policy, and action, or outcomes).

This chapter examines how leaders can think narrow frameworks that limit or prevent them from achieving an understanding of more viable options. The chapter concludes with examination of approaches to thinking that enable leaders to seek coherence rather than risk fragmentation.

THE NATURE OF THE PROBLEM AND FRAGMENTATION

Particularly challenging are those problems, such as the current COVID-19 crisis, that span traditional organizational boundaries and are increasingly global problems that cross the boundaries of nations and fractured states. Leaders today face sets of problems that have no clear definition, can be symptomatic of other problems, can be interdependent with other action, and are open to different levels of representation and explanation (Rittel & Webber, 1973).

Specifically these complex problems manifest in the areas of food and water security, biological threats (such as highly infectious viruses), human security in parts of the developing world, emerging impacts of climate change and environmental variability, managing global energy demands, an increasing world population and concomitant sustainability, addressing factors triggering mass migration across state borders, managing displaced communities, managing impacts of waste and pollution on the biosphere, distribution of resources and wealth between developed and developing countries (as well as within developing countries), aging populations in the developed world, the integration of AI into social systems and the economic, social, and political shocks associated with crises when they manifest rapidly (Costanza et al., 2007; Hanjra & Qureshi, 2010).

THE NEED FOR SALIENT LEADERSHIP

A key expectation of leadership in crisis contexts is that it tackles change and ideally creates a better situation. Leadership is seen as particularly pertinent for dealing with non-routine or those more challenging problems that frustrate managerial routines and evade the lessons learnt of prior organizational encounters (Grint, 2005; Heifetz & Linsky, 2002).

Leaders are involved as co-participants with other actors in the social construction of understandings of leadership and organizational settings that enable meaningful understanding of the actors' participation in organizational settings. The leader is likely to have a privileged role in these interactions due to the authority relationships and structures of power in organizations. Although the extent to which these meaningful understandings are related to organizational performance is contingent on a range of internal and external factors, leadership remains a vital force in shaping direction and understanding in the organization (Warn & Cox, 2014).

Crisis scenarios are not solved by fear, but by making sense of the context that enables leaders at all levels to bring about positive change. Traditional borders in this context are blurred and shaped by political, professional, and countervailing values, influence, and power. A starting point for leaders is in making sense of the context, meta-narratives of leaders and followers with different identities, ideology, motives, and intentions.

ASSUMPTIONS AND IDEOLOGICAL BARRIERS TO GLOBAL LEADERSHIP COLLABORATION

Recent experience of the various attempts at implementation of collaborative leadership approaches in crisis contexts reveals a gap between policy and practice (the *say-do* gap). The issues can be assembled under three broad headings. One concerns the dominance of a particular mental model, and usually this is driven by the circumstances surrounding the creation of the intervention as a means to ensure human security. The second relates to the ambiguity of the problem and the failure to address it as a complex problem that will require evolutionary understanding rather than a problem that can be solved with a narrow optic approach (Varhola & Varhola, 2006). Integrative approaches require a leadership perspective to see a crisis context through a wide, rather than narrow, spectrum. The final heading refers to the consequential nature of complex problems and inherent interconnectedness of the various components of these problems.

Dominance of One Mental Model

At first glance, a dominant mental model would appear to offer a cohesive set of interpretations and validate clear actions that would achieve coherency. In some circumstances, this might be the case. However, the very nature of a dominant mental model means that it serves as a filter to perceive the world from a particular perspective, in which information is selectively organized and interpreted. The selectivity protects the model from the emergence of dissonant information, a focus on congruent information and perpetuates it by its proponents engaging in self-confirmation bias.

Members of professional groups and institutions enact a mental model that makes sense of the world and enables their members to deal with certain sets of problems by applying knowledge in a systematic and proven manner. However, this professional optic can become a barrier to understanding complex problems where solutions cannot be constructed within the domain of any particular professional group. For instance, traffic congestion cannot be solved by building more freeways (i.e., adopting a traffic engineering lens) whilst ignoring related issues of urban planning, migration patterns, economic development policies, demographics, and housing availability.

Organizations by nature of their information hierarchies, power structures and pervasive cultures evolve these mental models, or what Bettis and Prahalad (1995) have described as dominant logics. Although this logic provides the organization with stability in its strategic environment, it can also impede the organization's capacity to adapt to a changing environment. Fragmentation emerges as the organization fails to adapt to changing environments in which its dominant logic becomes less accurate and less able to guide behaviors that achieve outcomes (Sull, 1999).

More pervasively in societies, ideological maps serve as the genesis of meta-narratives that reduce ambiguity and complexity by simplifying diverse events and experiences into a single comprehensive explanation. The meta-narrative acts as a schema that provides meaning and coherency to diverse events and experiences. Although a meta-narrative can serve as an organizing scheme for political stability or even political action, the actual everyday reality of individuals is likely to be more disjointed and discrete (Zompetti & Moffitt, 2009).

Ambiguity

In everyday understanding, ambiguity refers to inexactness or vagueness. It is generally seen as a negative characteristic in projects or as a source of confusion. For instance, a question identified in the management literature was, "Why is it that firms find it difficult to imitate the success of other firms?" This problem of correctly ascertaining the factors that have resulted in superior performance was defined by Steven Lippman and Richard Rumelt (1982) as causal ambiguity. Causal ambiguity refers to the uncertainty that exists in the relationship between inputs, actions, and outcomes. This phenomenon means that it may not be possible to provide clear causal explanations of events in complex social systems. In policy decision-making, it refers to the capacity to hold more than one interpretation of a policy problem

(Cairny, 2019). The implication is that decision-makers will need to tolerate and be aware of uncertainty in their planning. The leader must adapt a flexibility of mind to adapt to this uncertainty and be able to communicate understanding of this ambiguity to followers. Leadership strategy objectives require a robust form of scenario analysis and in-depth understanding of the locale of operation to assess the exigencies and level of risks and probability of opportunities to succeed.

Ambiguity is found in social planning where policy actions do not result in expected outcomes. That is, there is no simple correlation between policy initiatives and social outcomes. A sign that policies have failed to adequately address complexity occurs when additional expenditures result in diminishing returns (Redman et al., 2007). An example in Australia is where despite a real increase of 14% in Government funding for education, there has been no positive correlation at many grade levels for improvements in basic literacy, numeracy, and writing competency (Joseph, 2019).

An intolerance of uncertainty can result in binary thinking, which is an attempt to remove the presence of ambiguity when attempting to explain complex phenomenon. The binary constructs phenomena around two opposites, with one pole being perceived as good and safe and the other as bad and dangerous. Reliance on binary thinking creates anxiety since the world is seen as bad or dangerous place where one's own identity or safety is constantly threatened (Lukianoff & Haidt, 2018).

Binary thinking emerges when political opponents set up policy choice in terms of mutually exclusive opposites. This thinking is often evident in political discourse, news media and social media that projects a biased worldview of choices and options. In these binary worldviews, simple choices are amplified (Small & Warn, 2020). Neither of these opposites will provide a satisfactory explanation of events but political messaging aims to polarize individuals into either of one of two pre-determined camps. This approach is divisive since it accentuates the differences between people in society and attempts to fabricate antagonism between these two camps. Identity politics is a manifestation of this binary as it defines an individual in terms of set of exclusive identities. Fragmentation in society occurs as identity politics emerges as a dominant way of understanding issues in society (Fukuyama, 2018).

It is useful to distinguish between the concept of a binary opposition and binary thinking. The concept of a binary opposition has been used to explore the meaning of cultural narratives, where understanding is set up around paired meanings, where a word will be associated with another word, that acts as its opposite (Derrida, 1981a). However, this pairing is not neutral, since one pole is culturally subordinated to the other (e.g., male–female; nature–culture) (Derrida, 1981b). Although the structure of meaning between words is important for understanding cultural experience, an over-reliance on interpretation using binary oppositions is likely to constrain thinking about ambiguous phenomena.

Binary rhetoric can increase tensions and misunderstanding of opposing views in a crisis context. Binary sets up one side against the other, and typically one side is seen as good or at least better in some significant way to the other. Binary rhetoric can be used to shape a political discourse that imbues choices with moral implications. For instance, in the aftermath of the September 11, 2001, attacks, the United States President George W. Bush increasingly relied on binaries, initially "good versus evil" to contrast the United States against the terrorists, and later in the speech further developed his meaning with the binary of "Freedom and fear are at war" (p. 4). The use of these binaries in his rhetoric was intended to shape media reporting and public opinion (Coe et al., 2004). The initial US military action was directed against al Qaeda and other forces in Afghanistan but, as forecast by President Bush in an address in 2001, the war on terror would "not end until every terrorist group of global reach has been found, stopped and defeated" (Bush, 2001, p. 2). The speech foreshadowed further US military interventions and over a decade of the subsequent fragmentation of societies in the Middle East. Even today, the dynamics of complexity are being seen in the continued political instability in that region.

A sign that a social discourse has fallen into a binary is when three or four-word slogans have replaced discussion (Macmillan, 2019). A reliance on slogans and Twitter posts promote conflict, destroys harmony and, by presenting opposing views as existential threats, sets in motion the forces of fragmentation in society. To counter fragmentation, the role of responsible leadership is to work from principles that create dialogue rather than division.

Complex Interconnectedness

Public policy action can become fragmented in the face of complex problems, and poor policy responses can result in fragmentation across society. Fragmentation is likely to occur under conditions of social complexity, where there are diverse stakeholder views and interests, combined with the complexity (or wickedness) of the problem itself (Conklin, 2006). The notion of a wicked problem was developed by Rittel and Webber (1973) who defined 10 characteristics of such a problem. Important aspects of such problems are that they cannot be defined in any simple way, as such, it is not possible to find a definite solution. Furthermore, any attempt to solve them will set in train waves of consequences that cannot be predicted in advance.

The 2003 invasion of Iraq was militarily successful and was completed in a matter of weeks, concluding with the capture of Baghdad. A US-led administration was put in charge of rebuilding Iraq, but after the disbanding of the Iraqi army and the dismissal of many government officials, who had been members of the Baathist party, sectarian violence began to escalate. Eventually the continued violence become so destabilizing that it verged on being a civil war and in 2007 the United States sent 170,000 troops back into Iraq in order to regain military control. Many of the best officers in the Iraqi Army had been Sunni, and they increasingly became involved in the sectarian violence against the Shiite government of Iraq, and eventually many of them provided leadership for the rise of ISIS and its attack on Iraqi forces in 2014 (Thompson, 2015). The policymaking in regard to Iraq demonstrates an attempt to deal with single problems rather than addressing the situation as a complex interconnected problem. The tame solutions had unintended consequences and eventually contributed to destabilization and fragmentation.

The challenge of globalization has led to fragmentation of traditional stakeholders. While the globe only has the boundaries of shoreline, the map on the ground is shaped by borders, identity, passions, religions, and ethnicities. Reflection and perspective are required to assess perceived crises, opportunities, and threats. Increasingly, the existing map becomes blurred as former opponents share information systems and traditional gatekeepers are undermined by external gate-breakers using sophisticated algorithms and emergent technologies.

The consequential nature of complex problems and inherent interconnectedness of the various aspects of a problem pose a serious challenge for policymakers whose policy machinery assumes clearly defined problems (i.e., tame problems) that can be addressed with concrete identifiable actions. Complexity means that there are no simple cause and effects, and that impact of feedback loops in the system can drive unexpected outcomes. The danger is that policymakers attempt to tame a complex problem by oversimplifying it with the prospect of being able to take action with available tools and resources (Rittel & Webber, 1973). However, this policy action can set in train a sequence of events that blend the seemingly facile into a new set of problems.

THE CRISIS OF CORONAVIRUS

During the year 2020, the Coronavirus (COVID-19) pandemic has raged all over the world, and government and health authorities have struggled to keep it in check. Recently, there have been encouraging indications that vaccines would be available by early 2021. However, events are still unfolding, with increasing cases across many parts of the world, and much more needs to be understood about the origins of the virus, its epidemiology, and the toll that it has imposed on the world, along with the longer-term consequences. In the meantime, the three factors discussed above can be used as a lens to make some initial observations about the responses of key actors.

Reliance on a Simple Mental Model of the Context

Some responses to dealing with COVID-19 were construed very simply, as single step solutions, such as wait for herd immunity, wear masks, have extensive lockdowns, or wait for a vaccine. While each of these responses might have been effective if implemented within a wider epidemiologically focused strategy, by themselves they were likely to have only limited benefit. Other examples of a simple mental model being employed were the circulation of conspiracy theories, for example claims that the virus was a hoax or even a bioweapon (Imhoff & Lamberty, 2020).

Intolerance of Ambiguity

Ambiguity arose due to the time gap between being infected and the time to show visible symptoms, the variability in symptoms across different age groups, and incidence of testing in the community. Furthermore, non-aligned responses between different state authorities masked the spread and impact of the virus or in some cases impaired effective health responses for dealing with the virus (Abutaleb et al., 2020). Public uncertainty over the virus engendered amongst people a sense of fear which was intensified by the confusion and misinformation spread on traditional and social media by a plethora of commentators being promoted by as experts (Tagliabue et al., 2020). In response, politicians who imposed draconian lockdowns were perceived to be strong and decisive by many commentators as well as those in the electorate (Kerrissey & Edmondson, 2020). Rather than supporting people to manage the ambiguity, the political response tended to identify a simple message to allay fear.

A Failure to Recognize the Interconnectedness of Factors

The novel aspects of COVID-19 create a complexity of problems for state actors. Responses such as lockdowns that address one aspect of the problem (i.e., transmission) produce other effects that are quite adverse. The immediate effect of a lockdown is the cessation of economic and social activity, which in turn impacts on people's livelihoods, social cohesion, and mental health, and eventually the deterioration of the local economy and state budgets. There was a tendency for leaders to address the complexity of the problem by relying on a simple sequential plan, i.e., lockdown followed by a recovery roadmap (Howard & McElroy, 2020). However, such an approach ignores the systemic impacts as well as the amplification and feedback loops of the initial lockdown.

The Response to COVID-19 in Australia

It is worth noting the situation in Australia where, by the beginning of December 2020, there had been approximately 908 deaths (mainly in the aged care sector) related to COVID-19 and there were an estimated 61 active cases (Australian Department of Health, 2020). These are amazing numbers compared to the extent of the COVID-19 spread in most of the world.

A combination of external factors and quick government action mitigated the spread of the virus in Australia. Australia is an island nation with a federal government, and the Prime Minister acted quickly in early 2020 to stop most international flights into Australia, and to require mandatory 14-day quarantine in hotels for the reduced flow of overseas arrivals. Also, he offered the support of defense personnel to complement the state police in monitoring the restricted movement of people. However, the Federal government found that some of its policies could not be uniformly enacted as the State premiers activated their own emergency powers and pursued their own public measures in response to the virus. Notably, the state government in Victoria failed to set up a viable hotel quarantine scheme as well as failing to resource an effective contact tracing system to identify outbreaks in the community. As a result, the virus was transmitted into the wider community, and particularly in the aged care sector in Victoria, and over 90% of the deaths in Australia can be traced to this failure by the state government of Victoria. The state government responded to the crisis by imposing on the city of Melbourne a draconian 112-day lockdown, which restricted movement for essential shopping to a 5-km radius, closed schools, gyms, restaurants, religious gatherings, beaches, most retail outlets and imposed an unprecedented 8 p.m. to 5 a.m. curfew on its populace. The Victorian Government struggled to demonstrate how some of these measures were based on medical advice.

A useful comparison can be made with the situation in the bordering state of NSW where the Premier adopted an integrated policy approach that addressed epidemiological factors as well as maintaining economic and social activity. Initially, restrictions were placed on movement in public and public gatherings, but these were progressively eased within months. Health officials provided a clear health message to change social behaviors and to gain social cooperation (around social distancing, hand washing, use of sanitizers) and resourced a comprehensive contact tracing program and informed the public of precise locations of potential infection. Extra precautions were taken to prevent the spread of the virus into the aged care sector.

Although the full impact of the different policies between the two states remains to be seen the comparison offers opportunity to examine consequential impacts from a complex systems perspective. The situation in Australia compared to other countries attests to how unique factors can interact with policy responses to produce different outcomes. Small differences in policy and its implementation can result in drastic differences in outcomes. This complexity means that simple analysis of cause and effect may be beguiling but ultimately deceptive. However, some of the impacts are becoming apparent, and initial indications are that the COVID-19 and differing responses have impaired social and political cohesion within countries (Jani, 2020) and increased the likelihood of fragmentation of inter country arrangements (Marin, 2020).

OVERCOMING FRAGMENTATION

Fragmentation creates a challenge for leadership, since the influence of a leader is often derived from promoting the products of fragmentation (e.g., the fear evoked by the us vs them binary). Identity politics can provide a way for a leader to fuel fear and outrage around a social binary to gain traction with followers. Lukianoff and Haidt (2018) call this approach "common enemy identity politics" and distinguish it from leaders who can unify people through articulating a common identity. Martin Luther King Junior is a popular example of a leader who unified people through articulating a common identity (Lukianoff & Haidt, 2018). In contrast, common enemy identity politics attempts to define and distinguish groups based on a set of features, and to blame those not included in the groups for the perceived wrongs in the world.

Appealing to a common identity is not the same thing as proposing a form of universalism where everyone must subscribe to the same set of values and beliefs (Fukuyama, 2018). Rather, the work of the leader is to explore the tension between the two alternatives to explicate the concerns of people and the potentially unify understandings. The goal is to articulate the values and shared beliefs that enable coexistence and coherence.

A key role of leadership in countering fragmentation is the facilitation of making sense of things, or what Karl Weick (1995) has called "sensemaking," which is an ongoing and driven effort to understand linkages between people, places, events, and actions (Klein et al., 2006). Sensemaking can be understood as "a motivated, continuous effort to understand connections (which can be among people, places, and events) in order to anticipate their trajectories and act effectively" (Klein et al., 2006, p. 71). For Weick (1995), sensemaking is not simply interpretation, it includes "the ways people generate what they interpret" (Weick, 1995, p. 13). Sensemaking is triggered by the confusion or disorientation associated with an unexpected event and is ongoing as people attempt to make retrospective sense of events (Weick, 1995, 2010). The role of the leader is to guide the sensemaking process by creating a set of interactions which enable stakeholder sensemaking and sense-giving and at the same time contribute actively to the process (Maitlis & Sonenshein, 2010). The impact of leadership emerges in this interaction under tension and its value is dependent on the interconnectivity achieved and the possible actions identified (Kerr, 2014).

The sensemaking process can be guided by techniques and models that promote a shared understanding of the issues. For instance, dialogue mapping is a technique that provides a diagrammatic representation of different understandings of a problem, as well as listing the advantages and disadvantages of potential responses (Conklin, 2006). A number of dialogue methods have been used in the real-world problem-solving of complex problems with different methods (e.g., nominal group technique and appreciative inquiry) being more suitable for different types of questions (Bojer et al., 2006). Dialogue methods enable a more diverse and fuller understanding of a problem to be developed and shared amongst stakeholders. Additionally, by engaging in the dialogue process, participants are more likely to develop a sense of ownership on working together to tackle the problem.

Whilst tame problems can be addressed by managerial styles of leadership (Yukl, 1989), complex problems will require more adaptive leadership approaches (Heifetz et al., 2009). The Cynefin framework (Snowden & Boone, 2007) is an example of a framework that recognizes the need for different leadership approaches depending on the context of the problem. For instance, a complicated problem, such as a new software system for an airliner, might require leadership through a process of expert analysis; whereas a complex problem might require leadership that can facilitate a more evolutionary process of communication and understanding and involve higher levels of sustained collaboration, as well as maintaining the tension until patterns in the problem context can be discerned (Snowden & Boone, 2007). Rather than seeking cause and effect, leaders will need to adopt a systems perspective. The implications for leadership are the need to avoid hasty decision-making and manage distress from followers until some of the key dynamics of the complex system can be understood (Head & Alford, 2015; Heifetz et al., 2009).

The collaborative framework identifies a set of mindsets that can operate sometimes contemporaneously in the same geographical locale. These mindsets create a set of constraining assumptions and perceptions of opportunities for leaders operating in the same locale but with a differing mental model of that locale. The professional optic of the key actors will result in differing assessments over the rate and extent of progress and the efficacy of different actions. Also, stakeholders will have differing opinions based on their own personal situation and any particular ideological persuasion that they might adopt. Any outcome will be subject to a range of interpretations; and, in countries where there is independent and diverse media, this discussion could be both informative and critical.

Forming an overlapping understanding and shared commitment toward complex problem-solving requires integrative leadership that can create and maintain collaboration (Crosby & Bryson, 2010). The challenge for integrative leadership is to work across boundaries, bring diverse groups together to create shared meaning, and collaborate on specific projects directed at remedying complex problems. Integrative leaders can create spaces to enable dialogue between individuals as well as between groups. The process of dialogue is to share understandings so as to create a more comprehensive and differentiated understanding of complex problems (Senge, 1990). Tackling the complexity of problems depends on recognizing the interconnectedness between the elements of apparently different problems. Communication in shared spaces can make mutual knowledge possible (San Martín-Rodríguez et al., 2005). Collaboration founded on active communication enables leaders to achieve sensemaking and to build coherency through shared actions.

The contemporary leader is a key actor in a social construct where salient leadership sensemaking requires leveraging information and influence to engage followers by emotion, logic, and persuasion. Leadership in the contemporary context is to achieve understanding by making sense of a grammatical universe (Burke, 1969). This new leadership territory is a locale where understanding the actors, players, stage, and contextual stressors co-exist in shaping meta-narratives and sensemaking. To develop a constructive dialogue the leader needs to recognize opposing forces and requires a Hegelian dialectic (Wood, 2005) to understand and identify ways to reconcile to a higher truth to achieve mutual acceptance.

Although communication is important, the road to coherence requires groups and organizations to join together and work toward shared goals. In the public sector, there is increasing awareness of the need for evolving "whole of government" leadership approaches, especially when tackling problems that cross typical government department areas of responsibilities (Christensen & Lægreid, 2007). The "joined up" approach to policy implementation has been especially relevant for actors working in complex locales, such as restorative interventions in crisis scenarios in fragile states and in societal scenarios (such as a pandemic or an environmental crisis). These interventions typically involve a set of institutions, defense, diplomacy, development, and commerce required to operate in some unexpected and undefined ways with no clear outcome or end point (Warn et al., 2012). These organizational arrangements complement, and only are effective, if founded on the shared communication and sense of mutual purpose already formed by integrative leadership. It is, therefore, pivotal that policymakers clearly articulate the policy objectives and impacts on multiple stakeholders to guide leadership actions of those serving and leading in responding to crisis contexts.

CONCLUSIONS

It is posited that the theoretical understanding of leadership in the global crisis context requires more reflection, critique, and re-evaluation of the context to meet the challenge of leading in a changing inter-connected world. The research findings and chapter submission support the need for an integrative leadership framework for foregrounding the global crisis context to enable future leaders to adapt to an era of uncertainty and complexity. The framework would enable an assessment of leadership capability by identifying empirically justified linkages between the individual, organizational pressures, contextual factors, and the quality and impact of the leader's decision-making.

Crisis cannot always be solved and may not have a determined end point. Importantly, the leadership challenge requires emergent approaches for cooperation, collaboration, and communication to serve and lead in an unconquerable world. This chapter seeks to advance leadership education and leadership development in understanding the impact of mental models, ambiguity, and complexity in the contemporary global crisis context.

REFERENCES

Abutaleb, Y., Dawsey, J., Nakashima, E., & Miller. G. (2020, April 4). The U.S. was beset by denial and dysfunction as the coronavirus raged. The Washington Post. https://www.washingtonpost.com/national-security/2020/04/04/coronavirus-government-dysfunction/?arc404=true

Bettis, R. A., & Prahalad, C. K. (1995). The dominant logic: Retrospective and extension. *Strategic Management Journal*, 16(1), 5–14.

Bojer, M. M., Roehl, H., Knuth, M., & Magner, C. (2006). Mapping dialogue. A research project profiling dialogue tools and processes for social change: The German Technical Co-Operation (GTZ) Project: Support to the HIV/AIDS Programme of the Nelson Mandela Foundation, 10.

Burke, K. (1969). *A grammar of motives*. University of California Press.

Bush, G. (2001). *Address to a Joint Session of Congress and the American People*. The White House President George Bush. https://georgewbush-whitehouse.archives.gov/news/releases/2001/09/20010920-8.html

Cairny, P. (2019). *Fostering evidence-informed policy making: Uncertainty versus ambiguity*. National Collaborating Centre for Healthy Public Policy. https://www.ncchpp.ca/165/publications.ccnpps?id_article=1930

Christensen, T., & Lægreid, P. (2007). The whole-of-government approach to public sector reform. *Public Administration Review*, 67(6), 1059–1066.

Coe, K., Domke, D., Graham, E. S., John, S. L., & Pickard, V. W. (2004). No shades of gray: The binary discourse of George W. Bush and an echoing press. *Journal of Communication*, 54(2), 234–252.

Conklin, J. (2006). *Dialogue mapping. Building shared understanding of wicked problems.* John Wiley & Sons.

Costanza, R., Graumlich, L., & Steffen, W. L. (2007). Sustainability or collapse. In R. Costanza, L. Graumlich, & W. L. Steffen (Eds.), *Sustainability or collapse? An integrated history and future of people on Earth* (pp. 3–17). MIT Press.

Crosby, B. C., & Bryson, J. M. (2010). Integrative leadership and the creation and maintenance of cross-sector collaborations. *The Leadership Quarterly*, 21(2), 211–230.

Derrida, J. (1981a). *Dissemination.* (B. Johnson, Trans). University of Chicago. (Original work published 1972).

Derrida, J. (1981b). *Positions.* (A. Bass, Trans). University of Chicago Press. (Original work published 1972).

Fukuyama, F. (2018). *Identity: The demand for dignity and the politics of resentment.* Farrar, Straus and Giroux.

Grint, K. (2005). Problems, problems, problems: The social construction of 'leadership'. *Human Relations*, 58(11), 1467–1494.

Haidt, J., & Lukianoff, G. (2018). *The coddling of the American mind: How good intentions and bad ideas are setting up a generation for failure.* Penguin UK.

Hanjra, M. A., & Qureshi, M. E. (2010). Global water crisis and future food security in an era of climate change. *Food Policy*, 35(5), 365–377.

Head, B. W., & Alford, J. (2015). Wicked problems: Implications for public policy and management. *Administration & Society*, 47(6), 711–739.

Heifetz, R. A., Grashow, A., & Linsky, M. (2009). *The practice of adaptive leadership.* Harvard Business Press.

Heifetz, R. A., & Linsky, M. (2002). Leading with an open heart. *Leader to Leader*, 26, 28–33.

Howard, J., & McElroy, N. (2020, 27 September). Coronavirus Australia news: Victorian Premier Daniel Andrews details Melbourne's move into second step on COVID-19 recovery roadmap. *ABC News.* https://www.abc.net.au/news/2020-09-27/coronavirus-australia-live-news-covid19-melbourne-daniel-andrews/12707120

Jani, A. (2020). Preparing for COVID-19's aftermath: Simple steps to address social determinants of health. *Journal of the Royal Society of Medicine*, 113(6), 205–207.

Joseph, B. (2019). *We've set lower bars, not raised the results*. Centre for Independent Studies. https://www.cis.org.au/commentary/articles/weve-set-lower-bars-not-raised-the-results/

Kerr, F. (2014). *Creating and leading adaptive organisations: The nature and practice of emergent logic*. Doctoral dissertation, University of Adelaide, Adelaide. Retrieved from https://digital.library.adelaide.edu.au/dspace/bitstream/2440/91144/2/01front.pdf

Kerrissey, M. J., & Edmondson, A. C. (2020, August 13). What good leadership looks like during this pandemic. *Harvard Business Review*. https://hbr.org/2020/04/what-good-leadership-looks-like-during-this-pandemic

Klein, G., Moon, B., & Hoffman, R. R. (2006). Making sense of sensemaking 1: Alternative perspectives. *IEEE Intelligent Systems*, 21(4), 70–73.

Lippman, S. A., & Rumelt, R. P. (1982). Uncertain imitability: An analysis of inter-firm differences in efficiency under competition. *The Bell Journal of Economics*, 13(2), 418–438.

Lukianoff, G., & Haidt, J. (2018). *The coddling of the American mind: How good intentions and bad ideas are setting up a generation for failure*. Penguin.

Macmillan, J. (2019, August 7). Kenneth Hayne says trust in institutions has been 'destroyed' in scathing attack on modern politics. *Australian Broadcasting Corporation (ABC)*. https://www.abc.net.au/news/2019-08-07/kenneth-hayne-says-trust-in-political-institutions-has-eroded/11393488

Maitlis, S., & Sonenshein, S. (2010). Sensemaking in crisis and change: Inspiration and insights from Weick (1988). *Journal of Management Studies*, 47(3), 551–580.

Martin, N. (2020). COVID Pandemic and its Influence as Fragmentation of EU Market and Security. *International conference Knowledge-based Organization*, 26(2), 193–198.

Redman, C. L., Crumley, C. L., Hassan, F. A., Hole, F., Morais, J., Riedel, F., Scarborough, V. L., Tainter, J. A., Turchin, P., & Yasuda, Y. (2007). Group report: Millennial perspectives on the dynamic interaction of climate, people, and resources. In R. Costanza, L. Graumlich, & W. L. Steffen (Eds.), *Sustainability or collapse? An integrated history and future of people on Earth* (pp. 115–148). MIT Press.

Rittel, H., & Webber, M. (1973). Dilemmas in a general theory of planning. *Policy Sciences*, 4, 155–169.

San Martín-Rodríguez, L., Beaulieu, M. D., D'Amour, D., & Ferrada-Videla, M. (2005). The determinants of successful collaboration: A review of theoretical and empirical studies. *Journal of Interprofessional Care*, 19(sup 1), 132–147.

Senge, P. M. (1990). *The fifth discipline: The art and practice of the learning organization*. Doubleday.

Small, V., & Warn, J. (2020). Impacts on food policy from traditional and social media framing of moral outrage and cultural stereotypes. *Agriculture and Human Values*, 37(2), 295–309.

Snowden, D. J., & Boone, M. E. (2007). A leader's framework for decision making. *Harvard Business Review, 85*(11), 68–76.

Sull, D. N. (1999). Why good companies go bad. *Harvard Business Review, 77*(4), 42–52.

Tagliabue, F., Galassi, L., & Mariani, P. (2020). The "pandemic" of disinformation in COVID-19. *SN Comprehensive Clinical Medicine, 2*(9), 1287–1289.

Thompson, M. (2015, May 29). How Disbanding the Iraqi Army Fueled ISIS. *Time Magazine.* https://time.com/3900753/isis-iraq-syria-army-united-states-military/

Varhola, C. H., & Varhola, L. R. (2006). Avoiding the cookie-cutter approach to culture: Lessons learned from operations in east Africa. *Military Review, 86*(6), 73–78.

Warn, J., & Cox, M. (2014). The leader is leadership. In D. Svyantek & K. Mahoney (Eds.), *Organizational processes and received wisdom* (pp. 29–48). Information Age Publishing.

Warn, J., Okros, A., & Cox, M. (2012). The intellectual challenges of complexity in contemporary military missions. In H. Haas & J. W. Honig (Eds.), *Authentic leadership in extreme situations* (pp. 23–65). Peter Lang.

Weick, K. E. (1995). *Sensemaking in organizations.* Sage.

Wood, M. (2005). The fallacy of misplaced leadership. *Journal of Management Studies, 42*(6), 1101–1121.

Yukl, G. (1989). Managerial leadership: A review of theory and research. *Journal of Management, 15*(2), 251–289.

Zompetti, J. P., & Moffitt, M. A. (2009). Revisiting concepts of public relations audience through postmodern concepts of metanarrative, decentered subject, and reality/hyperreality. *Journal of Promotion Management, 14*(3–4), 275–291.

INDEX